W9-COX-919

doing business with

Libya

Published with the financial assistance of Shell Exploration and Production International Ltd

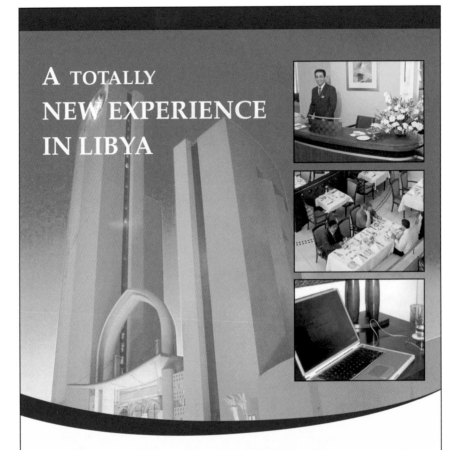

GLOBAL MARKET BRIEFINGS

doing business with
Libya

SECOND EDITION

CONSULTANT EDITORS:
JONATHAN WALLACE
BILL WILKINSON

Academy of Graduate Studies
Tripoli, Libya

CWCassociates
limited

BACB
البنك البريطاني العربي التجاري
British Arab Commercial Bank

Published in cooperation with The Academy of Graduate Studies, Tripoli, Libya

Cover photo courtesy of the Corinthia Bab Africa Hotel, Souk Al Thulatha-Al Gadim, Tripoli, Libya

Publisher's note

Every possible effort has been made to ensure that the information contained in this handbook is accurate at the time of going to press, and the publishers and authors cannot accept responsibility for any errors or omissions, however caused. No responsibility for loss or damage occasioned to any person acting, or refraining from action, as a result of the material in this publication can be accepted by the editor, the publisher or any of the authors.

This second edition first published in Great Britain and the United States in 2004 by Kogan Page Limited.

Kogan Page Ltd
120 Pentonville Road
London N1 9JN
UK

www.kogan-page.co.uk

ISBN 0 7494 3992 0

British Library Cataloguing in Publication Data

A CIP record for this book is available from the British Library

---

Typeset by JS Typesetting Ltd, Wellingborough, Northants
Printed and bound in Great Britain by Cambrian Printers Ltd, Aberystwyth, Wales

Contents

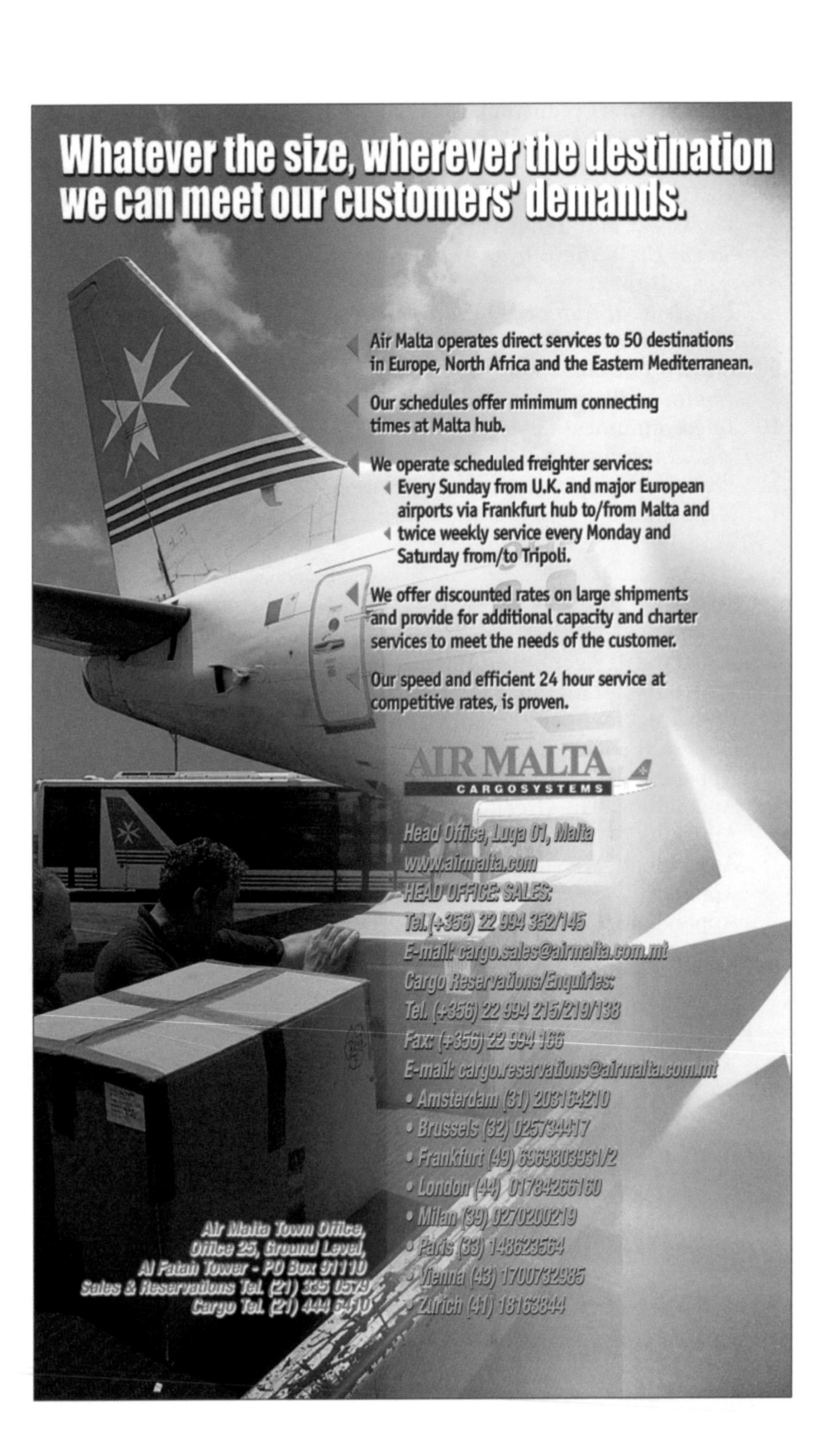

Whatever the size, wherever the destination
we can meet our customers' demands.
Air Malta operates direct services to 50 destinations in Europe, North Africa and the Eastern Mediterranean.
Our schedules offer minimum connecting times at Malta hub.
We operate scheduled freighter services:
Every Sunday from U.K. and major European airports via Frankfurt hub to/from Malta and
twice weekly service every Monday and Saturday from/to Tripoli.
We offer discounted rates on large shipments and provide for additional capacity and charter services to meet the needs of the customer.
Our speed and efficient 24 hour service at competitive rates, is proven.
AIR MALTA
CARGOSYSTEMS
Head Office, Luqa 01, Malta
www.airmalta.com
HEAD OFFICE: SALES:
Tel. (+356) 22 994 352/145
E-mail: cargo.sales@airmalta.com.mt
Cargo Reservations/Enquiries:
Tel. (+356) 22 994 215/219/138
Fax: (+356) 22 994 166
E-mail: cargo.reservations@airmalta.com.mt
• Amsterdam (31) 203164210
• Brussels (32) 025734417
• Frankfurt (49) 6969803931/2
• London (44) 01784266160
• Milan (39) 0270200219
• Paris (33) 148623564
• Vienna (43) 1700732985
• Zurich (41) 18163844
Air Malta Town Office,
Office 25, Ground Level,
Al Fatah Tower - PO Box 91110
Sales & Reservations Tel. (21) 335 0579
Cargo Tel. (21) 444 6410

The Air Malta Group

The Air Malta Group owns various subsidiaries such as The Crowne Plaza Hotel, the Grand Hotel Mercure Selmun Palace and the Hal Ferh Holiday Village.

Travel and tour operating subsidiaries also form part of the Group. These include Sterling Travel and Tourism in Malta, which handles both incoming and out-going traffic, and Holiday Malta which operates in various countries including the UK, Germany, Scandinavia, Russia and Greece and which specialises in selling Air Malta holiday packages to Malta.

The Group also owns Malta Air Charter, a subsidiary operating daily scheduled helicopter air-links between Malta and the sister Island of Gozo, as well as sightseeing tours over the islands.

Air Malta and Lufthansa Technik AG, set up a new joint venture, based in Malta. Lufthansa Technik Malta performs C-Checks on the Boeing 737 series – including the Next-Generation – and Airbus A320 family, for Lufthansa German Airlines and Air Malta as well as for external customers. Air Malta has a 49% shareholding in the company.
Other Companies owned by Air Malta are Osprey Insurance Brokers and Air Supplies, a company that specialises in duty-free sales at Malta International Airport and on board Air Malta aircraft.

Air Malta's products and services include Flyaway Tours which sells holiday packages to Air Malta destinations for groups as well as individuals.

Air Malta – Corporate Profile

Air Malta was set up by a Resolution of Malta's House of Representatives on 21st March 1973 and was registered as a limited liability company on 30th March 1973. Air Malta's primary aim is to establish, maintain, develop and operate air transport services to and from Malta which, by the carriage of passengers and cargo, serve the National interest.

Air Malta started flying operations with two wet-leased Boeing 720Bs on 1st April 1974 with scheduled services to London, Birmingham, Manchester, Rome, Frankfurt, Paris and Tripoli. Its schedule now serves around 45 destinations in Europe and North Africa.

Air Malta's current fleet includes five Airbus A320, seven Boeing 737-300 and two Boeing 737-200 A aircraft. In its last reported financial year (April 2001 – July 2002), Air Malta carried 2.3 million passengers on its combined scheduled and charter services.

Since its setting up, the airline has sought to diversify its activities through a number of subsidiaries that reflect the parent company's operation. The National Airline fully owns a tour-operating subsidiary in the UK. It also invested in hotels, tourist villages and self-catering complexes in Malta. Air Malta's two major hotels are the Crowne Plaza Hotel and the Grand Hotel Mercure Selmun Palace. The company's various subsidiary companies include Sterling Travel & Tourism and Holiday Malta. Sterling Travel & Tourism is a destination management company and a major tourism player as a representative and ground handler for foreign-based tour wholesalers. Holiday Malta is a tour-operating subsidiary based in London. It is the largest Malta specialist tour operator in the UK and Ireland and, as Air Malta Holidays in Scandinavia, Germany, Russia, Sicily and Greece, the company mounts a comprehensive year-round programme of inclusive holidays to Malta, Gozo, Comino and Sicily. Holiday Malta is also a leading incentive and group travel organiser. Other companies include Air Supplies & Catering

Co. Ltd, which provides duty-free goods on the ground and in flight, and Malta Air Charter that operates the inter-island helicopter service. The airline also has a stake in Middlesea Insurance, a State corporation writing insurance business.

In December 1997 Malta's House of Representatives unanimously approved a change in Air Malta's memorandum and articles of association. Air Malta was registered as Air Malta p.l.c. and the authorised share capital was increased from Lm5 million to Lm35 million.

Air Malta was awarded the JAR-145 Approval Certificate on 13th November 1997 by the French Director General of Civil Aviation after the European Joint Aviation Authorities delegated the French civil aviation authority to audit the airline's engineering facilities and procedures. Subsequently the Malta Department of Civil Aviation qualified as a full member of the Joint Aviation Authorities. Supervision of aircraft maintenance was taken over by the Maltese authority and following a second pre-qualification audit, the Malta Department of Civil Aviation awarded the JAR-145 Approval Certificate to Air Malta on 20th August 2001. This approval reflects the internationally-recognised maintenance standards of Air Malta's aircraft.

In June 2002 Air Malta and Lufthansa Technik AG setup a new joint venture by which, in January 2003, Lufthansa Technik Malta started performing C-Checks on the complete range of Boeing 737 and Airbus A320 family aircraft for Lufthansa German Airlines, Air Malta and third parties.

A month later Air Malta concluded a multi-million dollar agreement which involved International Lease Finance Corporation, Airbus Industrie and CFM International for the renewal of its fleet over a four-and-a-half-year period. Two major elements of the deal involve the sale and lease back from ILFC, a major American aircraft lessor, of Air Malta's own two A320-200s and three B737-300s, and the lease of twelve new aircraft from the Airbus A 320 family for a term of twelve years each. The aircraft will be powered by CFM engines.

AIR MALTA

Foreword

I am pleased to welcome readers to the second edition of *Doing Business with Libya.*

Recent developments, both on the international stage and within Libya, make the publication of this book very timely. Libya is ending almost two decades of isolation from the outside world and we are working to make investment an attractive proposition for foreign companies and institutions.

Libya's infrastructure is in need of repair. It is a huge country and all forms of the communications system need immediate attention. Other essential services must also be updated to meet the standards of the 21st century: hospitals, housing, schools, sanitation services, the water and power supplies, are all high on our list of priorities. Ports, airports and a rail system, linking Europe to Africa, all need building or upgrading.

Libya is traditionally Europe's gateway to Africa and an ideal entrepot for companies seeking to enter these exciting markets.

Libya has the longest coastline on the Mediterranean, 1,700 kilometres of unpsoilt beaches. Together with our unrivalled historical sites, beautiful desert oases and fine winter and spring weather, we can offer the visitor an unforgettable holiday. But first we need to build a tourism infrastructure and we are looking overseas for expertise and investment.

The openings that Libya offers the foreign company wishing to do business are presented in this excellent book and I must thank Kogan Page for its efforts in publishing it.

If this book raises your interest, I urge you to come to Libya and to see at first hand the exciting opportunities that will unfold for you.

Dr Shukri Ghanem
Prime Minister
Libya

Foreword

Bilateral relations between the UK and Libya have improved steadily since the re-establishment of diplomatic relations in July 1999. The recent lifting of UN sanctions now provides a new impetus for the bilateral relationship and for UK companies wanting to conduct business across a wide range of sectors. The UK should respond to the new opportunities on offer.

UK exports to Libya grew by 17 per cent in 2002 to over £215 million. Invisible exports (led by education) are estimated to at least match this figure. This increase was driven largely by the effective penetration of Libya's hydrocarbons market by small and medium sized UK-companies providing niche services and technology. The oil and gas industry remains the most crucial sector for the development of Libya's economy. But British firms are also exploring the potential in other areas such as healthcare, infrastructure, tourism and leisure, and education and training. Education and training merits special mention. The UK is the country of choice for Libyans wishing to study overseas. British providers are leading the way in meeting Libya's need for everything from English language to vocational and postgraduate training. The provision of product-related training is also a key tool in securing contracts.

Looking to the future, Libya's potential is vast. A welcoming and educated population, abundant natural resources and natural beauty combine to offer significant opportunities for rapid growth in the years to come. The reform process to make Libya more 'business friendly' still has some way to go to ensure that this potential is fully realized. But enterprising UK companies are already showing the commitment required to be successful in this market. We shall continue to encourage UK companies to take advantage of the many opportunities available in Libya and to play a full part in the future development of the country.

Mike O'Brien MP
Minister of State for Trade, Investment and Foreign Affairs

Academy of Graduate Studies

The Academy of Graduate Studies was established in 1988 and originally named the Institute of Higher Studies and Economic Research. It was composed of three major departments: the Department of Accountancy, the Department of Management, and the Department of Economics. The initiative was taken in response to fundamental challenges facing the Libyan state and society in economic, social, scientific and cultural fields. Its aim was to develop and enhance the programmes of postgraduate studies, and to create scientific cadres to meet the increasing demands arising from the spread of academic institutions and business activities. The initial number of students enrolled was 23, which rose to 500 in 1994, 1,566 in 1998 and 3,500 in 2003. Over the last 15 years the Academy has witnessed tremendous growth in terms of new departments and the number of students. The Academy is a unique institution in nature in that it is publicly founded yet self-financed, and flexible in management.

Recently, the Academy was restructured accordingly into three schools: the School of Humanities, the School of Management and Finance and the School of Applied and Engineering Sciences.

The degrees awarded are Graduate Diploma, MA and PhD. However, the emphasis is on the former two degrees. The students have to fulfil the academic requirements of the courses and write a thesis. The courses are divided into two terms. The minimum period of study is three years.

In addition, the Academy is engaged in the process of cooperation with national academic institutions, in economic and social activities, and in the organization of conferences and workshops in collaboration with foreign academic institutions and centres. In comparable Western terms, the Academy acts as a think-tank, offering consultancy to both state and private institutions.

The Academy has a leading role nationally in the field of publications, such as the Journal of Graduate Studies and a host of books and translations of various academic disciplines.

In 2001 the Centre of African and International Studies was created with the aim of enlarging, broadening and deepening the knowledge and understanding of developments in Africa. The Centre is composed of four departments: the Department of Politics and Strategy, the Department of Economics, the Department of Sociology, and the Department of Law. The Centre has initiated MA degree courses in 2003.

The library of the Academy has a vast number of books and journals distributed under many titles and disciplines.

Foreword

Libya is one of the most exciting of the emerging markets of Africa and the Arab world. The country is ideally positioned at the crossroads of Europe and Africa. It has been granted an abundance of natural resources, including a shrewd and well-educated population.

Economically, Libya's huge potential is only now being offered and opened to international markets for both trade and for investment. Both internal and external developments have accelerated a trend towards a liberalization of the national economy. The time has never been more auspicious for foreign enterprises to explore and to exploit these opportunities.

The political leadership has been engaged in a process of reviewing the philosophical assumptions behind the orientation of the national economy. Economic and human resources that have been restrained are being released to attract foreign investment to generate employment, training, products and services for the benefit of all Libyans. Laws covering a range of administrative and legal issues have been passed to facilitate economic and commercial ventures in Libya – especially in the tourism field.

The recent lifting of sanctions by the United Nations and a rapprochement with the international community have contributed greatly to a process of openness to outside organizations in an environment of increasing private enterprise.

We welcome investors to bring capital, technology and services to Libya. We are open to foreign enterprises to participate in the launching of a new phase of economic, political and social development in the country.

Dr Saleh Ibrahim
Director, Academy of Graduate Studies
Tripoli, Libya

List of Contributors

The **Arab Development Institute** (ADI) was founded in Tripoli in 1975 as a research centre devoted to research in issues related to socio-economic problems in the Arab world. A year later, it opened a branch in Beirut, Lebanon. The workforce in both Tripoli and Beirut was chosen from all parts of the Arab world. Its earlier administration was composed of a board of directors, a general director and a number of department directors. Later on, its administration took the same form as that which dominated the Libyan administration. Specialists from different parts of the Arab world were called upon to put together a long-term plan of research and other related intellectual activities. The plan was then divided into annual projects, which were carried out by specialized research teams. The institute publishes its research output in books and three journals: one for human sciences, the second for strategic studies, and the third for science and technology. Its list of publications contains more than 300 books. **Mustafa O Attir** began as a teaching assistant in 1963 at the University of Libya, and by the late 1970s was a member of the board of directors of the ADI, and its director from 1984 to 1986. **Khalifa Al-Azzabi** has published several articles and translated eight books from English into Arabic. He has been the director of the ADI since 1986.

British Arab Commercial Bank (BACB) was established in 1972 and is a leading provider of trade and project finance for Arab markets. BACB has expanded its market coverage in recent years and the bank is now able to handle business throughout the Gulf region, as well as transacting business in Algeria, Egypt, Libya, Morocco, Syria and Tunisia. BACB's largest single shareholder is HSBC Bank Middle East, a principal member of the HSBC Group. BACB specializes in trade services and can handle business from a wide range of issuing banks. Services offered by the bank include issuance and confirmation of documentary letters of credit, receivables discounting, bonding and guarantees, cross-border leasing, trade finance and project-related lending. BACB's expertise in Arab finance provides an opportunity to capitalize on opportunities in markets of growing significance – either for existing traders or for those contemplating Arab markets for the first time.

Salem El-Maiar has been working for Kellogg Brown & Root (KBR), a subsidiary of Halliburton, as a principal administrative and training specialist since 1992, when he attained his MBA. He is currently embarked on a part-time PhD programme at the University of London's School of Oriental & African Studies (SOAS). His research topic centres on the management of water resources in Libya in an era of changing technologies, with special reference to the Great Man-made River Project (GMRP). Renewable water and managing scarce water resources are a particular interest.

EWM operates from the Malta office of Ernst and Young. It has had a presence in Libya for more than 30 years, providing a wide range of professional services to international clients working in a variety of sectors. Its resident expatriates have accumulated a body of practical knowledge and experience of how to conduct business in the local environment. EWM is therefore positioned to provide appropriate solutions to business problems.

Eversheds Frere Cholmeley is an international law firm of more than 1,800 lawyers with offices in the UK, continental Europe and Asia. Its Paris office represents clients from all over the world, including the Middle East and Africa, in a wide variety of international transactions and disputes. **David Sellers** and **Nanette Pilkington** of the Paris office have particular experience of matters involving Libya, notably in the oil sector.

Azza K Maghur graduated from the Law Faculty, Garyunis University, Libya, in 1985 and obtained her DEA in international law and international organizations from the Sorbonne University in Paris in 1987. A member of the Tripoli Bar, Azza was the first female Libyan lawyer to appear before the International Court of Justice. She was also a member of the defence team before the Scottish Court in the Netherlands. Maghur & Partners was established in 1951 by Kamel H Maghur.

Dimitri V Massaras has been a regional manager for the Saharan Africa region since 1998 at the IHS Energy Group, based in Geneva, Switzerland. He received his BSc in geology in 1978 from the University of Massachusetts at Amherst, USA. From 1993 to 1998 he worked as a project geologist and petrophysicist for Pennzoil Exploration & Production Company in exploration, production, project management and property acquisitions. From 1986 to 1993 he worked as a senior geologist for Petrofina SA in project management and property acquisitions. From 1979 to 1986 he worked as a geologist for Gulf Oil Exploration & Production Company in exploration, production and well-site operations. He is a certified member of the American Association of Petroleum Geologists (AAPG) and a member of the Swiss Association of Geologists and Engineers. IHS Energy Group (www.ihsenergy.com) is the world's leading provider of global oil and gas information and decision support solutions to the industry.

MEC International Ltd, founded in 1983, is a business development company with strong links in the Middle East, Eastern Europe and Asia. The Board is chaired by Oliver Miles, former British Ambassador to Libya, Luxembourg and Greece. The Managing Director Ian Walker has a background in corporate communications and government relations. The two other Executive Directors are Geoffrey Hancock who founded MEC after a career with the Foreign Office in the Arab world, and Peter Thomson who has more than two decades of international banking experience. It draws on a large number of specialist consultants and has a network of contacts including strategic partnerships in Greece for example. MEC's services include Business Development (local partner identification, market entry strategy), Corporate Communications (government relations, event management), Finance (advising asset management companies on Middle East strategy, advising Middle Eastern financial institutions, access to individuals and companies in the Middle East), Publications (political risk, economic studies, market research), and Investigations (asset searches, due diligence, litigation support).

Oliver Miles is the chairman of MEC International Ltd. Oliver is a former British ambassador to Libya, Luxembourg and Greece. MEC, founded in 1983, is a business development company with strong links in the Middle East, Eastern Europe and Asia. The managing director, Ian Walker, has a background in corporate communications and government relations. The two other executive directors are Geoffrey Hancock, who founded MEC after a career with the Foreign Office in the Arab world, and Peter Thomson, who has more than two decades of international banking experience.

Mukhtar, Kelbash & Elgharabli is an independent law firm established in 1990 with offices in Tripoli, Libya. Its partners, **Mahmud R Mukhtar**, **Bahloul A M Kelbash** and **Abdudayem M Elgharabli**, and their associates advise foreign clients on all aspects of Libyan law.

Sahara (International Consulting) Libya was established in the early 1990s to offer services and consultation for tourists and business travellers coming to Libya, and to organize international investment conferences in promoting the country among the foreign business community both in Libya and abroad. Sahara Libya is also involved in the organization of trade fairs and provides comprehensive consulting services to foreign companies seriously interested in the Libyan market.

Dr Marat Terterov completed his doctoral thesis at St Antony's College, Oxford in 2002. His topic of research is the Egyptian privatization programme, specifically the politics of privatized companies and the Egyptian government. He has been travelling to, and living in, Arab and Middle Eastern countries since 1993 and has been conducting research into the political and business affairs of Egypt, Syria, Turkey, Jordan, Morocco and Libya during this time. He has visited Libya since the end of the UN sanctions and air embargo against Tripoli, and has explored the opportunity of providing consulting services to foreign companies interested in the Libyan market. Marat is an Australian national living in Oxford, England, although he was born into a Russo-Armenian family in Odessa, Ukraine, in the late 1960s.

Jonathan Wallace is a consultant publisher with Kogan Page with a responsibility for titles on the Middle East, Central Asia and Eastern Europe. He was, from 1965, the editor in chief and latterly chairman of the Middle East Economic Digest (MEED) Group, which he sold to the UK publishers EMAP in 1987. Since then he has worked as Middle East editor in chief for United Press International (UPI), as publisher for the Arab Bankers Association and as a consultant to a number of Arab and European companies. He is a frequent visitor to the region, with a particular interest in Libya and the Gulf Co-operation Council (GCC) states.

Bill Wilkinson spent 18 years as a marine engineer before becoming a consultant. In 1984 he joined an American management consultancy, having completed a two-year company turn-round assignment in Kuwait. Syn-Cronamics International specialized in rebuilding client profitability through direct intervention with front-line management systems and personnel. Bill formed Consultancy Support in 1990 to provide a more flexible consultancy response than specialist or accountancy-based practices were offering. He has also worked with further education colleges in the UK to help introduce vocationally based management development programmes. Consultancy Support is now focusing on supporting change in Libya and the MENA region.

Acknowledgements

My co-Editor Bill Wilkinson and I must first thank Dr Saleh Ibrahim and Milad Saad Milad of the Academy of Graduate Studies in Tripoli for their invaluable help and support in the preparation of the final text of the second edition of *Doing Business with Libya*. The first edition was largely put together by Kogan Page's editor Marat Terterov and I thank him for his pioneering work on which we have built this one.

There are many others I must thank. In no special order they are: Mohammed Abolhoul, Director of the Libyan Arab Foreign Investment Board; Mohamed Fezzani, British Arab Commercial Bank; Charlie Ghassoub of British Airways; Tim Clark, the CWC Group; Ray Borg and John Salibi, Air Malta; Dr Amjad Shaqrouni, JCS Translation; Ann El-Jorni, British Embassy; Capt. Bashir Tayari, Buraq Air; Mark Gaucci, Bab al Africa Corinthia Hotel; Hisham Fergiani, Fergiani's Bookshop; Mohammed Layyas and Faraj Roeid, Libyan Arab Foreign Bank; Mohammed Hureij, Libyan Arab Foreign Investment Company; Nanette Pilkington, Eversheds Frere Cholmeley; Sherif Mortgay, Shell; Jim Wilson, Black and Veitch; the staff and management of the Al Kabir Hotel; Joceline Bury, West Country Enterprise; Azza Maghur, Maghur & Partners; and last but by no means least, Linda Batham at Kogan Page for her forbearance and understanding of the unique difficulties that reporting on the Jamahiriya presents to all concerned.

Jonathan Wallace
London

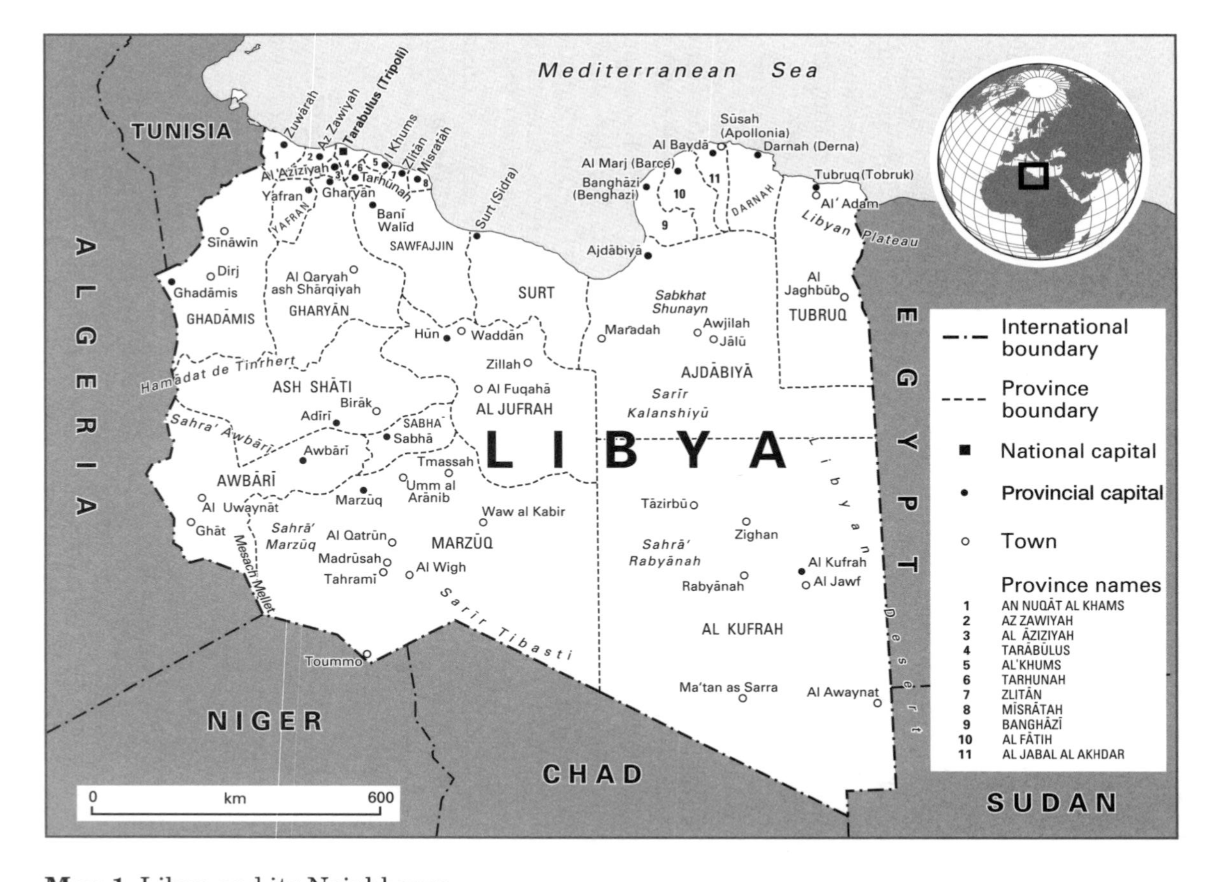

Map 1 Libya and its Neighbours

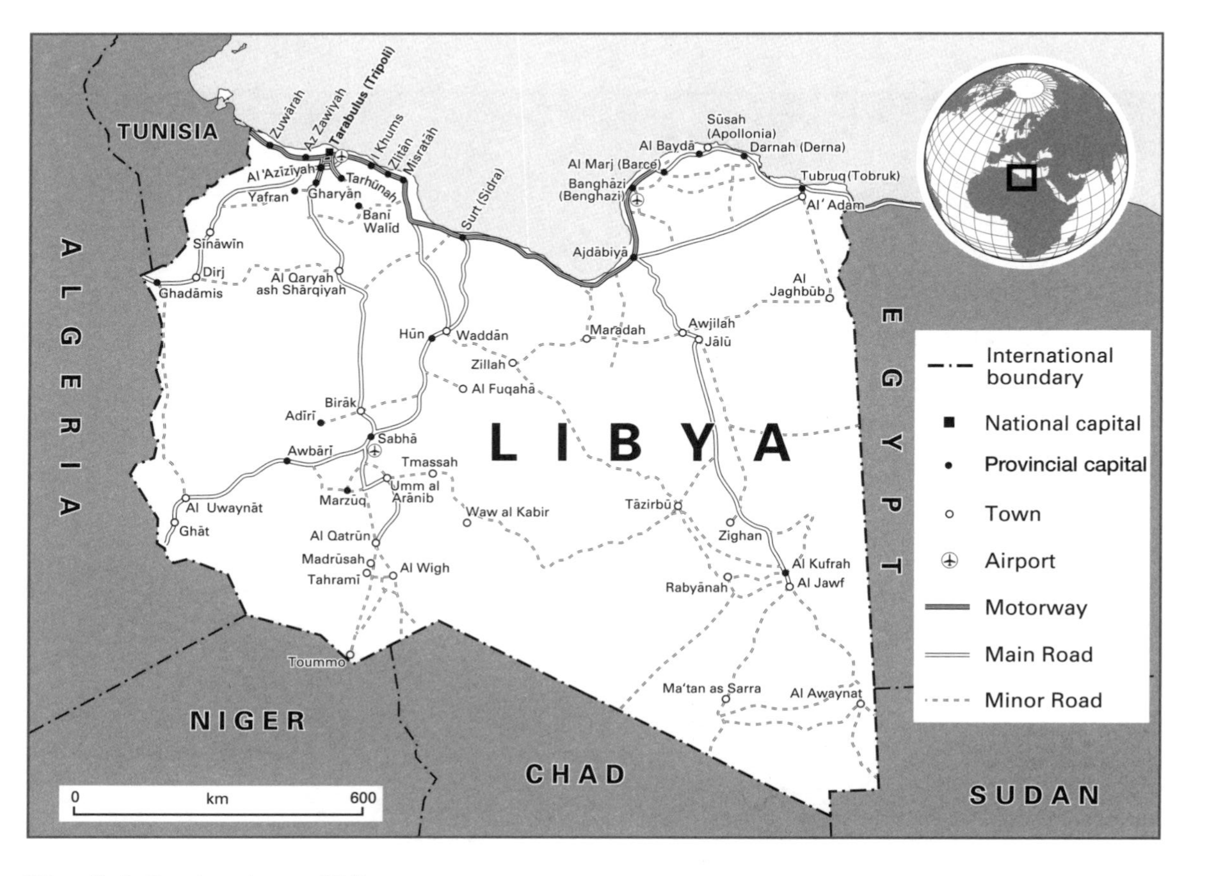

Map 2 Infrastructure of Libya

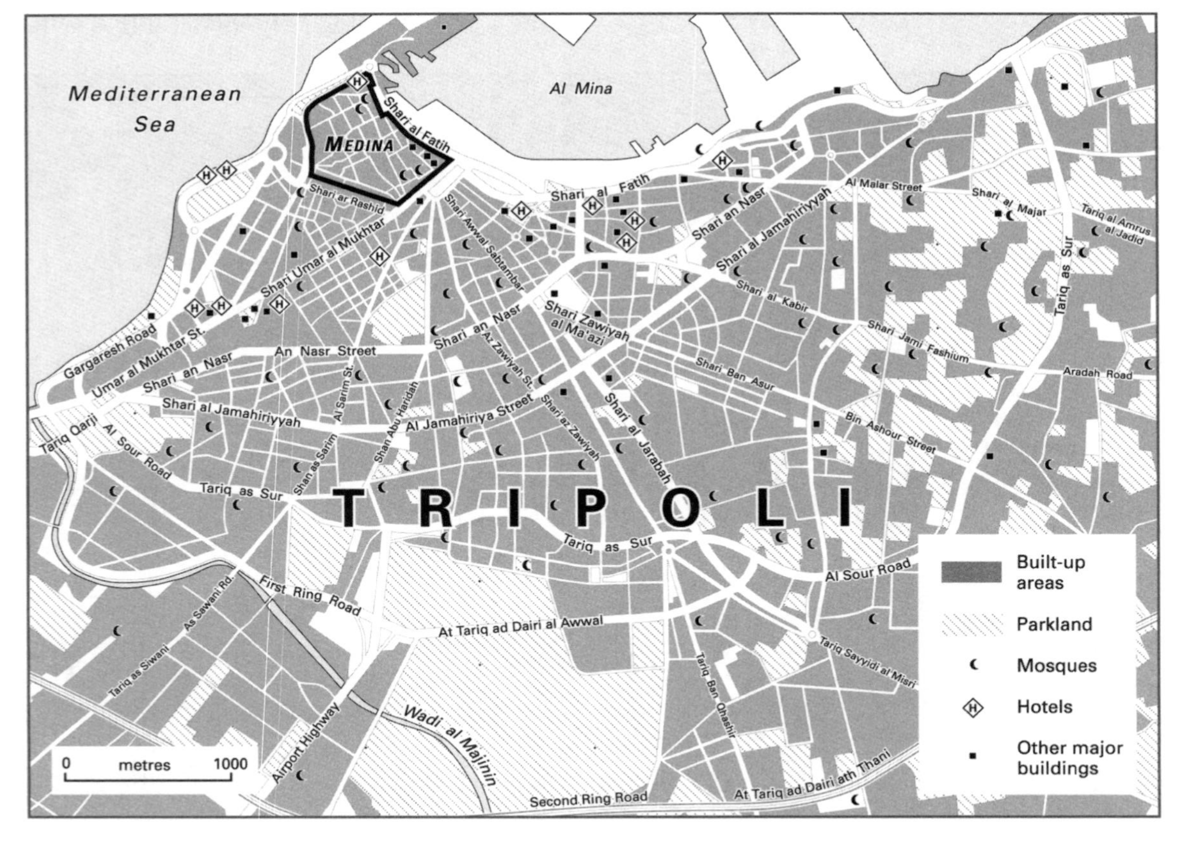

Map 3 Tripoli – City Plan

Introduction

> 'For Investment to succeed it should be based on agreements, wisdom, conditions and awareness.'
>
> Libyan Leader Muammar Qadhafi, *The Green Book*

> 'We speak of new beginnings.'
>
> Saif El Islam, Qadhafi son, London 2002

As we prepared the text in mid-June 2003 for this the second edition of *Doing Business with Libya*, the long-delayed meeting of the General People's Congress (GPC) took place. This meeting had been scheduled for November 2002 and had been heralded as a major event designed to change Libya's direction. It did.

Libyan Leader Muammar Qadhafi addressed the GPC and told it that 'soviet-style' economies had failed, urging Libya's citizenry to adopt a form of capitalism that functions within the concept of Jamahiriya. 'The system has failed, as it did in the Soviet Union and Eastern Europe. We need people of the highest skills with strong nationalistic beliefs and a dedication to the public interest,' the Libyan news agency JANA reported Qadhafi as saying on 14 June.

The GPC also announced a new government, in which the modernising internationalist Dr Shukri Ghanem was appointed Prime Minister. Younger men representing a more modernist approach replaced other long-serving members of the 'old guard'. (See box.)

To signal that these moves are more than rhetoric, the Central Bank announced a unified foreign exchange rate on 19 June in a move designed to stimulate foreign investment and to reform Libya's command economy. The bank had devalued the Libyan Dinar (LD) by 51 per cent in early 2002. On 25 June 2003 the rate was US$1 = LD1.372/1.365.

The GPC appointed former Prime Minister Amar al-Litaif as Minister of Tourism. High on the government's priority list is the development of tourism and his appointment was then seen as significant. Sure enough, on 19 June Al-Litaif announced an investment programme of US$7,000 million over five years to attract three million tourists a year.

Soon after the Sirte meeting of the GPC news started to leak out that a finalization of the Lockerbie affair was near, that a compensation settlement had been agreed with the families of the crash victims and that a final removal of the UN's sanctions was imminent.

Other reforms are also in the wind, as we go to press. Chief among these is a change to the tax laws for foreign enterprises.

The mood in Tripoli is one of expectation that two decades of isolation and privation are coming to an end and that foreign participation in a re-energized economy, with or without American involvement, is on the horizon.

Despite the privations endured by Libya's citizens, they have a standard of living that is better than that of all their neighbours in North Africa. Libya enjoys a per capita annual GDP of US$6,500 – way above the Arab world's average of US$4,140 and of Algeria's US$1,800, Morocco's US$1,200 and Egypt's US$1,500. With the changing international environment and a new willingness to open the economy domestically, Libya's task is now to put its wealth to work within the economy.

Jonathan Wallace and Bill Wilkinson
November 2003

New government appointed 14 June 2003

At the end of its sessions in Sirte on 14 June 2003, the General People's Congress (GPC) issued the following resolution for the re-selection of the GPC:

Dr Shukri Mohammed Ghanem, Secretary GPC (Prime Minister)
Abdallah Salem al-Badri, Assistant Secretary GPC
Dr Al-Baghdadi Ali al-Mahmoudi, Assistant Secretary for Production
Eng Ma'atoug Mohamed Ma'atoug, Assistant Secretary for Services
Abdelrahman Mohamed Shalgam, Secretary GPC Foreign Liaison
Dr Al-Taher al-Hadi al-Juhaimy, Secretary GPC for Planning
Amar al-Mabrouk al-Litaif, Secretary GPC for Tourism
Mohammed Ali al-Misrati, Secretary GPC for Justice
Al-Ogaili Abdelsalam Barini, Secretary GPC Finance
Abdelgader Omer Belkhair, Secretary GPC Economy and Trade.

The GPC also issued the following resolution to re-select the Secretariat of the GPC:

Al-Zanati Mohamed al-Zanati, General Secretary

Ahmed Mohamed Ibrahim, Assistant General Secretary
Ibrahim Abdelrahman Ibjad, Secretary for People's Congresses Affairs
Ibrahim Ali Ibrahim, Secretary for People's Committees Affairs
Suliman Sassi al-Shohoumi, Secretary for Foreign Affairs
Abdallah Idris Ibrahim, Secretary for Unions and Federations
Amal Nouri Abdallah Safar, Secretary for Social Affairs

Dr Shukri Mohammed Ghanem
Appointed Prime Minister 14 June 2003
2001–2003: [Minister] of Economy and Trade
1998–2001: Acting Deputy to the Secretary General of OPEC, Vienna
1993–1998: Research Director, OPEC, Vienna
1987–1993: Economics lecturer at Al-Jabel al-Gharbi University, Gharayan
1984–1987: Director of the Economic Studies Centre, Tripoli
1982–1984: Visitor, School of African and Oriental Studies, Univ. of London
1977–1982: Head of Economics, The Arab Development Institute
1975–1977: Adviser to the Oil Ministry
1975: Acting Oil Minister
1970–1975: General Manager, Economic Management, Oil Ministry
1968–1970: Director of Marketing, Member of the Management Council in the NOC
1966–1968: Deputy Manager of the Libyan news agency JANA, translation department
1963–1965: Head of American and European Affairs, the Economy Ministry
PhD in Economics, Fletcher School of Economics, Boston, USA, 1975
MSc in Economics, Fletcher School of Economics, Boston, USA, 1973
BSc in Economics, [University of Libya], Benghazi, 1963
DoB 9 October, 1942.

Source: Libyan News Agency JANA, 14 June 2003

We are privileged to work in this way with:

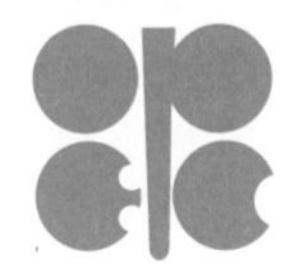

NATIONAL OIL CORPORATION

Kuwait Petroleum Corporation

مؤسسة البترول الكويتية

www.thecwcgroup.com

Part One

Background to the Market

1.1

Libya Reconsidered: Towards a Closer Relationship between Libya and the Foreign Business Community

Oliver Miles, former UK Ambassador to Libya

'The brother leader pointed out that the holding of the first and second investment conferences in Libya. . . indicated that Libya was serious about encouraging foreign investment.'

Libyan TV report of Qadhafi's address to an international investment conference, 15 November 2000

In the first 20 years following the Libyan Revolution of 1969, Qadhafi's Libya established itself in a role which brought it sharply into conflict with the West, and in particular with the United States. Libya saw itself as the champion of anti-imperialism, intransigently hostile to Israel and ready to support virtually any liberation movement, however violent. In the eyes of Western governments and the Western media, Libya was the prime example of a rogue state, dedicated to the support of worldwide terrorism and subversion. There were a number of bloody incidents, in which both Libya and others suffered shocking casualties.

From rogue state to moderation

The rhetoric of this period survives in the Revolutionary Committees, the Libyan media and some of the utterings of Qadhafi himself, and also in foreign attitudes towards Libya, most particularly in the United States. However, the reality is that since 1989 there has been a process of stabilization, healing and partial normalization. Even the Americans, in recent terrorist outrages, have detected no Libyan hand. Libya has expelled the many extremist groups, particularly Palestinians, which had previously been welcomed and supported. The construction of weapons of mass destruction seems to have been abandoned, although Libya continues to seek to arm itself. Libyans now have open access to information through satellite television and the Internet. The population is no longer cowed. Qadhafi's own reforms have led to a substantial improvement in the position of women. There are signs that sensitive issues that were previously swept under the carpet, such as drugs and crime, or the existence of an ethnic minority of Berbers, are now being addressed in a more open and adult fashion.

The problem of Islamic fundamentalism appears to have receded, and freedom of Christian religious practice continues, as it has since the Revolution. Qadhafi's reaction to the atrocities of 11 September 2001 was immediate, denouncing the attacks and offering sympathy and support to the Americans, support which took the practical form of providing information about Libyans and others involved in such actions. It came as a surprise to many to learn that Libya had issued a warrant through Interpol for the arrest of Usama bin Ladin two years before the Americans.

Sanctions have discouraged investment

A variety of trade sanctions had been imposed on Libya in reaction to the events of the 1980s, including US government sanctions, EU sanctions and, in a series of Security Council resolutions, UN sanctions. The main impact was felt in defence goods, civil aviation and the expansion and development of Libya's oil and gas fields. In practice, the main impact on ordinary Libyans was through the ban on civil aviation, which meant that all Libyans wishing to travel abroad – for example, for medical treatment or to make a pilgrimage to Mecca – had to go by land or sea to a neighbouring country before travelling onward. This also acted as a serious discouragement to foreign businessmen who wished to visit Libya.

However, even when all these sanctions were fully in force, they did not amount to anything like a total interruption of trade relations between Libya and the outside world. Exports of Libyan oil and gas, as well as trade in most sectors including both capital and consumer goods, were not directly affected. Libyan oil production remained substantial, somewhere below 1.5 million barrels per day (bpd), and Libya continued to earn oil revenue depending on variations in oil price. Trade with the United Kingdom remained fairly steady, with UK exports totalling up to a quarter of a billion pounds annually; during the period in which diplomatic relations were broken off, the British government did not provide the usual services in support of exporters, yet made no attempt to deter UK companies from trading with Libya. Several thousand UK citizens continued to live and work in Libya, some of them replacing Americans, but many of them working for UK companies. Many companies avoided publicity for their legitimate Libyan operations, which contributed to the impression that sanctions had effectively stopped normal trade, though this was never the case.

Normalization of foreign relations

Following the relative normalization of Libya's relations with the rest of the world described above, UN sanctions were suspended in 1999. They cannot be re-imposed except by a decision of the Security Council, which would require a majority of Security Council members and would be subject to veto. It is a racing certainty that there will be no such decision.

The present situation, therefore, is that while an EU (but not UN) ban on defence sales remains in place, civil trade and investment are no longer subject to sanctions; the exception is that unilateral US sanctions remain strictly in place, subject only to the exemption of food and medical supplies introduced by the Clinton Administration in 1999. A solution to the remaining problems has been sought through a series of meetings between Libyan, US and British officials, as a result of which a Libyan offer which includes payment of compensation to the families of Lockerbie victims has been put on the table. The US reaction is awaited. It is not possible to forecast when it will come, given the opposing pressures within the United States. Meanwhile, the absence of US companies from a marketplace in which they played a very large part creates an opportunity for UK and other companies to replace them.

Encouraging foreign investment...

In the past few years, Libya has made considerable efforts to encourage foreign companies to trade and invest. These efforts have coincided with a period of higher oil prices, which has enabled Libya to accumulate reserves that are now available for spending on development projects and current needs. Libya has for some years spoken of an investment programme estimated at US$35 billion over five years, of which some 30 per cent will be sought outside Libya. Law no. 5 of 1997 (Encouraging Foreign Investments) seeks to offer an attractive package of legal, administrative and economic incentives. Starting in 1999, Libya, and Qadhafi personally, organized a number of high-profile events with the same objective. The terms offered for new concessionary acreage make Libya an attractive territory for oil and gas exploration and production. The cumbersome multiple exchange rate has finally been abandoned in favour of a unified rate, and efforts are being made to modernize the banking system.

. . . but disappointing results

To date, however, the impact of all this on business has been disappointing. The reason probably lies mainly in the failure of the Libyan administration to adapt to the new situation, and to take the necessary operational decisions. An attempt in 2000 to decentralize decision-making and strengthen the position of local governorates did not produce the results expected of it. In June 2003 the General People's Congress announced some ministerial changes aimed at further reform of the government framework in which the Libyan economy operates. The private sector is still very small, although it is now officially encouraged and can be expected to develop quickly – at the Congress Qadhafi spoke of 'abolishing' the public sector and pointedly referred to the way that 'it collapsed in the Soviet Union and the whole of Eastern Europe because it relied on incompetent officials who disregarded the interests of the nation'.

The published trade figures for Libya should not be taken at face value; there are too many distortions, such as routing trade through Malta during the period of sanctions, and disguising what are really US exports as those of other countries. Nevertheless, the United Kingdom has remained an important supplier of the Libyan market, not far behind Italy, the market leader. The balance of trade is heavily in the United Kingdom's favour; Italy and Libya's other main suppliers in the Mediterranean import very large quantities of Libyan oil, which the United Kingdom does not, since it is similar in quality to North Sea oil. There have been a number of trade missions to Libya from the United Kingdom since the restoration of diplomatic relations in 1999 and these have been consistently well received. Trade is multi-sector, but UK consultants have a particularly high reputation. UK consumer goods have been excluded in some cases, for what are apparently political reasons, but the ban has not been consistently applied. In general, Libya is used to buying in the international market, and factors such as quality and price carry far more weight than politics.

Expectations exceed results

In nearly 41 years since the discovery of oil Libya has made very considerable progress because of major structural changes that have taken place since this discovery. It has developed from one of the poorest countries in the world into one whose physical and human infrastructure compares favourably with that of its neighbours. Indeed, Libya has begun to experience some of the problems of prosperity, such as the inflow of an army of unqualified and destitute immigrants looking for work in what is for them an Eldorado. Qadhafi's achievements include the Great Man-Made River (GMR), which brings fresh water from beneath the Sahara to the cities and populated areas along the Mediterranean. Whatever view one takes of its economic fundamentals, and some people both within and beyond Libya's borders question them, it is a practical achievement on a gigantic scale, and one that brings tangible benefit to the population. Inevitably, however, expectations are running ahead of achievements, and with a population 50 per cent of whom are below the age of 20, Libya will have to move very fast if the aspirations of the young for employment and a decent role in society are to be satisfied.

1.2

The Libyan Jamahiriya: Country, People, Social and Political Development

Mustafa O Attir, Professor of Sociology, and Khalifa Al-Azzabi, Assistant Professor of English Literature, Arab Development Institute

Geography

Libya is located in the centre of North Africa with a Mediterranean coastline of close to 2,000 kilometres. To the north, the country is bounded by the Mediterranean Sea; to the east by Egypt and Sudan; to the south by Niger, Chad and Sudan; and to the west by Algeria and Tunisia. In terms of size (1,775,500 square kilometres), Libya is the fourth largest country in Africa, and seven times the size of the United Kingdom. However, over 90 per cent of the land is either desert or semi-desert, and the country's climate is affected by the Mediterranean Sea to the north and the Sahara to the south. The coastal region is the most fertile but is so narrow in some places that it does not exceed 50 kilometres; in other areas, however, it expands to a few hundred kilometres. The coastal strip is under the influence of the Mediterranean, while the rest of the country is under the influence of the Sahara. Therefore, the northern part of the country enjoys warm and sunny weather for most of the year. The temperature reaches the 20s and 30s during most months. Of the winter months, January is the coldest. The mean monthly maximum and minimum temperatures range from 19°C to 8°C for coastal cities, and between 25°C and minus 1°C in the oases of the Sahara.

The Libyan desert is part of the Great African Sahara. It has its own climate, with hardly any rain, is warm throughout most of the year, and can get extremely hot during the period from May to September when temperatures can reach close to 50°C.[1]

[1] The highest temperature ever recorded in the shade was 48°C in the town of Azizia, some 38 kilometres south of Tripoli.

Religion

All Libyans are Sunni Muslims of the Malikite rite and are fundamentally attached to their Islamic faith. Religion permeates all facets of life. Thus, Libya differs from many other Arab countries that have more than one religion and more than one rite. However, there are more than one million foreigners living in Libya, many of whom belong to different Christian sects or to an Indo-Chinese religion. There are churches and places of worship for the majority of these religious groups.

Population

Libya's population is estimated to be 5.4 million, including numerous foreign residents, and is said to be growing at a rate of 3.5 per cent, one of the highest population growth rates in the world. The population is young – almost 50 per cent are under 20 years old – and 86 per cent urban, one of the highest urbanization rates in the world. According to the UNDP's 1995 Human Development Report, Libya's urban population grew on average by 4.2 per cent annually between 1960 and 1992. Education and health care have improved under the impact of oil wealth. In 1992, 72 per cent of the adult population was literate, while the ratio of doctors to patients from one per 3,860 people in 1965 to one per 690 people by 1992. Nevertheless, these indicators are poor in comparison with other similar-income countries in the region and with OPEC countries. The infant mortality rate at 61 per 1,000 live births exceeds the average for the region.

Historical background

Throughout history, several nations, political systems and leaders have left their mark on the country and its history. The Phoenicians arrived from the shores of Lebanon and built a few coastal trading centres, with three of them, on the western shores, eventually becoming the major cities of Tripoli, Leptis Magna and Sabratha. The Greeks settled on the eastern shores, where they developed an elaborate system of irrigation, which helped develop agriculture, and built five major cities including Benghazi and Cyrene. Most of these became thriving trade and cultural centres, and their ruins still bear testament to their previous glory. Next came the Romans in c150 BC, from which time they ruled Libya until their empire finally declined and the Byzantines took over from the 5th century AD to the 7th century AD, at which time Libya became part of the Arab Islamic Empire. It was later to become part of the Ottoman Empire. Since that time, Libya has stayed true to her Arabic

Islamic identity, despite several attempts from Christian Europe to change this – namely, the Spanish and the Knights of St John from Malta who ruled the north-western shores for half a century during the 16th century, and the Italians who invaded the country in the early years of the 20th century. The war between the Libyans and the Italians lasted more than 20 years before Libya became an Italian colony.

Italian colonization

When the Italians arrived in Libya, they found a very poor and backward country but were intent on staying forever. As a result, they constructed many aspects of material modernization. The construction work was not intended for Libyans, but for those Italian settlers who came from Italy. However, when the Italians finally left, they left behind all that they had built of the infrastructure. They also left a society that was economically poor, with a mostly illiterate population, who lived a life of bare subsistence, and who continued to do so until the second half of the century when the country took some major steps on the road to modernization.

However, the process of modernizing the society has its roots in different time periods. It is possible to trace the early roots of modernization in Libya to the second half of the 19th century. During this time, Libya was under the rule of the Ottoman Empire and the country experienced, for the first time, modern schools, hospitals, municipal facilities, a publishing house, newspapers and a number of new regulations. Most of these facilities were restricted to one city. However, the major cultural change came when Italy invaded the country during the 1920s. This change was many-sided: Libyans saw modern war equipment for the first time and this was their first contact with modern forms of technology. For many years, this was the only modern technology that Italians brought into the country; other institutions and ideas were to follow later. However, except for a small minority, the majority of Libyans had very little, if anything, to do with this aspect of modernization (Attir, 1992: 245–248).

The Italian colonization came to an end when Italy was defeated in World War II. The country then remained under British and French military administration for almost a decade. Although the military administration did very little in the way of modernization, it allowed Libyans to go to school and the figures on student numbers in Table 1.2.1 demonstrate clearly how education, an important mechanism of modernization, developed. Although modern education had been introduced during the 18th century, only a very small group had benefited from it. The Italian administration made it possible for Libyans to send their children to school. However, the Italians did not provide school facilities for everyone, and did not allow Libyans to go beyond elementary education. Therefore, the rise in student numbers gained momentum only after the country became independent at the end of 1951. As the century drew to a close, more than one-third of the population were students. In addition, women's education, which was once lagging behind, grew more rapidly and finally closed the gap (GSESR, *A Report on the Development of Education*, 1999).

Jamahiriya

Libya was granted independence by a UN Resolution, independence was proclaimed on 24 December 1951 and Libya became a kingdom following the British model. On 1 September 1969, Libya was transformed from a constitutional monarchy into a revolutionary republic. The Revolution was led by a group of young military officers. Qadhafi, then only 27 years old, became the head of a 12-man Revolutionary Council. The country underwent a number of far-reaching social,

Table 1.2.1 Development of education and other demographics as indicators related to modernization in Libya

Year	Total students ('000)	% female students	University students only ('000)	% female students	% of women in labour force	Income from oil (US$ million)
1876/77	0.06	–				
1911/12	0.1	–				
1921/22	0.6	–				
1931/32	4.4	–				
1938/39	6.9	–				
1943/44	6.7	0.5				
1948/49	25.1	1.2				
1950/51	32.8	11.0				
1955/56	70.1	16.0	0.03	–		16.0
1960/61	136.4	18.0	0.7	3.3	2.1	6.6
1965/66	227.5	26.0	1.9	8.9	3.3	179.8
1970/71	407.4	34.0	5.2	10.7	6.2	1,351.2
1975/76	743.5	43.0	13.4	17.6	7.6	8,848.0
1980/81	973.8	44.0	19.5	21.6	11.1	22,527.2
1985/86	1,224.3	46.0	36.6	28.1	–	6,091.8
1990/91	1,492.4	48.0	62.2	43.2	17.6	4,181.1
1995/96	1,603.3	48.0	129.2	44.0	22.3	11,401.5
1998/99	1,990.7	49.0	165.7	47.7		11,988.9

Source: UNDP, *Human Development Report 2000*

political and economic changes, the most important being the declaration of the Libyan 'Jamahiriya' in March 1977. The Jamahiriya is a state of the masses involving the transfer of both legislative and executive powers, to the people. Libya was divided into several small communities, each with its own legislative group (Basic People's Congress) and an executive team (People's Committee). The basic congresses – and at a later stage the people's congress at the municipal level – were expected to debate issues ranging from the maintenance of local roads to international issues such as the reconstruction of the UN. The various issues debated at both these levels were later grouped together in the melting pot of the General People's Congress, where they became national policy.

Throughout its history, Libya played a vital role in international relations, especially in relation to countries with shores on the Mediterranean Sea, which throughout history has been the cradle of various civilizations. As indicated earlier, the country was invaded by almost every major international power. Each has attempted to include Libya within its boundary. Sooner or later, each has left but not before leaving its mark. In addition, Libya has always played a major and important role in world trade, especially between central Africa and Europe. The size of trade expanded after the introduction of the camel to Africa. Although modern transportation made it possible to transfer goods between European and African cities directly, Libyan cities can still play an important but not yet fully explored role in economic relations between Europe and Africa since Libya is on good terms with nearly all African states and groups.

State of development

When Libya was granted independence in 1951, it was described as one of the poorest and most backward nations of the world. The population at the time was approximately 1.5 million, and only 15 individuals finished university that year, almost all of whom were majoring in humanities. There were only two working hospitals in the whole country, together with a number of small medical units. Electric power could be found only in major cities and even so did not reach all homes in those cities. Water and sanitary facilities were equally limited.

In the late 1950s, the World Bank sent a team to assess the socio-economic situation of the country and her people. The team published its report in early 1960, concluding that:

> 'Libyans live a very simple life, their food is simple, their necessities are limited, and their knowledge of twentieth-century technology very limited. The majority are farmers who consume most of their production. Their

living quarters are very poor, and the majority live in shacks, hamlets or caves. They use donkeys, camels and horses for transportation.'

The International Bank for Reconstruction and Development, The Economic Development of Libya, 1960: 1

The development of modern societies in the Third World is due to an increase in the scope of government activity. Libya is no exception. Therefore, from its earliest days, the Libyan Government made the search for economic resources its major priority. It was assumed that the Libyan desert might hold important resources and thus the search for oil began during the early 1950s, and it was soon obvious that Libya would become an oil producing country. A development council was created in 1956 as a consulting agency to suggest ideas for development. Its primary objective was to provide the country with the structures and functions of a modern society. However, the most pressing problem was a lack of funds. The United Nations and a number of Western nations provided the Government with financial assistance, which was directed by foreign bodies and agencies. The amount of money and the way in which it was spent was decided by foreign experts. As the number of Libyan university graduates increased and they took higher government jobs, it was felt that foreign aid determined by foreigners was not always in the best interests of the country, and thus by 1961 all functions of foreign agencies were suspended.

Oil and development

Oil was discovered in large quantities and by 1961 the development council was transformed into a planning body ready to implement national policies. The first five-year plan was prepared for the years 1963–68, followed by a three-year plan and another five-year plan. Through such development plans, the Government succeeded in introducing major changes related to the quality of the individual's life. These included education, health, electricity, housing, communication facilities, mechanization of agriculture, industry and a variety of consumer goods, etc. Naturally, these are empirical indicators of modernization which can be observed and measured. In the area of education, measuring the indicators can be achieved through the number of schools, their different levels, the number of classrooms, the number of teachers, the number of students and their ratio in each age category. In the area of health, indicators include the number of hospitals, the number of medical centres, the number of hospital beds, and the number of doctors and nurses. For housing, references are made to the number of housing units made available every year, and the percentage of these units with electricity, running water and adequate sanitation.

Table 1.2.2 Indicators related to modernization in Libya (2)

	Electricity consumption (per capita kilowatt hours)	Population per doctor	Under-five mortality rate (per 1000 live births)	Telephone lines (per 100 people)
1959	35	7250	290	0.7
1964	60	4755	–	1.1
1969	130	2611	87	–
1974	260	1100	69	1.5
1980	1600	960	56	2.4
1995	3300	715	30	5.9

Source: UNDP, *Human Development Report 2000*

Tables 1.2.1 and 1.2.2 show the development of major indicators over time. The construction of infrastructure and the provision of all aspects of modernization reached every corner and every human settlement no matter how small. Thus, there was no difference between rural and urban communities in this sense, which makes Libya different, especially among Third World countries where per capita spending in rural areas does not match the amount spent in urban areas. It was one of the most important goals of the plans to reach people even in the most remote villages. Therefore, when cross-national comparisons are made, Libya's achievement today puts the country among the most advanced (UNDP, *Human Development Report 2000*: 158–166).

Urban and rural life

Reports prepared during the Italian occupation classified the population of the country into nomads, semi-nomads and settled population. In 1917, the nomads were estimated at approximately 10 per cent of the population, semi-nomads at 30 per cent, and the rest of the population were classified as settled. A similar classification appeared in the 1964 census, in which 9 per cent of the population were classified as nomads, 12 per cent as semi-nomads, and 79 per cent as settled. According to a 1973 census, only 0.04 per cent of the population were classified as nomads, with 3.2 per cent as semi-nomads. The last official census was taken in 1995 and its definitive results put the population close to 4.5 million belonging to just over 700,000 families. Only 54 families were nomads and 284 families were semi-nomads (Attir, 1992: 225–230; Population Census of 1995).

Traditionally, the population in general has kept to their places of residence for many generations, and even the nomads and semi-nomads who moved to certain areas did not go far. However, two major events changed this pattern. The first was related to the Italian invasion, when thousands were forced to leave their usual homes. The second was the voluntary movement of thousands of people from rural areas to cities. Accordingly, the relationship between the rural and urban population has changed through time. During the early 1950s, three-quarters of the population were living in rural areas. By the 1964 census, the proportion of urban population had increased to 40 per cent. This percentage grew to 60 per cent in 1973 census. Today, close to 80 per cent of all Libyans live in urban centres, and more than half of them live in the two main cities of Tripoli and Benghazi (Attir, 1995:125–126).

Emancipation of women

Women in modern Libya enjoy an important social status. Fifty years ago, urban women were confined to their homes and had to wear the veil whenever they ventured out. Of course, rural settlements were organized along extended family and tribal lines and thus women were allowed to work in the fields in the company of male relatives. Most aspects of a woman's affairs were left to men: first the father, brother or cousin, then later the husband or son.

Basic women's rights were provided for in the Constitution and the laws of the newly independent state. Thus, women were granted equal rights to men in terms of education, equal pay for similar jobs, and equal rights to engage in different activities. However, this does not mean that all such rights are exercised in real life. Many traditional customs are still stronger than the law. The 1 September Revolution made the emancipation of women among its topmost priorities, and a plan was developed to fulfil such a priority. The first step was to implement the Law of Compulsory Education, which made it compulsory for all children – male and female – to attend nine years of schooling. The next step was to facilitate the entry of women into the job market, allowing them to work next to males, and to open all fields of work to women, including the police force and the army with all its specializations (Attir, 1985).

However, the single most important change lay in the field of education. Women's education prior to the second half of the 20th century was a subject that few dared discuss, but once the country became an independent state, education for both sexes was given utmost priority. Yet parents, in both urban and rural areas, remained suspicious and resisted the education of girls. As can be seen from Table 1.2.1, women's education lagged behind for many years. Finally, however, it moved rapidly ahead and bridged the gaps in the different educational levels.

During the 1950s and early 1960s, the percentage of women in elementary education was between 11 and 19 per cent. By the early

1970s, it rose to 37 per cent, and by 1990 it had rocketed to 48 per cent. Women's education scored the same success at all levels and types of education – for example, the percentage of women at university level developed from a low 3 per cent in 1961 to 8 per cent in 1966, then to 20 per cent in 1981 and to 43 per cent by 1996. Thus, even though women's education moved very slowly initially, the situation changed dramatically during the 1970s. By the mid-1980s, women's education was developing at full speed. By the early 1990s, the number of women at all levels of education became equal to the number of men.

Women working outside the home is a phenomena strongly associated with the expansion of modern education. In Libyan society, women, except in rural areas, rarely work away from home. Until the mid-1960s, only a small group of pioneers dared leave home to work as teachers or nurses. Gradually, however, increasing numbers of women began to work outside the home. By 1970, their proportion in the Libyan labour force reached 6 per cent. This percentage grew slowly to reach 11 per cent in 1980 and 22 per cent in 1996. No dramatic change in this respect is expected in the near future.

Relations between the sexes

Many laws have been passed to regulate modern relations between the sexes. Laws dealing with women's emancipation include their right to participate freely and equally in all legal, social, political and economic activities. Their right to choose a spouse or to request an ending of a marriage is guaranteed. Contrary to tradition, the family home belongs to the wife and thus, in the case of a divorce, it is the husband who has to leave and look for an alternative place to live. Polygamy is legal in Islam and was and still is widely practised in the Arab world. However, according to Libyan personal laws, a man can rarely take a second wife as he would even have to go so far as to secure the written approval of his first wife! According to traditional Islamic law, divorce is a simple practice and is among the privileges of husbands. A wife can be divorced if her husband says so, loudly, in front of two witnesses. Today, however, divorce is a very complicated issue. Both husband and wife have to file a complaint. There are lengthy legal procedures and the couple have to wait for a court decision.

References

Attir, Mustafa O. 'Ideology, Value Changes and Women's Social Position in Libyan Society' in Elizabeth Fernea, *Middle Eastern Women: New Voices of Change*, Austin: University of Texas Press, 1985.

Attir, Mustafa O. *The Road Toward Modernization of Libya: The Mixture of Old & New*, Beirut: Arab Development Institute, 1992.

Attir, Mustafa O. *Direction of Urbanization in the Arab Society*, Casablanca: Innovation Publishing Co, 1995.

General Secretariat for Education and Scientific Research (GSESR), *A Report on the Development of Education*, 1999.

National Authority for Information & Documentation, *Population Census of 1995*.

The International Bank for Reconstruction and Development, *The Economic Development of Libya*, Baltimore: Johns Hopkins University, 1960.

UNDP, *Human Development Report 2000*, New York: Oxford University Press, 2000.

1.3

The Current Status of Sanctions

David Sellers and Nanette Pilkington, Eversheds Frere Cholmeley, Paris

Introduction

Libya has been unique in the range of sanctions to which it has been subject. Like Iraq, it has been subject to stringent UN sanctions. Like Iran, it has been the subject of the US sanctions embodied in the Iran–Libya Sanctions Act (ILSA), also known as the D'Amato Act. The importance of these is that, although embodied only in US legislation, they are designed to affect US and non-US companies alike. Finally, Libya has been subject to a wide range of US sanctions since 1986, affecting only US companies and individuals (but also foreign subsidiaries of US parents and, for example, foreign branches of US banks).

This chapter looks briefly at each of these in turn with a view to (i) explaining their current status, and (ii) assessing to what degree they affect companies wishing to invest in Libya.

UN sanctions

Main elements

The UN sanctions against Libya imposed following the Lockerbie bombing in 1988 included the following:

- a flight ban, and restrictions on assistance (provision of spare parts, etc) to the Libyan aircraft industry;
- a ban on the sale of weapons and military assistance generally;
- a reduction of Libyan diplomatic missions and restrictions on their freedom of movement;

- an assets freeze;
- a prohibition on the financing of Libyan interests;
- prohibitions on the supply of certain pipeline and refinery equipment.

These sanctions are wide-ranging, but less elaborate than those that were imposed against Iraq. Indeed, some trade and some investment projects, particularly in the oil sector, were able to continue despite the sanctions. Moreover, an exception was made for sales of crude oil and petroleum products, providing payments were made into special bank accounts.

Conditions for suspension and lifting

The UN established certain conditions for the suspension and eventual lifting of sanctions, which was envisaged as a three-stage process. First, the UN made it clear that sanctions would be immediately suspended if the Lockerbie suspects were delivered for trial, and if the French judicial authorities were satisfied with regard to Libya's cooperation in their inquiries relating to the bombing of UTA 772 in 1989 over Niger.

Second, the UN provided for a 90-day period following suspension, by the end of which the Secretary-General was to report on Libya's compliance with a series of conditions.

These conditions are important. They did not simply cover surrender of the suspects for trial, but also required Libya *inter alia* to cooperate with the trial, pay compensation in the event that the suspects were found guilty, and, more generally, confirm the country's lack of support for terrorist actions.

Stage three would depend on the Secretary-General's findings – either a full lifting or, in the event of non-compliance, the UN reserved the right to take further measures against Libya.

Recent events

After several years of what seemed to be permanent deadlock, in August 1998 the proposal for trial in the Netherlands in what was effectively a Scottish court acting in accordance with Scottish law was accepted.

At the beginning of April 1999, after several months of negotiations to make this proposal concrete, the two suspects arrived in the Netherlands. Sanctions were duly suspended. Following the 90-day time limit, on 30 June the Secretary-General rendered his report, and on 9 July 1999 the Security Council welcomed Libya's 'satisfying progress' in complying with the UN Resolution, but did not formally lift the sanctions. Thus, the sanctions remained suspended.

The reasons why the sanctions were not formally lifted can be found in the Secretary-General's report. The Secretary-General noted first that the French were satisfied with regard to Libya's cooperation in their investigations into the UTA incident.

Second, he noted that Libya had given assurances at the highest level that it would cooperate in the trial and pay compensation in the event that the suspects were found guilty. However, he also noted the difficulty he found himself in in reporting on these aspects as, logically, full Libyan compliance could not be guaranteed until the trial was over.

Finally, he also noted Libya's assurances that it did not support terrorism, and the satisfaction of the French and British governments in this regard. However, he was also forced to note the United States' reservations in the same regard.

The US State Department made it clear that 'assurances were not enough' with regard to Libya's cooperation with the trial, payment of compensation and renunciation of terrorism. For the United States, 'suspension' has a legal significance. It is 'provisional', and thus not the equivalent of 'a clean bill of health'.

The trial ended in January 2001, with one suspect found guilty and the other acquitted, and an appeal court confirmed the sentence in March 2002.

The future

Sanctions have remained suspended since the end of the trial. Although it has been reported that Libya has declared itself ready to accept civil responsibility for the incident and to pay substantial compensation to the victims' families, no formal agreement has yet been reached. Reports suggest that if such agreement is reached, it is likely that the various sanctions will be lifted in different stages.

While sanctions are suspended, companies are effectively free to do business.

Iran–Libya Sanctions Act (ILSA)

Scope

The Iran–Libya Sanctions Act (ILSA), commonly known as the D'Amato Act after its main proponent Senator D'Amato, came into force in 1996. This Act targets Iran and Libya for their deemed support of terrorism and efforts to acquire weapons of mass destruction, and Libya specifically for its failure to comply with UN resolutions relating to Lockerbie. The importance of the Act is that it applies to any person, whether US national or otherwise, and whether present in the United States or not. The Act was due to expire in August 2001, but was renewed for a further five years until August 2006.

This Act originally made sanctionable any investment by any person (US national or otherwise) of US$40 million or more (or any combination of investments of at least US$10 million that equal or exceed US$40 million in any 12-month period), which 'directly and significantly contributes to the enhancement of Libya's ability to develop its petroleum resources'. This threshold has been decreased to US$20 million in the renewed Act.

The definition of 'investment' in the Act is rather wide. It covers agreements by 'any person' entered into with the government of Libya or a non-governmental entity in Libya dealing with the following activities:

- the entry into a contract which includes responsibility for the development of petroleum resources located in Libya;
- the entry into a contract providing for the general supervision and guarantee of another person's performance of such a contract;
- the purchase of a share of ownership, including equity interest, in that development;
- the entry into a contract providing for the participation in royalties, earnings or profits in that development, without regard to the form of the participation.

'Investment' does not, however, include 'the entry into, performance or financing of a contract to sell or purchase goods, services or technology'. Thus, the purchase of oil or gas from Libya is not a sanctioned activity in and of itself.

The Act provides that 'development' includes the exploration and extraction phase of petroleum operations, in addition to refining and transportation by pipeline.

If any person is found to have made any such 'sanctionable investment', at least two of a set of possible sanctions will be imposed. These include:

- denial of EXIM bank assistance for exports to the sanctioned person;
- restrictions on US exports to the sanctioned person;
- restrictions on loans by US financial institutions to the sanctioned person;
- special sanctions applicable to a sanctioned 'person' that is a financial institution;
- the US government will not procure from a sanctioned person;
- restrictions on imports from a sanctioned person.

International opposition

ILSA has been widely condemned in the international community. Its extraterritorial element – the application of US law to non-US entities carrying out business outside the United States – is considered illegal in international law. It has also been seen as contrary to free trade rules and both the EU and Canada have threatened WTO proceedings if the United States were ever to seek to apply the Act against their nationals.

The EU has put into place a blocking statute calling on EU companies not to comply with the Act.

ILSA in practice

It is questionable, however, how effective ILSA can be in the long run against non-US companies. EU opposition forced the United States to back down in considering sanctions against a very significant investment by Total, Gazprom and Petronas in Iran. In April 1998, an understanding was announced between the EU and the United States in which the US administration made it clear that the president would use his special authority to waive the application of sanctions against these companies on the basis that it was contrary to US national interests. This authority is enshrined in Section 9(c) of ILSA and may be the pattern for future investments in Iran and Libya.

The future

The current expectation is that ILSA may be reviewed if an agreement is reached with regard to the acceptance of responsibility and the payment of compensation in connection with the Lockerbie incident.

Other US sanctions

US sanctions have been in force since 1986 in response to Libya's deemed involvement in terrorism. They are draconian (with criminal penalties for breach) and wide-ranging, covering all US nationals and prohibiting almost any kind of transaction.

It is these sanctions that remain most relevant for US companies and make the return of such companies to Libya almost impossible. They remain relevant to non-US companies in a number of ways: they affect any US national wherever located; and they affect foreign subsidiaries of US parents unless no US national or resident has any role in the relevant transaction (although it should be noted that facilitating actions by a US parent of a foreign subsidiary would remain subject to the various prohibitions).

The prohibitions are very wide-ranging and cover:

- imports and exports;
- financing by US banks, including foreign branches of US banks;
- any contracts, loans or transactions with Libyan entities, or which benefit Libyan entities directly or indirectly;
- travel restrictions.

1.4

Establishing a Presence

Bill Wilkinson, Consultancy Support Ltd, UK

This section has been written to offer help to those wishing to find new contacts, or re-establish old ones, in Libya. There are other sections of this book that cover the legal aspects of working in Libya, so we would like to offer a few words to help the reader understand more about establishing those all-important new contacts.

History

Libya has a long history of international trading and providing a bridgehead between sub-Saharan Africa and the seafaring nations of Europe. The legacies of ventures past are scattered across the whole of Libya and are well worth visiting in off-duty moments. Historically, travellers from the West Coast of Africa used the coastal fringe as their favoured East–West route; today we can recommend that any visiting executive adds a refreshing dip in the sea to their travel schedule.

Although Libya has many historical links with Europe, the people, products and environment on both sides have changed considerably in recent years. We hope the following will encourage the reader to take a fresh look at the opportunities for developing strong and healthy business links with Libya.

The current situation

Libya has emerged strong and healthy from the sanctions era: sanctions have in effect strengthened the country's self-sufficiency and national pride. Today, the Jamahiriya has two focuses of attention: modernization of all industrial sectors and a commitment to African unity. Libya sees its geographical position – as the gateway for Europe–Africa trade – as essential in helping to generate economic growth in other African states.

Although oil and gas drive the Libyan economy, there are numerous other natural resources ready for exploitation. The energy sector conducts its business in a professional and modern manner and energy projects enjoy much higher priority than those in other sectors. In the non-energy sectors you will find a mix of management expertise and ability: some managers will have made significant achievements within the strict budget controls imposed upon them, but many are less motivated than their energy sector counterparts.

Newcomers and those wishing to re-establish old links in Libya should not be misled into thinking they have to follow the traditional methods of their predecessors to establish new business there. Modern thinking and practices are evident in many areas.

Finally, you should keep in mind the following facts:

- Libya has no overseas debt and has large overseas investments.
- Fifty per cent of the 6 million population are currently undertaking some form of education in a system mainly based on that of the United Kingdom.
- The majority of senior and aspiring managers have been educated abroad; many completed their higher education and professional training in the UK.

Where to find information

For the British, a good place to start gathering information is the Libya desk at the UK government's Trade Partners UK (who have also sponsored this book). The Trade Partners UK Web site – www.tradepartners.gov.uk – will help to identify trade associations, chambers of commerce and trade mission organizers who are active in the region. Few investors rely entirely on the written word, so why not pick up the phone and talk to your counterparts in the businesses known to be working there? We have found there is great camaraderie between people working in the Libyan market. The London-based Middle East Association provides excellent opportunities for meeting politicians, finance house personnel and businesspeople who are actively involved in Libya. There are several Web sites providing up-to-the-minute information relating to Libyan current affairs and culture.

Many governments have reopened embassies in Tripoli. An evening's stroll around the shopping streets and upmarket restaurants will bring you into contact with overseas contractors and other resident or visiting businesspeople. Libya has recently developed a habit of looking for what it wants and then building alliances outside its borders. The net result is an increasing number of contracts being signed at the end of high-profile trade visits either to or from Libya. The message here is to do your homework, identify and use every access point available to you and do not rely too heavily on local diplomatic patronage.

Making the first contact

Writing unsolicited letters or faxes asking for invitations can be a very unproductive activity. Reverse the roles and you know how you would react to such an approach! If you don't already have an invitation to visit Libya, you can often take advantage of a trade mission or similar organized business trip to make the first contacts. We participated in the last two Britain and Libya: Partners in Progress exhibitions in Tripoli and were impressed by the interest generated and the valuable contacts made.

Since presenting similar ideas in the first edition of this book, we have noticed a lessening of Libyan interest in non-specialist or poorly targeted trade missions. Consider the relatively small number of Libyan decision-makers who can attend missions and the number of outward missions per year planned from your own country and others; subtract holidays (both formal and informal) and Libya's own outward missions programme, and you will start to understand the decline in enthusiasm. Slow decision-making and limited tangible outcomes are additional causes for frustration.

Current market opportunities

If you are looking to compete for tenders, then Internet-based bulletin boards and specialist publications will provide leads. But an active in-country agent may win more business for you.

If you are introducing a new product or service, you will need to do more groundwork yourself. No one else will have a better understanding of what you are offering or looking for than yourself, so ideally you should initially talk direct to your customers.

Personal contact

If your interests lie in the more modern technology sectors, such as IT and the Internet, which are now blossoming in Libya, you may well find yourself dealing with young technocrats who are extremely well educated and upwardly mobile.

There are many new and second-generation traders in white goods, fashion accessories and a full range of domestic products that can offer advice based on their experience of trading in Libya, as importers. Valuable information can be extracted from every conversation you have – but only you can decide its value to your business.

The Libyan people, with very few exceptions, are among the most open and friendly we have met. One should, however, take care to apply a liberal pinch of salt to some claims of 'having good connections' and keep an open mind when criticisms are made of 'the system'. You will meet the whole range of expert critics, fence-sitters and enthusiasts as you sift through your new contacts and it is up to you to decide whom to take note of, whom to ignore and whom to cultivate.

Be wary of anyone whose opinions are rooted in the past – we regularly encounter such characters, both inside and outside Libya. By all means sift through their dialogue for its historical interest and regional trends, but to make business judgements based on such guidance alone would be folly. Be assured that the desire for and pace of change in Libya is accelerating. The Libyans have several unique challenges to resolve before they will be able to meet international expectations in every sector.

No one Arab community is like another. Each has its own idiosyncrasies. But Libya has a particularly distinctive social, political and business climate that should be understood before embarking irrevocably on any serious business initiative.

To date, we have yet to meet anyone who has misrepresented himself or herself or been less than open and honest with us. Indeed, during a recent exhibition in Tripoli, one young man asked for help importing printing equipment and materials. After gentle interrogation we were able to persuade him to use his budding entrepreneurial talents in some form of legal enterprise, rather than to risk his freedom printing counterfeit money. 'I want to make millions of dollars,' he said. That, we found, was very honest!

Keeping in touch

Keeping in touch can be a very one-sided and frustrating activity but it is very important. Faxed messages seem to take precedence over letter writing and Libyans have a habit of replying to correspondence only when they see the need. If you do not get a reply, it does not imply any discourtesy, merely that they have nothing to say at this time. Be assured that when they want to contact you, they will.

It is sometimes difficult to get telephone and fax connections routed through British landline systems. Whether this is because of restrictions in the UK or Libya we are not sure, but be patient, check your numbers and try again when there is less demand or when you know someone is there to answer you.

Libya is a potentially lucrative market for European goods and services. Now sanctions are being lifted, it is well worth exploring.

Appointing an agent

The same basic rules apply for appointing an agent in Libya as elsewhere. Be careful, take your time and, above all, follow your instincts. An assortment of professionals, 'wannabes', bullies and agency collectors will present themselves to you at some time or other. What you are looking for is someone who already has the knowledge, resources, contacts and attributes to match your requirements and who can demonstrate current ability to deliver.

I was attending a Middle East Association function recently and was asked by a prominent international executive if I could assist his team to make a new start in Libya. They had until now relied on a large UK partner company with 'the best connections in Libya' to make all the moves and win contracts, but, sadly, after four years the results were zero. When I followed up our conversation a few days later, he reported that they had started to win small but important contracts through a subsidiary working with a less prominent, but obviously very effective, local agent. Keep your agency business simple, direct and free from corruption and you will be well rewarded.

Conclusion

In conclusion, we suggest you do not pay too much heed to the melodramatic reports of yesterday's Libya. While the new government is still being installed, we can see significant decisions being made and changes being implemented that will be good for investment and for the economy.

Go and see Libya as it is today. Who knows? You may be joining the growing number of new entrants to the market that come away with instant success. The worst that can happen is that, like us, you will have to make several visits before finding that success – but believe me, visiting Libya is always a pleasure.

1.5

The Libyan Economy and International Trade Relations

Marat Terterov

Introduction

The Libyan economy is dominated by the hydrocarbons sector, which accounts for one-third of national output and generates more than 95 per cent of total foreign exchange earnings. However, this sector provides employment for only about 2 per cent of the country's workforce of some 1.2 million. The service industry contributes an equal share in GDP, while the contribution of agriculture has remained negligible, despite government efforts to promote this sector and achieve self-sufficiency in food production. Libya has a comparatively high GDP per caput, of approximately US$7,500 per year.

Exploitation of major oil and gas reserves has formed the backbone of the Libyan economy for the past 40 years. This has led to significant development in other sectors of the economy, although investment in all sectors has been undermined by seven years of UN sanctions (1992–99), which led to periodic shortages of basic goods and food inside the country. Libya's large oil exports, not interrupted by the sanctions regime, ensured the country's economic survival during the 1990s. Infrastructure deficiencies are now being addressed on a large scale with the installation of a railway system, gas distribution network and, most prominently, the US$30 billion Great Man-Made River (GMR) project designed to deliver sub-Saharan water resources to inhabited northern areas. Some industrial diversification into petrochemicals, iron, aluminium and steel has been realized, but often through extensive government subsidization, such as the steel complex at Misratah.

The suspension of UN sanctions in April 1999, combined with the US maintenance of the Iran–Libya Sanctions Act (ILSA) of 1996, provides a unique opportunity for non-US oil and gas majors to participate in highly prospective Libyan acreage without competition from US firms. The seven-year period of UN sanctions initiated in 1992 is reported to have cost Libya US$26 billion in hydrocarbon revenues. The low Libyan operating-cost profile and ready access to European markets make Libya one of the oil industry's most attractive development prospects. Unlike its ambivalence towards foreign investment in general, the Libyan government has fostered stability in this critical sector. Foreign direct investment (FDI) in energy is expected to be directed towards downstream projects.

Economic policy

From early 1988, Libya moved towards liberalization of its economy, exemplified by the greater scope allowed to private enterprise in the retail trade, and to small-scale industries and agricultural businesses. However, the abolition of state export and import companies remains confined to trade in consumer goods, while large-purchase items such as cars are still controlled by state purchasing companies. In September 1992, a Privatization Law was passed providing for the sale of state assets to private interests and for private sector participation in the economy. To date, however, little progress has been made in implementing the new law. In essence, the template for economic development remains the 'Green Book' written by Libyan Leader Muammar Qadhafi. (See Appendix 4.) A number of sources suggest that the Libyan leadership's emphasis on a shifting, primarily external, political focus and reluctance to develop the private sector are constraining substantial economic potential following the suspension of debilitating UN sanctions in 1999.

A wide range of reform measures will be necessary to stimulate the Libyan economy to achieve its potential. Banking and investment regulatory reform, alteration to tax rates, trade laws and incentives for further exploitation of energy resources are envisioned. The inadequate legal structure, bureaucracy and unpredictable government decision-making process continue to place limitations on development, particularly with a view to attracting foreign investment in the non-hydrocarbons sector.

The government's primary objective is to improve agricultural self-sufficiency once the benefits of the GMR water project are realized. Additional areas for future development are tourism, fisheries and Africa–Europe transit industries. Since the suspension of UN sanctions, Libya has actively sought greater economic cooperation with a wide range of nations, of which one of the most promising near-term partners appears to be Russia. However, disputed Libyan debts of between US$3 billion and US$4 billion for prior military obligations from Russia may somewhat limit the extent of cooperation between the two countries.

Economic performance

Really up-to-date statistics for Libya are hard to come by. We do know that the economy revived in mid-1999 in direct correlation to the rise in world oil prices. Oil revenues of US$5.6 billion in 1998, a year in which the economy contracted by 1 per cent, more than doubled to an estimated US$12 billion in 1999. Libya's GDP grew by about 2 per cent in 1999, and real growth was estimated at 6.2 per cent in 2000. GDP was US$32.3 billion in 1998 according to the government, but is likely to be considerably higher in purchasing power parity terms, estimated by some economists to be approximately US$55 billion in 2000. Increasing government consumption probably slowed growth to around 5.5 per cent in 2001 and 4.8 per cent in 2002. Inflation, which was estimated at approximately 18–25 per cent in 1999, most probably fell to an estimated 12 per cent in 2000–01 and around 10 per cent in 2002 as goods which were in short supply under UN sanctions became increasingly available.

The Libyan Government has managed to avoid accumulating large external debts and long-term borrowing. Non-military foreign debt stood at US$2.6 billion in 1997 and US$3.8 billion in 1998, rising to an estimated US$4–5 billion at the end of 2000.

Foreign reserves fell from US$14 billion in 1981 to US$3.8 billion in 1998, before rising to US$4 billion at the end of 1999, and were estimated at US$7.2 billion at the end of 2000, excluding frozen assets in the United States. These reserves are managed abroad and investments include those in international financial institutions, real estate, other productive assets, and in petroleum refining and marketing operations abroad.

The budget

Much authority over budgets has been delegated to Sha'biyat (regional authorities), but there is still central control of various services. The government budget for 2000 aimed for a balanced fiscal account and provided for a cut in recurrent spending in the main budget, from US$7.6 billion in 1999 to US$6.7 billion in 2000. This reduction in expenditure is more than offset by a doubling of the development budget. On the revenue side, the contribution of oil to spending is reduced, to be compensated for by an increase in income and other taxes.

It is clear that oil will continue to provide the bulk of government revenue. The reforms may prove politically sensitive, both in terms of a change to taxes and because a large part of the population relies on public-sector wages and state subsidies for its relatively comfortable standard of living. The authorities are likely to reverse expenditure cuts if there are signs of concerted political resistance.

Balance of payments

Supported by import restrictions, Libya has managed a steady nominal merchandise trade surplus in recent years. The current account slipped into deficit in 1998 due to low oil prices, but rebounded in 1999 with a surplus of US$2.1 billion. The current account registered a further surplus of US$3.2 billion (6.7 per cent of GDP) in 2000, declining to US$268 million (0.5 per cent of GDP) in 2001. Conversely, the capital account has deteriorated sharply since posting its last surplus in 1996 to a deficit of slightly more than US$1 billion in 2000.

Libya has suffered negative annual FDI of between US$80 million and US$150 million during recent years (Tables 1.5.1 and 1.5.2). Portfolio investment activity is minimal. The balance of visible trade will continue to have the most significant impact on the current account.

Table 1.5.1 The FDI outflow, 1989–2000 (US$ million)

1989–94	1995	1996	1997	1998	1999	2000
-47	83	63	282	304	226	271

Source: Adapted from The United Nations World Investment Report (2001: 296)

Table 1.5.2 The FDI inflow, 1985–2000 (US$ million)

1985–95	1996	1997	1998	1999	2999
25.2	–134.9	-82.0	–151.9	–128.1	0.0

Source: UNCTAD, FDI/TNC Database

Foreign trade

Libya reported a trade surplus of US$3 billion in 1999 and between US$1 billion and US$2 billion in the previous two years. Libya's main trade partners are Italy, making up about 40 per cent of the export market and 18 per cent of the imports, Germany with 20 per cent and 12 per cent, France with 7 per cent and 4 per cent, and the United Kingdom with 6.5 per cent and 3 per cent. Other sources of imports are Tunisia (5 per cent) and Belgium (4 per cent), while Sudan accounts for a further 4 per cent of exports. The distribution between products is uneven, although dominated by petroleum exports to Europe and imports of technology products. Sanctions caused a shift over to imports from other countries (eg China), although Libya is closely tied to its neighbours in the Arab Maghreb Union (AMU), which also includes Algeria, Morocco, Tunisia and Mauritania.

The UN-imposed embargo had a sharp effect on non-oil-industry-related trade. Libya's economically vital oil industry was largely exempt from the embargo, although imports of oil maintenance supplies have been insufficient, as the country is heavily reliant on US-manufactured oil industry spares and equipment. In November 1999, the United States modified its unilateral economic sanctions to allow for commercial exports of food, medicine and medical equipment. After the suspension of UN sanctions there is political will to strengthen trading ties with sub-Saharan African countries, partly in gratitude for political support.

Libya is presently being courted by invitations and high-level delegations from Japan, Russia, Italy, the United Kingdom, France, South Africa, Malaysia, China and Saudi Arabia, among others. Russia is keen to resolve the issue of Libya's debt (incurred as a result of military aid) so that trade can flow more freely. Italy wrote off US$260 million of debt in October 2000, reportedly in compensation for the country's actions during the period of harsh colonial rule. Malaysia has suggested that Libya might become involved in making car components and selling the Proton car in Libya. The Kuwait-based Arab Fund for Economic and Social Development has lent Libya US$81 million (at 4.5 per cent annual interest, for a period of 22 years, with a five-year grace period) to increase and improve production in the industrial, services and other sectors of the Libyan economy. This deal brings total loans so far extended to Libya by the Arab Fund to approximately US$350 million.

Libya: macroeconomic activity

Table 1.5.3 Real GDP per capita

	1995	1996	1997	1998	1999
Real GDP (million 1995 US$)	36,453	36,891	37,370	36,249	36,974
Total population (million, mid-year average)	4.654	4.686	4.760	4.875	4.993
Real GDP per capita (1995 US$ per capita)	7,832	7,872	7,851	7,436	7,405

Table 1.5.4 Global ranking

GDP (million 1995 US$)		Population (million)		GDP per capita (1995 US$)	
Rank	**1999 GDP**	**Rank**	**1999 Population**	**Rank**	**1999 GDP per capita**
70	36,974	106	4.993	57	7,405

Table 1.5.5 Economic overview

Currency	Libyan Dinar (LD)
Exchange rate (1 August 2003)	US$1 = LD 1.21; EU1 = 1.36; GBP 1 = 1.94
Gross domestic product (GDP)	(2000E): US$55.1 billion
Real GDP growth rate	(1999E): 2%; (2000E): 5%
Inflation rate	(Consumer prices, 1999E): 18%; (2000E): 12%
Unemployment rate (1998E)	around 30%
Current account balance (1999E)	–0.35 billion
Major trading partners	Italy, Germany, United Kingdom, France, Turkey, Greece, Spain
Merchandise exports	(1999E): US$13.4 billion; (2000E): US$14.2 billion
Merchandise imports	(1999E): US$11.4 billion; (2000E): US$12.1 billion
Merchandise trade balance	(1999E): US$2 billion; (2000E): US$2.1 billion
Major export products	Crude oil, refined petroleum products, natural gas
Major import products	Machinery, transport equipment, food, manufactured goods
Total external debt (non-military) (1998E)	US$3.8 billion
International reserves (2000E)	US$7.2 billion

Table 1.5.6 General statistics

Life expectancy at birth (1999)	70.3 years
Total population (1998 est)	5.3 million
Forecast population, 2015	7.6 million
Annual population growth rate (1975–99):	3.1%
Urban population (1999)	87.2%
Urban population (2015 est)	90.3%
Population aged 60 and over (1999)	3.3%
Population aged 60 and over (2015 est)	5.1%
Doctors per 100,000 people (1990–99 avge)	128
Nurses per 100,000 people (1992–95 avge)	334
Adult literacy rate (1999)	79.1%
Combined primary, secondary and tertiary education enrolment rate (1999)	92%
International travel departures per '000 (1997–98 avge)	650
Telephone lines per '000	84
Cellular mobile subscribers per '000 (1996–98 avge)	3
Television sets per '000 (1996–98 avge)	143
Per capita electricity consumption (kilowatt-hours, 1980)	1,588
Per capita electricity consumption (kilowatt-hours, 1997)	3,677

Sources for all tables: US CIA *World Factbook*, IMF *World Outlook*, US Census Bureau International Database, UN *Statistical Yearbook*, CountryWatch.com calculations

1.6

Business Culture

Hakim Nageh, Sahara (International Consulting) Libya

Historical perspective

The name 'Libya' is among the oldest geographic denominations in antiquity. According to the Greek writer Herodotus, it referred to almost the whole of Africa.

Over the millennia, a number of civilizations have lived in what is today known as Libya. The Gannant people were the desert-dwellers whose civilization reached its apogee about 4,000 to 6,000 years ago. They developed administrative and transport systems designed to enhance trade with their African neighbours, the Egyptians and, later, the Romans.

The Romans maintained trading points along the Libyan coast, such as Sabratha and Leptis Magna. Trading paths led from Sabratha to the Phoenician town of Carthage (in Tunisia), and caravans left from Ghadames to other African towns. The Greeks founded the trading base of Cyrenaica in eastern Libya, engaging in trade with Athens and neighbouring Egypt, as well as with other Greek towns in the Mediterranean region.

Both during the height of Islamic civilization and during the time of Byzantine rule, cities such as Tripoli, Benghazi, Misurata and Ghadames were thriving trading posts. Huge fleets protected the trade routes in the Mediterranean Sea. Being positioned in the middle of the Arab-Islamic world – between Mashreq and Maghreb – the region known today as Libya fulfilled the role of a trading bridge between Chad, Sudan, Niger, Mali and the remaining Islamic regions, as well as the Mediterranean.

During Italian colonial rule, the green coastal belt served as a granary for Rome. After independence in 1951, the country was locked in a developmental impasse, which was overcome with the discovery of oil reserves and the start of oil exports. Since then, the country has developed its oil industry and, with the support of foreign technology and know-how, has built up an enormous infrastructure. Libya has also launched an educational offensive both within the country and abroad.

Cultural tourism

Originally, the idea of fostering tourism sprang from the need to reduce Libya's dependence on oil. Given neighbouring countries' negative socio-cultural and ecological experiences of mass tourism, Libya decided to concentrate on cultural tourism, leading to meaningful exchange between different cultures.

Libyan tourism specialists are predicting an increase in tourist numbers over the next few years, in particular those interested in visiting the archaeological sites. There has also been a rise in business and conference tourism.

In order to be able to cater to this demand, it is necessary to expand the existing infrastructure. Many investment opportunities can be found in such areas as hotel construction close to ancient sites, and in health tourism. Businesspeople who come to Libya for a few days are well advised to relax in the Roman cities near Tripoli and the Greek ones close to Benghazi.

Libyan national character

Libyans are known for their hospitality, sociability, adaptability and flexibility – all features that have their roots in the nomadic-Arabic past. They communicate easily and pay much attention to communication and verbal agreement. The family is of great importance to the individual. There are many small family enterprises. The importance of belonging to a social group is reflected in all levels of social and professional life. Usually, Libyans can be met in small or large groups in cafés, clubs, the working environment and parties. They are very proud of their historic achievements, their struggle against Italian colonial fascism and their independence.

Work culture

Libya's work culture is very different from that of Western Europe and the United States. As is the norm in Arab and Mediterranean countries, meetings do not start immediately with the first point on the work agenda; first, there will be an element of small talk, something to eat – and only then will work commence.

Planning is short-term, pragmatic and not fully strategy oriented. Only when it comes to large-scale projects will there be strategic thinking.

Because of the Libyans' propensity to act within groups, business does depend on friendship and, indeed, is geared towards generating friendly relations among people. In such an environment, trust and reliability are important factors: riding roughshod over them may endanger the successful completion of any business venture.

Working hours differ between the public and private sector. In the former, working hours are 8 am to 2 pm (winter) and 7.30 am to 2.30 pm (summer). In the private sector they may be 8 am to 2 pm and 4–6 pm or 9 am to 2 pm and 3–8 pm.

Despite assertive leadership in some enterprises and administrative boards, employees tend to enjoy a great deal of freedom. The leadership styles of higher-ranking personnel who have studied abroad, or who have management experience, reflect their British, German, Italian or American training. Because of the traditional unity of the family and of groups, Libyans are equipped with a high degree of social competence and the ability to think collectively. This makes the establishment of teamwork in firms and the public administration easier.

As regards day-to-day communication, the exchange of information between employees or private enterprises is mostly informal. This is not the case with state entities, which follow formal and bureaucratic procedures – a fact that demands patience and perseverance. Flexibility is an important element of the Libyan professional world – as it is in Africa and the Mediterranean generally. Specialization is common among both employees and firms; indeed, it is regarded as a factor for success.

Local–regional outlook

Libyan society holds local cultural traditions in high esteem. Foreign businesspeople, and tourists, are expected to respect the prevalent cultural-religious values. On a regional level, Libya's strategic orientation towards African countries represents an important element in its trade relations. There are many examples of successful business ventures and projects between Libya and African nations. Moreover, Libya is keen to promote and participate in foreign investment elsewhere in Africa. During a summit meeting with European heads of state, Qadhafi has made it clear that Libya is interested in promoting joint European–Libyan investment in Africa.

Global outlook

The volume of international business communication and information exchange has been continually increasing over the past few years, as has the number of international economic conferences dealing with African economic integration and foreign investment in Libya. One example was the international conference on emerging markets held in Tripoli in November 2000. A similar event took place in London in July 2001. In addition, a number of new business fairs are being held, such as the International Tripoli Fair held in 2000 and 2001. A number of foreign business delegations have also visited Libya during the past year or two.

Numerous Internet sites concerned with Libya and its business affairs, economic institutions and private enterprises have been created. Through encounters with tourists, foreign business, study programmes abroad and work, most Libyans have come into contact with foreigners. In particular, long-term study visits to Europe and the United States serve to transfer knowledge and experience back to the home country. This constitutes one of Libya's great potentials: its people are ambassadors of global culture, management and science, capable of globalizing local knowledge and culture without losing sight of their roots.

Qualifications and international cooperation

There is a close relationship between the quantity and quality of economic actors and the chance for success in international economic cooperation. Libya's educational system has been upgraded by means of a broad expansion of school and university education, as well as the creation of other institutes. Moreover, this large educational campaign includes sending Libyan students and postgraduates abroad. The aim is to increase the number of highly qualified professionals in all sectors. Compared with the rest of North Africa, Libya has the highest number of academically trained and highly qualified citizens.

Many Libyans have completed study programmes at well-known foreign universities; they are well educated, but not sufficiently well trained, in particular with regard to management and leadership techniques. New investors are therefore well advised to equip their projects with a training strategy in order to enhance the chance of success of joint ventures. There is a shortage of competent, technically trained employees. Vocational training needs to be modernized in terms of curricula and learning techniques.

Development and culture-oriented investment

International investors will encounter a highly attractive market in Libya's oil, gas and agricultural sectors, natural resources, infrastructure expansion, telecommunications, education and tourism. Legislative security and guarantees, such as those accorded to investors under Law no. 5 of 1997 (Encouragement of Foreign Capital Investment, see Appendix 2), are geared towards creating a profitable, low-tax environment for foreign investors. Moreover, the rights of investors are internationally safeguarded. However, it is important that foreign businesspeople respect the following ethical and cultural aspects:

- acceptance of the relationship between investment and development;
- integration of training measures into project planning and implementation;
- ecological soundness of investment projects;
- rejection of corruption;
- reinvestment of part of the profits obtained in the Libyan market;
- integration and support of domestic economic sectors;
- adaptation of management and leadership style to the domestic national and business culture.

1.7

Practical Reasons for Investing in Libya: Incentives and Guarantees

Eversheds and Mukhtar, Kelbash & Elgharabli

While the United States' unilateral sanctions regime remains in place, European companies have been quick to seize the opportunity offered by the suspension in 1999 of UN sanctions against Libya. Libya's infrastructure suffered considerably during the sanctions period, but now offers significant opportunities for foreign investors. A five-year development plan of US$35 billion has been announced, identifying significant priority areas for investment, including water projects, oil and gas, electricity and power generation, transport (including roads, airport infrastructure, aircraft, ports and marine fleets and railways) and telecommunications.

In the United Kingdom, the Department of Trade and Industry strongly supports companies investing in Libya and it is generally perceived that Libya represents a good investment opportunity for UK companies.

Incentives to investment

Foreign investment in Libya is governed by two sets of legislation: one for the oil sector and one for other sectors. Investment in the oil sector is governed by Petroleum Law no. 25 of 1955, as amended, and various decrees, regulations and ordinances issued under it, including Decree no. 10 of 1979, which reorganized the National Oil Corporation of Libya (NOC). This is more fully discussed in Chapter 3.2. Investment outside the oil sector is governed by the Foreign Capital Investment Encouragement Law no. 5 of 1997 (Foreign Investment Law) and the related executive regulation which has the aim of attracting foreign capital to investment projects within the framework of the general policy of the State and objectives of economic and social development. In addition, further incentives to investment are to be found in certain legislation on specific subjects such as the Law on Free Zones and various customs regulations.

Foreign Investment Law

Article 8 of the Foreign Investment Law lists the sectors to which the Law is applicable. The oil sector is not included in the list, which comprises the industrial, health, tourism, service and agricultural sectors and any other sector that may be determined by a decision of the General People's Committee upon a proposal by the secretary for planning, economy and commerce. Article 26 of the Law expressly states that it shall not apply to foreign capital invested in petroleum projects, both upstream and downstream. This is because it is believed that the oil sector has already established a regime that provides all necessary incentives. However, companies that are involved in the provision of services to the oil sector, but which are not directly related to exploration or production of oil or gas, may come within the ambit of the Foreign Investment Law. For example, a company manufacturing drilling rigs might be considered as belonging to the industrial sector rather than to the oil sector.

Projects coming within the ambit of the Law enjoy various advantages, including customs and tax exemptions:

1. Exemption from customs duties, fees or taxes on the importation of everything required for the project, including machinery, instruments, materials, spare parts and raw materials.
2. Free export of all products involved with the project.
3. Exemption from stamp duty on all commercial documents.
4. A five-year exemption from income tax.

All of the above advantages are also enjoyed by any reinvested profits.

5. Repatriation of profits.
6. Ownership and/or leasing of real estate as required for the construction and operation of the project.
7. Repatriation of the invested capital upon expiry of the project's period, its liquidation, the sale of the project, or after a lapse of at least five years from the date of the granting of the licence.
8. Repatriation of the uninvested capital after a lapse of at least six months from the date of transfer if the investor can prove that he or she was unable to invest because he or she was unable to attain a

licence, or where circumstances beyond his or her control prevented the investment (eg non-availability of water or electricity).

9. If the investment involves the establishment of a company in Libya, such a company is exempt from the usual requirements regarding registration with the Commercial Register and the Ministry of Economy and Commerce.
10. The investor is entitled to employ and import the foreign manpower and technical expertise necessary for the establishment and operation of the project.

Applications for investment projects to come under the ambit of the Foreign Investment Law can be submitted to the Foreign Investment Board directly or through any Libyan People's Bureau (embassy). The applications are then referred by the Foreign Investment Board along with their recommendations to the General People's Committee for Economy and Commerce for approval before the Foreign Investment Board can issue authorization for the investment project.

A number of projects are now established under the Foreign Investment Law, despite the complexity of the investment approval process and certain lacunae in the law. At present, there are a number of proposals to issue new regulations to fill some of these lacunae. In particular, the Executive Regulation of the Law is under review with the aim of amending it to accommodate some of the concerns expressed by potential investors, and the Law itself may also be changed in the same direction.

Import/export and customs legislation

The Government has recently announced the formation of a special team to reconsider customs legislation for the purpose of promoting investments.

Under the current general legislation, which applies to sectors not covered by the special regime of the Foreign Investment Law or the regime for petroleum projects, personal goods, including furniture, may be imported into Libya without duty but within a certain limit as to value. In certain cases, an import licence may be required, but this is easy to obtain, especially if there is no concomitant transfer of funds from Libya.

Petroleum and its derivatives may be exported free of duty. The re-export of any goods that have been imported free of duty is also free of duty, provided that certain formalities are complied with.

Transit trade and free zones law

Although a law establishing free zones dates back to 1959, it was only recently that such a zone was established adjacent to Misurata port, which is a busy port located 220 kilometres east of Tripoli.

Law no. 9 of 2000 for the Transit Trade and Free Zones provides that free zones are established by a decision of the General People's Committee and are managed by the Administration for Free Zones. The following activities may be exercised in free zones:

1. Storing of transit goods and goods ready for export.
2. Sorting, cleaning, mixing and repackaging of goods as required for trading.
3. Any manufacturing, assembly and commissioning of goods as required by free zone operations.
4. Such professions as are required by activities and services in free zones. These include banking, insurance and other services. In addition, terminals and airports may be established in free zones.

All licensed activities and investments within a free zone enjoy the same benefits and exemptions as provided for by the Foreign Investment Law above.

Intellectual property

The various Libyan laws relating to intellectual property are currently under review. Until such a review and accompanying updating has occurred, foreign investors should be aware that, while laws do exist concerning the protection of trade marks, patents, industrial drawings and models, and copyright, only patent law has really been developed and is enforced in Libya.

Support services

Foreign Investment Board

Article 6 of the Foreign Investment Law and Executive Regulation 186 of 1998 pursuant to the Foreign Investment Law set out the role of the Foreign Investment Board. Article 6 states that the Board is to work for the encouragement of foreign capital investment and the promotion of investment projects by various means. The Board provides support to foreign investors in Libya by supervising all investments which come under the ambit of the Law. It also recommends exemptions, facilities or other benefits for projects that are considered important for the development of the national economy. It considers the petition and litigation of complaints or disputes lodged by investors relating to the application of the Foreign Investment Law. More generally, it is useful for foreign investors as it gathers and publishes information and conducts economic studies relevant to potential investments in projects that contribute to national economic development.

Banking and project financing

Following a recent development in Libyan law, private individuals and companies may now hold accounts in foreign currency as well as Libyan dinars with Libyan commercial banks.

Although foreign banks are now permitted to open representative offices or branches in Libya, no branches have been opened to date.

Until recently, project financing in Libya has been somewhat limited, but it now appears to have begun to take off. Both ABC and APICORP have provided financing for projects in Libya. Islamic project financing is practised by some Islamic banks from the Gulf and the Islamic Bank of Development. Under such schemes, the lender takes a part of the profit in lieu of interest, or, where a procurement contract is involved, it buys the material in its own name and then sells it on with a mark-up.

Investment guarantees

Constitution and quasi-constitutional legislation

While the Constitution does not provide for specific investment guarantees, it does provide that no tax will be imposed or modified except in accordance with the law, and that expropriation will take place only in accordance with the law. It further provides for independent judicial protection of rights. The 1988 Charter on Human Rights provides that 'Property is sacred and protected; it may not be touched save in the public interest and against fair compensation'. Similarly, Law no. 20 of 1991 (Enhancement of Freedom) provides that private property cannot be confiscated except in the public interest and with fair compensation.

Foreign Investment and Free Zones Laws

For projects falling under the Foreign Investment Law of 1997, investors are protected against arbitrary expropriation, etc, and are entitled to fair and immediate compensation in the event of nationalization or expropriation. A similar provision for fair compensation is contained in the Free Zones Law of 2000.

Guarantee organizations

The Multilateral Investment Guarantee Agency (MIGA) of the World Bank can provide coverage against non-commercial risks, such as transfer restrictions preventing investors from converting local currencies into foreign exchange or transferring capital or dividends abroad, expropriation (including nationalization and 'creeping' expropriation), breach of contract by the host government, and war and civil disturbance resulting in the destruction, damage or disappearance of tangible assets. Such insurance is available to cover new investments and the expansion, modernization or privatization of existing investments in Libya. Eligible investments include equity, commercial bank loans, shareholder loans, technical assistance and management contracts, originating in any other MIGA member country (MIGA members include all EU member states).

Guarantees against political risk, etc are also available from national export credit guarantee companies. The willingness to provide guarantees varies depending on the guarantee company involved. Thus, it appears that, to date, guarantees are more readily available from French and Italian companies than from the United Kingdom. However, the Export Credit Guarantee Department (ECGD) is currently reviewing its policy on Libya with a view to possibly easing insurance cover rules governing UK exporters. It is believed that a technical paper on restoring medium-term cover is currently in the process of being prepared.

In the case of investors from other Arab countries or with majority Arab shareholdings, guarantees may be obtained from the Inter-Arab Investment Guarantee Corporation.

Bilateral investment treaties

Libya enjoys a traditionally strong relationship with Italy, and in December 2000 Libya and Italy signed a bilateral investment protection treaty.

Relations between Libya and Germany have also traditionally been strong and it would appear that a bilateral investment treaty is soon to be signed between the two countries.

Part Two

The Legal Structure and Business Regulation

2.1

The Legal Framework

Eversheds and Mukhtar, Kelbash & Elgharabli

Government and the judiciary

The legislature

The legislative branch of the Libyan government is formed by a hierarchy of People's Congresses (Basic People's Congresses at local level, delegates from which form the Municipal Branch Congresses and, above them, Provincial Congresses, culminating with the General People's Congress). The General People's Congress carries out a parliamentary role. It has its own Secretariat, chaired by the Secretary-General of the People's Congress, which is one of the most senior positions in the state, and its official task is to set the agenda for the meetings of the Basic People's Congresses, including draft laws. These legislative proposals, regarding such matters as the budget, laws, regulations and even treaties, are passed from the General People's Congress down the hierarchy to the Basic People's Congresses for their comment and approval. Once laws have been approved by all the Basic People's Congresses, they are issued by the General People's Congress. The General People's Congress also makes nominations for appointments to the Executive.

The Executive

The executive branch of the government, the Cabinet, is the General People's Committee (usually abbreviated to 'GPC'). The head of the government (the Prime Minister) is the Secretary of the General People's Committee, while the other Secretaries (or ministers) are responsible for the routine running of their ministries. At the time of going to press, there were only five ministries in Libya (Foreign Affairs, Economy and Commerce, Finance, Justice and Internal Security, and African Unity). In addition, there are two Assistant Prime Ministers, responsible for services and production.

The court system

The Libyan court system is similar to that of civil law countries such as France and Italy. In Libya, courts are classified by function, with trial courts and appellate courts. Trial courts hear disputes initially and there is usually a single judge who controls the trial and determines the outcome. Appellate courts review the decisions of trial courts where a party is dissatisfied with the decision rendered by the trial court. At the top of the hierarchy is the Supreme Court, which is divided into specialist chambers. Its decisions are binding upon all courts and authorities in Libya.

Overview of the legal system

The Libyan legal system is a civil law system similar to that of France. In Libya, as in other civil law countries, there is a hierarchy of legislative texts with, in descending order of authority, the Constitution, laws (including various codes), executive regulations, and executive and ministerial decisions. In the absence of applicable legal provisions, a judge refers to other sources of law and will apply the following principles:

1. Islamic law (the Shari'a).
2. Prevailing custom.
3. Principles of natural law and rules of equity.

Laws are issued by the General People's Congress, executive regulations and executive decisions are issued by the General People's Committee and ministerial decisions are issued by the individual ministries.

The Constitution

On 11 December 1969, a Constitutional Proclamation was issued 'to provide a basis for the organization of the national and democratic revolution'. Although a 'Declaration on the Establishment of the Authority of the People' was issued on 2 March 1977, which supersedes certain of the provisions of the original Constitutional Proclamation, a new Constitution has not been issued to date, and the provisions of the Constitutional Proclamation of 11 December 1969 that have not been superseded remain in force.

The Constitutional Proclamation contains only very general principles, which give little by way of clear guarantees or protections to the foreign investor, although mention may be made of the provision protecting private ownership (on condition that it is non-exploitative) and stating that expropriation will take place only in accordance with the law. On the other hand, a number of provisions may be perceived as unhelpful to the foreign investor, such as those declaring the intention to liberate the national economy of foreign influence or the primacy of public ownership.

Human rights legislation

The 1988 Charter of Human Rights and Law no. 20 of 1991 (Enhancement of Freedom), which contains similar provisions, are quasi-constitutional texts.

The provisions of Law no. 20 go somewhat further than the Constitutional Proclamation and the 1988 Charter in identifying the specific rights that are protected. An important provision for the foreign investor is Article 12, which states that private property shall not be confiscated, except in the public interest and against fair compensation. Among the other rights protected are freedom of expression, freedom to form trade unions, private property and the right to resort to the courts. Certain of these rights are, however, subject to exceptions.

Codified legislation

As Libya is a civil law country, it has a series of codes. After 1969, the codes were reviewed and revised to harmonize them with the Shari'a. It should be noted that the codes are now rather old and have not always been updated by the incorporation of more recent legislation. Therefore, although they may be relied upon insofar as they lay down basic principles of Libyan law, it is important to verify whether their detailed provisions have been supplemented or superseded by subsequent legislation on specific matters. The main codes are as follows:

Civil Code

The Civil Code was issued in 1953. It is based on the Egyptian Civil Code, which in turn was based on the French Civil Code. It is considered to be the main law for civil transactions relating to both personal and real rights. The provisions of the Civil Code deal with sources of obligations such as contract, unlawful acts, unilateral undertakings and unjust enrichment. It goes on to deal with specific performance, damages and evidence. The Civil Code also deals with specific contracts such as sale, exchange, partnership, agency and insurance.

The Civil Code provides that a contract is created from the moment that two people exchange concordant intentions. A contract may be verbal or in writing, and a declaration of intention may be implied when neither the law nor the parties require it to be expressed. An agreement by which the parties or one of the parties agrees to enter into a contract in the future is only binding if the essential terms of the contract are agreed clearly. The contract may be concluded by a representative, although such a contract is only considered valid if the representative has acted within the limits and provisions delegated to him or her by his or her principal. All obligations arising as a result of the contract are governed by the terms of the contract, and the contract cannot be revoked or amended unless by the mutual consent of the parties or for reasons provided by law.

Commercial Code

The Commercial Code also dates from 1953. In general, it deals with commercial transactions between commercial entities. A transaction is considered to be commercial if it is listed under the Commercial Code, is carried on by a commercial entity, and is based on the concepts of 'speculation, circulation and enterprise'. The Commercial Code also deals with a number of specific subjects such as the commercial register and requirements for registration thereon, commercial contracts such as sale, supply, lease, transportation and shipment, bank transactions, commercial credit instruments such as bills of exchange and promissory notes, and bankruptcy.

Civil and Commercial Procedure Code

This Code again dates from 1953. It deals with the hierarchy of the various courts and their respective jurisdiction, procedural rules, enforcement of judgements, and arbitration.

A *Criminal Code* and a *Criminal Procedure Code* also exist.

Administrative Contracts Regulation

The Administrative Contracts Regulation of 2000 applies to all administrative contracts entered into by governmental departments, public authorities, public corporations and public organizations.

Administrative contracts are defined in the Regulation as contracts that are concluded by public entities for the purpose of carrying out projects approved in the state's development plan and budget, developing or managing public utilities, or providing public services, whenever such contracts contain certain exceptional provisions not normally found in civil and commercial contracts, and which might be onerous for the contractor. Examples of such exceptional provisions are:

- where the contractor's scope of work may be increased by up to 15 per cent without any corresponding increase in the contract price;
- where subcontracting is restricted and, in the event of subcontracting, priority is given to Libyan nationals;
- where the contract price may not be increased in the event of an increase in market prices;
- where all payments due to the contractor must first be approved by the Popular Monitoring Authority;
- where all disputes are subject to the jurisdiction of the Libyan courts.

Foreign investors should be aware that this Regulation might apply to their contracts with public authorities or organizations, and thus that they might be subject to rather onerous conditions.

2.2

Privatization: The Environment for Reform and Legal Aspects

Azza K Maghur & Partners, Tripoli

Introduction

Libya gained independence in December 1951. On 28 November 1953, the Libyan Commercial Code (LCC) was promulgated. This Law contains seven parts. Each part is divided into chapters. In all, the LCC contains 913 articles and regulates the definition of commercial activities and commercial entities, trade names and marks, the commercial register, commercial contracts, bank transactions, documentary credits; bills of exchange, commercial companies and bankruptcy.

Athough the LCC was the main piece of legislation that regulated the private sector at that time, there are other parallel pieces of legislation that cover various economic activities, including Law no. 40 of 1956 regarding trade marks and Law no. 10 of 1959 relating to free zones. After the 1969 revolution, more legislation was brought in, notably Law no. 55 of 1970 relating to traders, commercial companies and their supervision; Law no. 33 of 1971 concerned with the organization of commercial agencies, and Law no. 869 of 1975 regarding the functions of commercial agencies.

Over the past half century, Libya has been through major reforms in all aspects of life, including a major political reform, the 1969 Revolution and the establishment of a new political system on 2 March 1977 by the Declaration of the People's Power. But the commercial code, although subject to limited amendment, continued in force. However, the LCC is now facing major political, economic and social changes. Indeed parts of it have been neglected and have, *de facto,* ceased to be applied.

With the full reactivation of the private sector in 1991, legislation relating to private activities started to flourish again. Major reforms were established in the private sector, either by way of legislation to regulate new fields in economic activities, or by regulations to reactivate legislation already in force, but out of use at the time.

Commercial and civil codes

Article 2 of the Commercial Code states: 'In case the provisions of this present code fail to deal therewith, the provisions of the Civil Code shall be applied to certain commercial matters. However, application of the said provisions shall be made only in such measure as they agree with the principles recognized by the Commercial Code.'

Thus, there is a strong link between Libya's commercial and civil codes. In addition to the Civil Code provisions being complementary to the Commercial Code, the latter also attributes importance to customary rules in commercial dealings.

In short, the private sector is regulated by different codes and pieces of legislation, and regulations pertaining to the application of legislation.

Other recent legislation and regulations: the need for reform

Evaluation of any reform in the private sector can be measured by both legislation and the application of legislation. The General People's Congress (Parliament) promulgates legislation in Libya, while the executive body that issues regulations is the General People's Committee (Cabinet).

Since the 1950s, Libya has passed numerous laws regulating economic activity in the private sector. However, the late 1970s/early 1980s witnessed a retreat of the private sector in the face of a dominant public sector. But legislation regulating the private sector continued in force, and was neither radically amended nor abrogated, so the process of reactivating and reviving the private sector has been quite straightforward.

The process of reform has been one of reactivation, rather than initiation. Nevertheless, new legislation was issued to cover or regulate fields in the private sector, which the existing legislation did not cover. The best example of this is Law no. 5 of 1997 (Encouragement of Foreign Capital Investment) and its regulations.

The process from a dominant public sector to a compatible and active private sector was gradual, but constructive.

On the legislative side, the process of reform can be summarized as follows:

1. Changes started with the promulgation of Law no. 9 of 1985, regarding a limited form of economic activity. This law permits limited economic activity as long as it takes two forms: individual (commerce) or a simple partnership (Tasharykia).
2. In June 1988, the Great Green Charter of Human Rights was issued by Decision no. 11, adopted by the General People's Congress. This

remarkable event led to an active process of general legislative reforms. Article 11 of the Charter – considered among jurists to contain constitutional principles – referred to the right to practise private activities, either individually or in the form of a partnership. It also provided protection to private activities. Further, Law no. 5 of 1991 (implementation of the principles of the Great Green Charter of Human Rights) indicated in Article 1 that all current legislation in force should be reviewed and amended in the light of the Charter, and that it is prohibited to issue any legislation incompatible with the Charter.

3. Law no. 9 of 1992, relating to the exercise of economic activities, was a significant step in the reform process. Article 2 opened the door to unlimited private sector activities; Article 3 outlined structures for economic activity: individual, family, or through partnership and stock companies.

4. In 1997, a major piece of legislation in a new area of the private sector was issued. This was Law no. 5 of 1997, relating to the encouragement of foreign capital investment; it was followed by regulations, enacted by Decision no. 186 of 2002.

5. In 1999, the General Organization of Free Zones was established by General People's Committee Decision no. 20. Law no. 9 of 2000, regarding the regulation of transit trade and free zones, was promulgated – abrogating Law no. 10 of 1959, relating to free zones.

6. On 28 December 2001, law no. 21, relating to certain rules with regard to the exercise of economic activities, was promulgated. The major innovation is found in Article 10, which permits any authority designated by the General People's Committee to establish a stock market. Executive regulations were issued by General People's Committee decision no. 49 of 2002.

7. In 2001, the General People's Committee issued Decision no. 178 regarding commercial agencies. This revived the application of previous legislation on commercial agencies, specifically Law no. 33 of 1971 (organization of commercial agencies) and Law no. 869 of 1975 (functions of commercial agencies).

8. Reforms have also extended to the banking sector. Law no. 1 of 1993, regarding banks, currency and credit, permits foreign banks to open branches, agencies or representative offices in Libya. Article 53, as amended by Law no. 2 of 1995, indicated that all Libyan commercial banks should take the form of Libyan joint-stock companies and that individual, private and public entities are allowed to hold shares in them. Thus, private commercial banks and private local banks (Ahlia) were established all over Libya, and foreign banks also opened offices.

In 1994, the General People's Committee issued Decision no. 537 on the rules for holding shares in a commercial bank.

Conclusion

The private sector in Libya has existed since independence. Just as any other sector, it has been influenced by political, social, economic and other factors. Private sector legislation in Libya has undergone several changes. Before the 1969 Revolution, it was governed mainly by commercial and civil codes. After 1996, both codes continued to be in force under limited amendments. Meanwhile, other laws relating to specific economic activities were issued. The period between 1978 and 1985 was marked by a dominant public sector. The promulgation of the Green Charter of Human Rights in 1988 led to several major legislative changes in all fields, including economic activities.

Major reform in the private sector took place in 1992, through Law no. 9, relating to the exercise of economic activities. The current principal law governing economic activities, in addition to codes and other legislation mentioned above, is Law no. 21 of 2001, relating to the exercise of economic activities, and its regulation.

2.3

Incorporating a Company

EWM, Malta

Introduction

Foreign companies wishing to perform work or supply services within Libya must register a branch in accordance with the provisions of Law no. 65 of 1970 (Company Law), or must register and obtain a licence to conduct a specific project under Law no. 5 of 1997 (Encouragement of Foreign Capital Investment; the Investment Law).

Upon approval of an application to register a branch under Law no. 65 of 1970, the Secretariat of Economy will issue a five-year renewable business licence.

Upon approval of an application to register a branch under Law no. 5 of 1997, the Investment Promotion Board will issue a licence for the duration of the approved project, subject to the approval of the Secretariat of Economy. Projects related to investment in the oil sector are excluded from the provisions of Law no. 5 of 1997.

Foreign companies entering into joint ventures with a Libyan entity have historically formed joint venture companies abroad that have subsequently established branches in Libya. This is the norm for 'joint operating companies' within the oil sector. Such joint venture companies must fulfil the requirements applied to any other branch of a foreign company established under the provisions of Law no. 65 of 1970.

Foreign companies entering into joint ventures with a Libyan entity under the provisions of Law no. 5 of 1997 generally form joint stock companies in which they have a majority shareholding.

Business licences

A foreign company may only register a branch to work in Libya if it has a contract with a Libyan government agency or company. It is not possible to establish a foreign-owned entity in Libya in order to seek work prior to having a contract, nor is it possible to work only for other foreign-owned entities.

The business licence issued by the Secretariat of Economy is specific, and therefore the application to the Secretariat should set out the whole range of services that the branch would seek to provide. Should work be performed beyond the terms of the licence, the branch would face a variety of exposures and penalties. The licence is renewable at five-yearly intervals for a further five years or for the duration of a remaining contract or contracts.

The licence issued by the Investment Promotion Board is valid for the duration of the approved project.

In addition to requiring a business licence, it is necessary to renew annually various other registrations, including that with the Companies Immigration Department of the Ministry of Justice, which issues a certificate confirming that work continues to be performed for a Libyan government agency or company. If this is not so, the branch will be required to close, despite the fact that its business licence remains valid.

Registration with the Secretariat of Economy

The application to the Secretariat of Economy comprises:

- completed Application Form 7, which includes details of the name and address of the branch in Libya and its proposed activities;
- an original or authenticated copy of the company's articles of association;
- an original or authenticated copy of the company's memorandum of association;
- a board resolution stating each of the following:
  - an affirmative decision to establish a branch in Libya;
  - a detailed statement of the objectives of the branch in Libya;
  - a decision to allocate at least LD70,000 as branch capital;
  - a decision to appoint a branch manager accompanied by his or her power of attorney, and details of his or her qualifications and experience;
- a certificate of deposit from a Libyan bank confirming the receipt in foreign currency of branch capital of LD70,000;
- four performance certificates for projects completed at home and abroad, listing in detail contract values, commencement and completion dates, and a summary of work performed (as a matter of practice these may be supplied by the ultimate parent). The Chamber of Commerce in the country where the document was issued should endorse these;

- a declaration from the board of directors to abstain from any involvement in Libya's political affairs;
- a declaration from the board of directors undertaking to prepare an annual balance sheet and profit and loss account for the branch;
- an original certificate issued by the Chamber of Commerce in the country of origin, confirming the company's registration number and date of registration;
- a certificate issued by the Boycott of Israel Office in Tripoli, confirming that the company is not blacklisted for violation of rules governing the boycott of Israel.

Occasionally, the following are also requested:

- head office accounts for the prior year;
- a certificate of 'no bankruptcy'.

A fee of LD13,000 is payable after a favourable decision has been made.

Boycott of Israel Office application

The certificate issued by the Boycott of Israel Office in Tripoli must be included as part of the application documentation submitted to the Secretariat of Economy. The application comprises:

- a covering letter requesting a certificate;
- an original or authenticated copy of the company's memorandum and articles of association;
- an original of the company's certificate of membership of its local Chamber of Commerce;
- a board of directors' decision appointing the manager of the branch, an original of his or her power of attorney, and a copy of his or her passport;
- answers to a one-page questionnaire;
- a list of branches abroad;
- a board of directors' declaration that the company was not and is not dealing with Israel;
- a board of directors' declaration that the company will not deal with Israel in the future;
- a letter of authority for the company's Libyan representative employee or professional adviser to deal with the application for the Boycott Certificate (the representative must be Libyan).

Registration with the Investment Promotion Board

The application to the Investment Promotion Board comprises:

- a certificate of the company's nationality;
- a detailed statement of the capital to be invested;
- a statement of local materials which the project will exploit or develop;
- a detailed feasibility study;
- a certificate issued by the Chamber of Commerce in the country of origin, confirming the company's registration therein;
- project accounts if the project to be carried out in Libya is an extension to an existing project;
- a certificate of 'no bankruptcy';
- a detailed project timetable.

The Board has issued Circular no. 1 of 2002 setting out procedures to be followed regarding import of equipment and materials, export, recruitment, and suchlike.

General comments

All documents submitted for all applications set out above must be endorsed by the appropriate authorities in the country in which the documents were issued. This requires notarisation by a public notary, authentication of the notary's signature by the Foreign Office, translation into Arabic, and stamping by the Libyan People's Bureau (Embassy) in order to confirm the authenticity of all documents.

In addition to the primary registration with either the Secretariat of Economy or the Investment Promotion Board, branches of foreign companies must register with a number of other authorities. Companies that have achieved the primary registration would be able to provide what is required for these subsidiary registrations:

- All foreign entities must register with the Libyan Chamber of Commerce and with their local Municipality (Shaabiyat).
- All foreign entities must register with their effective 'sponsor', the governmental agency responsible for the economic sector in which they work. For example, all foreign oil service companies must register with the National Oil Corporation of Libya (NOC) in order to be placed on their list of approved contractors. This 'sponsor' will

usually require regular statements of contract status, number of employees, and so forth.

The registration process is time consuming and will usually take at least six months.

Although it was noted that unregistered foreign companies might not perform work in Libya, in practice companies offering a specialised service for a short time and with a small team may be granted temporary visas by an employing party, if the work to be performed is regarded as strategic. This is exceptional.

Registration with the tax and social security authorities

All foreign companies must register with the tax and social security departments. It is not necessary for a company to have achieved branch or project registration in order for it to register as a taxpayer and pay relevant taxes.

2.4

Employment Law for Libyan and Foreign Employees

Eversheds and Mukhtar, Kelbash & Elgharabli

The basic law in this field is Labour Law no. 58 of 1970, the provisions of which are applicable to all employees working both in the private sector and for state-owned companies. It deals with the employment of both nationals and foreigners, employment contracts, working hours, the resolution of disputes, and procedures and conditions for the termination of employment contracts. It lays down minimum requirements for salaries and benefits. Employers are free to offer more favourable conditions unless the employees are subject to Law no. 15 of 1981.

Wages and salary in the state sector – Law no. 15 of 1981

Salaries of civil servants and employees of state-owned companies are subject to a special scheme under Law no. 15 of 1981. The provisions of Law no. 15 are also applicable to Libyan companies where there is any Libyan public ownership of any part of the share capital. Under Law no. 15, salaries have been more or less frozen, with a very minimal annual increase and no merit increases or allowances since 1981.

Branches of foreign companies are free in principle to offer any salary they wish to their Libyan employees. In the oil sector, however, the application of Law no. 15 may cause problems in the context of an exploration and production sharing agreement (EPSA) that reaches the development stage, since it is the policy of the National Oil Corporation of Libya (NOC) to require the salary scale of Law no. 15 to be applied to all operations where the NOC makes a contribution to the funding, regardless of the NOC's percentage share and regardless of whether or not the operating company is wholly foreign-owned.

Working hours

Labour Law no. 58 of 1970 states that:

- An employee cannot be engaged in actual work for more than eight hours per day, not including breaks for meals or rest.
- If daily hours of work exceed six, there must be a break or breaks of at least one hour in total and the employee must work no more than six continuous hours.
- Juveniles are not permitted to work more than six hours per day with a break or breaks of not less than one hour.
- Juveniles are not permitted to work between 8 pm and 7 am.

Leave

Labour Law no. 58 of 1970 states that:

- Each employee is entitled to one paid day off in every week.
- An employee who has worked for one year is entitled to fully paid annual leave of 16 days.
- Juveniles and employees who have worked for five years are entitled to fully paid annual leave of 24 days.
- An employee who has worked three consecutive years with the same employer is entitled to fully paid special vacation not exceeding 25 days in order to perform his duty of pilgrimage. This is allowed only once in a lifetime.
- In the case of normal sickness, an employee is entitled to 60 per cent of his or her income for a period of up to one year. Where the sickness is the result of a work injury, he or she is entitled to 70 per cent of that income for the same period.

Female employees

Labour Law no. 58 of 1970 states that:

- Women are not allowed to work between 8 pm and 7 am or for more than 48 hours each week.

- In the 18 months following childbirth, women are entitled to two rest intervals a day, each of not less than half an hour. These form part of working hours and do not result in a reduction in pay.
- With regard to maternity leave, a female employee receives her full basic income for a three-month period, including pre- and post-delivery days.

Termination

An employment contract can be for a fixed or unfixed term, or it may be for a specific project or assignment. If the parties to a fixed-term employment contract continue to use the same contract after the expiry of the term, it will be considered as a renewal for an unfixed term. If the term of the contract is not fixed, at least one month's notice must be given before termination of the contract.

An employment contract for a fixed term may not exceed five years; thereafter the term of the contract becomes unfixed. An employment contract is for a fixed term if it states the duration in the contract or if a fixed-term contract is characteristic of the particular assignment.

An employer may terminate the contract where work is wholly or partially suspended for a period of two consecutive months, or if the work is temporary by nature. An employer may also terminate the contract where an employee's disability or illness prevents him or her from performing his or her duties for a continuous period of not less than 120 days or a total number of 200 days over the course of a year.

Dismissal

An employer may dismiss the employee without notice and without indemnity or compensation in the following situations:

- The employee lied about his or her identification or submitted false certificates or references.
- The employee was appointed on probation.
- The employee committed a mistake leading to grave material loss to the employer, provided the event was reported by the employer to the labour office within three days of it coming to his or her attention.
- The employee failed to comply with safety instructions, in spite of personal written warnings, provided the instructions were written and posted in an obvious place and a copy of the personal warning was sent to the relevant labour office.

- The employee was absent without legitimate reason for more than 20 days in total over one year or more than 10 consecutive days, provided written warnings were sent after 10 and five days respectively, with copies sent to the relevant labour office.
- The employee fails to perform his or her basic obligations under the employment contract.
- The employee disclosed secrets relating to his or her work.
- The employee is found guilty of a criminal act or misdemeanour relating to honour, integrity or public morality.
- The employee is found drunk or under the influence of drugs during working hours.
- The employee attacks or assaults a colleague or manager.

Social security

Social Security Law no. 13 of 1980, as amended by Law no. 1 of 1991, requires non-Libyan employers to pay 75 per cent of each employee's social security contributions. Employees' contributions are withheld from their salary by the employer, who is responsible for payment. The total contribution corresponds to 15 per cent of the employee's gross salary and is payable monthly. The employer must declare and pay his or her contributions by the 10th day of the month following the month to which they relate. Late payments carry a penalty of 5 per cent per year. In exchange, employees receive certain benefits in kind and in cash, such as a retirement pension and compensation in case of injury.

Health and safety legislation

The Industrial Security and Labour Safety Law dates from 1976. It places upon the employer the general obligation to take all necessary precautions to protect his or her employees from work-related danger, harm and disease. In particular, the employer is obliged to take all necessary steps to ensure his or her employees' safety when using instruments and machines and when handling harmful materials, and to provide necessary medical and first aid facilities.

Where the number of employees exceeds 200, the employer must appoint a specialized employee to be responsible for labour safety in the establishment and for the enforcement of the provisions of the law.

Libyan and foreign employees

It should be noted that certain jobs are reserved for Libyan nationals, such as accountants, typists, drivers and guards. Foreign companies must employ a certain number of Libyan trainees, corresponding to at least 20 per cent of the total personnel of the company. If a company fails to employ the requisite number of Libyans, an amount is payable to a vocational training fund.

A decision of the assistant prime minister for services, issued on 1 August 2000, has placed a ceiling of 46,523 (about 1 per cent of the national population) on all foreign workers in government departments and national and foreign companies. A ceiling has also been established for each sector.

Under the Foreign Investment Law, the investor is entitled to employ and import the foreign staff and technical expertise necessary for the establishment and operation of the project, although 'the import of normal labour should be avoided as much as possible'.

Foreign employees are subject to the same employment laws as nationals outlined above.

Work permits

Foreign workers must obtain a work permit from the Immigration Department before they apply for a residence visa. Work permits are strictly controlled in order to preserve the local workforce.

The process for obtaining such permits may be somewhat difficult and changes from time to time. Sometimes applicants are required to produce original documents giving evidence of their qualifications, education and experience. In the oil sector, the process is facilitated by a letter of support from the NOC. In general, it is easier for executive personnel to obtain permits than it is for technical personnel.

2.5

Arbitration and Dispute Resolution

Eversheds and Mukhtar, Kelbash & Elgharabli

Arbitration

Arbitration is governed by Articles 739 *et seq* of the Civil and Commercial Procedure Code. These provisions are applicable to all arbitrations taking place in Libya, whether purely internal or international.

In general, contracting parties have the right to agree to subject disputes under their contract to arbitration. However, there are circumstances where arbitration is not permitted under Libyan law – for example, where the dispute concerns public order, or disputes between employers and employees with respect to social security and industrial accidents.

Libyan law provides various safeguards for parties wishing to arbitrate in Libya. For example, the agreement to arbitrate must be made in writing and the subject of arbitration must be specified either in the agreement or in the pleading. There must always be an odd number of arbitrators. Where there is disagreement as to the appointment of arbitrators, provision is made for assistance by the competent court. Where an arbitrator withdraws from the procedure without just cause, he or she becomes liable to pay damages to the parties. The parties are free to determine the rules of procedure, failing which the arbitrators can determine the rules that they consider suitable. Arbitrators do not have the power to order conservatory measures. The award of the arbitrators must be made in writing and provide reasoning. It must be given within the territory of Libya, otherwise it will be subject to the rules provided for judgments rendered in a foreign state. All awards must be deposited with the court that would normally have had jurisdiction over the dispute in the absence of an arbitration agreement. Awards are subject to appeal unless the parties have waived the right to appeal, and the right to request nullification of the award cannot be waived. Nullification is possible on various grounds, which are largely procedural.

In practice, contracts between Libyan and foreign parties commonly provide for some form of international arbitration, referring any dispute under the contract to arbitration outside Libya. In such cases, they may provide for the application of the Rules of Arbitration of the ICC (the International Chamber of Commerce in Paris), the LCIA (London Court of International Arbitration) or any other set of arbitration rules. It should be noted, however, that the approval of the General People's Committee is required to include such a clause in administrative contracts.

It is recognized that the provisions of the Civil and Commercial Procedure Code relating to arbitration would benefit from modernization, especially as regards the right of appeal, and the procedures for enforcement of foreign arbitral awards, discussed below. The system is therefore currently under review, as is the possible establishment of an arbitration centre in Libya.

Court system

In the absence of an arbitration agreement, Libyan courts would have jurisdiction to hear a claim of a foreign investor against a Libyan contractual partner. Libya is a civil law country with a court system similar to that of other civil law countries such as France, both as to the hierarchy of the courts and to their jurisdiction. In order of seniority, the court system is made up of the Supreme Court, the Courts of Appeal, the Courts of First Instance and the Summary Courts.

All courts convene in open session, unless public morals or public order require a closed session, and all judgments are delivered in open session.

Jurisdiction over the subject matter of a case is usually determined by the amount and/or nature of the claim involved in the case.

Summary Court (Small Claims Court)

The Summary Court has jurisdiction for first instance civil and commercial claims that do not exceed LD1,000 (approximately US$800). There is no right of appeal if the value of the claim does not exceed LD100. In other cases, there is a right of appeal before the Court of First Instance. Proceedings before the Summary Court are heard by a single judge.

Court of First Instance

The Court of First Instance has two roles. First, it hears appeals from the Summary Court and, second, it has jurisdiction for civil and commercial claims that fall outside the remit of the Summary Court. When it sits in its appellate function, there are three judges and the judgment can be appealed only before the Supreme Court. In other instances, the court has a single judge, and judgments are subject to appeal before the Court of Appeal. The Court of First Instance is divided into chambers (civil, labour and commercial) and there are no commercial courts as such.

Court of Appeal

Appeals from judgments of the Court of First Instance are heard by the Court of Appeal. There are four such courts in Libya: at Tripoli, Benghazi, Misurata and Zawia. Disputes before the Court of Appeal are heard by specialized chambers for civil, commercial, employment or administrative matters. The Court of Appeal is made up of three judges. Administrative acts may be challenged before the Court of Appeal directly. New arguments and new evidence are admissible at appeal. A normal legal dispute going before a trial court and an appeal court can be expected to last for a period of two years, but may require a longer period where they involve experts and witnesses. Judgments rendered by the Court of Appeal are subject to appeal before the Supreme Court.

Supreme Court

The Supreme Court is based in Tripoli. In common with the Court of Appeal, this court is also divided into specialized chambers such as civil, commercial, criminal and administrative. Each chamber consists of either three or five judges. Within the Supreme Court, the Department of Prosecutors represents the state or public interest. The Supreme Court rules only on issues of law and not on fact, and thus any appeal from the Court of Appeal must be based on a violation of substantive law or alternatively of the procedure applicable before the lower court. The decisions of the Supreme Court are binding upon all courts and authorities in Libya.

Enforcement of foreign judgments and arbitral awards

Libyan law allows the enforcement of foreign judgments and arbitral awards subject to certain substantive rules and judicial procedures set out in Chapter 6 of the Civil and Commercial Procedure Code. As regards judgments, it states that their enforcement is permitted under the same conditions required for a Libyan judgment to be enforced in the foreign country. It also specifies that in order to apply for the enforcement of such a foreign judgment, a party should file it with the Court of First Instance according to normal procedures.

The judgment will be enforced, provided it satisfies the following four conditions:

1. The judgment was issued by a judicial body which had competence according to the laws of the country in which it was issued and has become final and enforceable in that country.
2. The parties were notified to appear and were duly represented.
3. The judgment does not conflict with any judgment or order previously issued by a Libyan court.
4. The judgment does not violate morality or public order rules in Libya.

Libyan arbitral awards are enforceable by virtue of an enforcement order issued by the judge of urgent procedures in the court where the award has been deposited. Before issuing the order, the judge must first examine the award and the arbitration agreement, and must ascertain that there are no obstacles to execution. Appeals are admissible against refusals to issue enforcement orders.

With regard to foreign arbitral awards, Libya is not a signatory to the New York Convention on the Recognition and Enforcement of Foreign Arbitral Awards, which means that enforcement of such awards is subject to the relevant provisions of the Civil and Commercial Procedure Code, which state that arbitral awards issued in a foreign country may be enforced if they are final and capable of being enforced in the country in which they were issued. In other words, the beneficiary of a foreign arbitral award who wishes to enforce that award in Libya must first obtain an enforcement order in the country of origin of the award. It must then demonstrate to the Libyan court that Libyan public order was not violated, that due process was respected with regard to the proceedings, and that the country of origin of the award grants Libyan awards reciprocal treatment.

2.6

The Regulatory Framework for the Oil and Gas Industry

Eversheds and Mukhtar, Kelbash & Elgharabli

Relevant laws and regulations

Petroleum Law and Regulations

The Petroleum Law (Law no. 25 of 1955, amended up to 1983) remains the most comprehensive piece of legislation regulating Libya's oil and gas sector, together with Decree no. 10 of 1979, which reorganized the National Oil Corporation of Libya (NOC) and empowered it to enter into all kinds of petroleum exploitation agreements.

Various regulations have been issued under the Petroleum Law. The only regulations remaining in force are: no. 1, dividing the territory of Libya into four zones; no. 8, regarding the standard practices to be followed in oilfield operations; and no. 9, for financial, administrative and technical control over the preservation of oil wealth.

The Petroleum Law and Regulations were issued with concession agreements in mind. However, while there remain a number of oil companies operating under concessions in Libya, these are now essentially a thing of the past. No new oil concessions have been granted in the past 30 years and the existing concessions will begin to expire in 2005. However, it is believed that, among other contracts, the new draft law (discussed below) will continue to allow for concessions. At present, the usual way for a foreign oil company to undertake oil operations in Libya, unless it takes over an existing concession interest, is to enter into an exploration and production sharing agreement (EPSA) or a development and production sharing agreement (DEPSA).

In this context, the Petroleum Law and Regulations remain important, since the governing law of the EPSAs expressly includes the

Petroleum Law as amended, and the regulations issued thereunder, except as otherwise provided in the EPSA itself.

While it appears that the new draft Petroleum Law aims to deal with gas exploitation agreements, the existing legislation does not contain specific provisions for gas, and the current EPSA model does not incorporate clauses allowing the development of a gas project. However, foreign companies are able to negotiate an amendment of their EPSA to provide for such projects if so required. To date, there have been no operations in Libya specifically directed at gas, but gas has now become a priority area.

Other relevant legislation

Further general legislation also has an impact on the oil industry. Mention may be made of company law, tax legislation, employment law, housing regulations, etc. However, the Foreign Investment Law of 1997, which offers various incentives to foreign investment in Libya, is not applicable to the oil sector.

Other legislation that is directly relevant to the oil industry includes environmental legislation, some of which deals specifically with oil-related activities. Law no. 7 of 1982 relates, *inter alia*, to the prevention of pollution of the sea by oil. It prohibits the disposal of oil or the washing of tanks within Libya's territorial waters, and lays down the procedures to be followed in the event of accidental pollution by oil.

Further legislation relates to the use of fresh water in oil-related activities. In principle, the use of potable water for injection into oil reservoirs is prohibited. However, licences may be granted in cases where the use of potable water is necessary, but only on a temporary basis until an alternative source of non-potable water is found, and only by agreement between the NOC and the Public Authority for Water.

Libya's rich archaeological heritage has led to the enactment of various legislative provisions for the protection of antiquities. The Petroleum Law itself prohibits any work within the precincts of cemeteries, places used for religious worship and places of antiquity. In addition, Law no. 3 of 1994 provides that it is forbidden to establish mining or industrial camps or any other facilities or buildings at a distance of less than 500 metres from immovable antiquities without the approval of the Antiquities Department.

Role of the Secretariat of Petroleum

The Petroleum Law, as amended, provides for certain functions to be exercised by the Secretariat (Ministry) of Petroleum. Under the Law, the Secretariat of Petroleum is both the regulatory authority for the technical aspects of operations and the tax authority. It is also the contractual partner of the foreign companies under the concession agreements. It was abolished in 1986, and until it was reinstated in 1989, its technical and regulatory functions were assigned to the NOC, while its sovereign functions remained with the government. The Secretariat was again abolished in 2000 and, at the time of going to press, its functions have not been officially reallocated. However, as on the previous occasion, the NOC has *de facto* taken over its technical and regulatory functions.

Role of the NOC

In addition to its assumption of the Secretariat of Petroleum's technical and regulatory functions, the NOC (referred to as the 'First Party') is the contractual partner of all foreign companies (referred to as the 'Second Party') under the EPSAs or any other agreements that may be entered into for the purpose of exploiting the country's oil resources. The NOC has the power to negotiate any such agreement and to agree upon its terms, but all agreements and amendments thereto must be referred to the government for ratification. Within the NOC, special committees have been established for the negotiation of exploration agreements, for development (ie enhancement of recovery from existing producing fields) and for attracting foreign participation in downstream activities.

EPSAs

As noted above, the EPSA is at present the most usual way for a foreign company to engage in oil exploitation activities in Libya. There have been three generations of EPSAs, dating back to the early 1970s. The second generation was entered into at the beginning of the 1980s, when the NOC was able to obtain for itself more favourable contractual terms in the circumstances prevailing on the international oil market after the second oil shock. Those EPSAs were generally regarded by foreign companies as too heavily weighted in favour of the NOC and against the Second Party. The present generation of EPSAs (EPSA III) was introduced by the NOC in response to subsequent changes in the international oil market and in an attempt to attract more participants in its new exploration efforts. In this model, the NOC has adopted flexible contractual terms and has recognized the right of the Second Party to recover its costs and achieve a reasonable return on its investment. The major features of EPSA III are as follows.

Term

The model EPSA provides for a contractual term of 25 years. A certain number of years is agreed upon as the 'exploration period', during which time the Second Party must conduct exploration operations in accordance with an approved exploration programme. At the end of the exploration period, the EPSA terminates in respect of all parts of the contract area other than the exploitation areas – in other words, the areas in which a commercial discovery has been made – unless non-associated gas has been discovered in any block that would otherwise have been terminated. In the latter event, the parties must enter into negotiations to agree on how to proceed with the appraisal and development of the gas field. A right of withdrawal is provided for the Second Party on condition that its exploration obligations have been met or otherwise paid for.

Distribution of costs and expenses

The Second Party undertakes all exploration and appraisal expenditures at its own risk. Development expenditure and exploitation capital expenditures are usually shared 50–50 by each party. The NOC and the Second Party share the exploitation operating expenditures, generally according to the initial sharing of production. A parent company guarantee is required to cover all the Second Party's payment and other obligations under the EPSA. The Second Party is guaranteed an initial share of production with a view to enabling it to recover the expenditure it has incurred during the exploration, development and production phases. However, actual cost recovery is never guaranteed.

Allocation of production

An initial sharing is agreed that gives the Second Party a share of between 25 and 35 per cent of production. Production from each block or group of blocks constituting one zone within the contract area is then allocated to the parties in accordance with this percentage. Once the cumulative value of crude oil produced from this area equals the cumulative petroleum operations expenditures incurred by the company in respect of the same area, the remaining amount of crude oil, if any, is allocated between the NOC and the Second Party according to a formula that is designed to allow the Second Party to take a share of the net profit. The same formula also allows the agreement to continuously reflect market conditions without the need to review and adjust the initial terms, and to deal with varying sizes of exploration projects. Application of the formula ensures that small discoveries will still secure an acceptable return to the Second Party, but that windfall profits will not result from unexpectedly large discoveries.

Management

The Second Party acts as operator, under the supervision and control of an owner's management committee composed of three members, two (including the chairman) appointed by NOC, and one by the Second Party. This committee decides on the major issues relevant to petroleum operations (approval of budgets and work programmes, the contractors' list, and contracts above a certain value, etc).

Following the declaration of a commercial discovery, the operator is managed by an operator's management committee that acts as the board of management, under the supervision of the owner's management committee. This committee also has three members, two (including the chairman) appointed by NOC and one by the Second Party. Decisions are taken by simple majority vote.

Operator's obligations

The operator has a range of obligations, of which the most significant are:

- to follow proper industry practices;
- to have work programmes approved;
- to provide proper information, allow inspection and keep records, etc, including accounts in US dollars and Libyan dinars;
- to obtain proper insurance;
- to hire and train Libyan nationals;
- to give priority to Libyan contractors and suppliers.

Commercial discovery

If the owner's management committee decides to proceed with the development of a field where a discovery has been made, it must declare a commercial discovery and adopt a development plan for the field. The operator must, without unreasonable delay, implement any development plan adopted by the committee.

However, a sole risk clause provides that in the event that the Second Party reasonably disagrees with the first development plan, on the basis that the plan is uneconomic for it, it is not obliged to participate in the plan. In such circumstances, the NOC may proceed with the plan through the operator, but for its own sole benefit and at its own sole risk, expense and liability. The Second Party is not entitled to participate in any subsequent development plan related to the same field.

Once a commercial discovery is declared, the NOC has the option to change the operatorship to a joint operating company or to one of its affiliated companies (although to date it has never availed itself of this opportunity).

Production and lifting programmes

Six months prior to the expected commencement of regular commercial production, and annually thereafter, production programmes are to be submitted by the operator to the owner's management committee for approval. The production rate is set by the regulatory body in Libya. In the event that it is set below the maximum efficient rate of the individual wells and the reservoir, the parties are to discuss whether an extension of the term of the EPSA would be appropriate.

After a commercial discovery has been declared, the parties enter into a separate detailed agreement providing that each party shall endeavour to lift its share of crude oil regularly throughout each calendar year. In the event of under-lifting, the shortfall is to be made up subsequently, unless otherwise agreed.

Associated gas

At its option, the NOC may take and freely utilize, for its sole benefit and at its sole cost, all associated gas that is not used in petroleum operations under the EPSA.

Taxation

No income taxes are levied on the Second Party's share of production. This may raise an issue with regard to tax creditability in the Second Party's home country. In such an event, the NOC is usually willing to adopt a different clause according to which taxes are levied on the Second Party's share of production, and to agree that this tax liability will be discharged by the NOC.

Customs duties

The foreign company is subject to customs duties in accordance with the Petroleum Law. As a result, it is exempt from duties on the import of plant, tools, machinery, equipment and materials used for petroleum operations.

Title to purchased items and data

All material, equipment, machinery, articles and supplies purchased by the Second Party for use in petroleum operations under the EPSA become the property of the NOC immediately after purchase if purchased in Libya, or when landed at a Libyan port if purchased outside Libya. The NOC also has title to all original data resulting from operations under the EPSA.

Applicable law and dispute resolution

The EPSA is governed by the laws and regulations of Libya, including the Petroleum Law, as amended, and the Petroleum Regulations, except as otherwise provided in the EPSA. Disputes are to be referred to arbitration to be held in Paris in accordance with the ICC Rules.

New draft Petroleum Law

A commission formed to review the existing Petroleum Law has made a number of recommendations for the updating of the law. It recommended, *inter alia*, that:

- the new legislation should deal with all aspects of the oil industry, including refining, petrochemicals and gas;
- there should be open bidding rounds for oil and gas exploitation agreements;
- more acreage should be released from the hands of the national companies and made available for bidding;
- steps should be taken to encourage foreign participation in the refining and petrochemical industries.

It was further recommended that provisions relating to customs duties, taxes, salaries, the employment of expatriates and the training of human resources be modernized and simplified.

In response to these recommendations, the drafting committee has made considerable progress in identifying and analysing the areas that need to be updated, changed or added. Its aim is to draft comprehensive new legislation to include both a new Petroleum Law and the required technical, administrative and financial regulations.

At the time of going to press, however, the new law has not been issued, and it is not yet known when it will be issued. In the absence of a new law, foreign companies can present proposals for the treatment under new EPSAs of certain issues that are not dealt with in the existing legislation.

Part Three

Finance, Accountancy and Taxation

3.1

Banking and Insurance

Marat Terterov and the Libyan Insurance Company

Banking sector

The Libyan banking sector comprises the Central Bank, six state-owned commercial banks, several private banks and several state-owned development banks. The six state-owned commercial banks are all supervised by the Central Bank of Libya and include Gumhouria Bank (formerly Jamahiriya Bank), National Commercial Bank, Sahara Bank, Umma Bank, Wahda Bank and the Libyan Arab Foreign Bank (LAFB), which is the largest of the group. The banking sector is heavily dominated by the state, and inward investment into the sector is currently being sought for the first time.

In 1996 the country's only privately owned commercial bank, the Bank of Commerce & Development (BCD), was opened.

The Central Bank

The Central Bank of Libya was established in 1955 and started operations in 1956. Initially it operated under the name of the National Bank of Libya, but its name was changed to the Central Bank after the Revolution of 1969. The Central Bank owns the majority of the share capital in the commercial banks and has established rules for their control and supervision. The main provisions for regulation of the banking sector are spelled out in Law no. 1 for Banking, Currency and Credit (1993), which replaced Law no. 4 of 1963. The provisions of the new law cover reserves, liquidity, monthly reporting and the day-to-day running of the banks and their business strategies. Article 2 of Law no. 1 provides that the authorized capital of the Central Bank of Libya will be LD100 million. The new law also allows for foreign banks to open branches in Libya so long as permission is granted from the Central Bank and the Cabinet.

Libyan Arab Foreign Bank (LAFB)

The Libyan Arab Foreign Bank (LAFB) is by far the largest of the Libyan banks and is the only bank in the country with an offshore status. It provides facilities and advisory services to several national companies, while its main role is to provide support for trading with Libya. To this end, it provides money market and foreign exchange services, trade and project financing and investment banking, in addition to the usual commercial banking and ancillary services. It has a large network of subsidiaries and affiliates located in more than 30 countries throughout the world, while more concentration of equity participation is found in the Arab world, Africa and Europe.

Being wholly owned by the Central Bank of Libya with the above-mentioned role, the LAFB's investment decisions are often politically driven – such as to support certain overseas development programmes or to provide support to the economy of certain countries. Hence, it consistently reports low levels of performance, especially relative to its size.

Commercial banks

Five other commercial banks operate in Libya, three of which are of a similar size in terms of total assets, while two are smaller. All these banks are owned by the Central Bank of Libya. However, each bank is independently run by its management and has its own board.

As the economy in Libya is centrally planned, the activity of the commercial banks is rather restricted and the banks provide limited services to individuals and state-owned enterprises. In more recent years, private businesses have been encouraged and commercial banks have begun to play a role in this field; however, their services remain constrained by the stringent credit policies and procedures to which they must adhere.

To individuals, the banks provide a means of payment of their salaries through their current accounts and provide loans for the building of residential homes. However, these loans are restricted to LD15,000 (US$12,400) against a mortgage over the land. No credit or debit cards are issued by any of the banks in the country. For corporations, the banks provide payroll services, current accounts, lending and issuance of letters of credit for imports, while the LAFB provides an undertaking for all the commercial banks' foreign commitments. Although none of the commercial banks are specialized in specific areas, historically these banks dealt in larger volumes with their main corporate customers.

The major customers of each bank are:

- **Gumhouria Bank**: National Company for Plastics; National Company for Textiles; National Company for Stationery; Benghazi Food Products Company; Al-Mamoura Food Products Company.
- **The National Commercial Bank**: National Supply Corporation (Nasco); National Cement Company; National Company for Tyres and Batteries; National Company for Pipes; Ras Lanuf Petrochemical Company.
- **Sahara Bank**: National Company for the Post Office; National Company for Electricity; National Company for Agricultural Supplies.
- **Umma Bank**: National Company for Trucks and Buses (Iveco); National Company for Beverages; Abou Kamash Project (Chemicals); National Company for Marketing.
- **Wahda Bank**: National Company for Household Goods; National Company for Electronics; Al-Ethad Al-Arabi Company for Building Materials.

Management

Article 53 of Law no. 1 of 1993 requires that commercial banks are organized as joint-stock companies and managed by boards of directors. Members of the board of each bank should be of Libyan nationality, enjoying civil and political rights, and no member is allowed to be a member of the board of another bank. Directors of the banks owned by the Central Bank are appointed by the General People's Committee (Council of Ministers) on nomination from the secretary of finance. Directors of the privately owned bank are appointed by the general assembly of the shareholders.

The board of each bank is responsible for the management of the bank. It is authorized to take all actions and measures that it deems necessary to fulfil the objectives of the bank. These include, but are not limited to:

- setting the rules for the provision of banking services within the limits of the banking law and the instructions of the Central Bank;
- determining policies for the investment of the bank's funds within the limits of the law;
- appointing and dismissing agents, representatives and correspondents, as well as accepting to act as agents or representatives for other banks;
- approving the establishment of branches or offices of the bank inside and outside Libya;
- laying down the internal rules and regulations for the bank;

- purchasing or renting real estate property for the bank's activities, and selling or leasing such property, or investing it;
- appointing and dismissing branch managers and other employees and fixing their salaries according to the relevant rules and regulations.

Decisions of the board with respect to the general rules for work organization, salaries and the appointment of key positions require the prior approval of the Central Bank and the secretary of finance. Decisions relating to long-term investment and the opening and closing of branches and offices inside and outside Libya require the prior approval of the Central Bank. The chairman of the board is the chief executive (managing director) and the legal representative of the bank.

Accounts

It is possible to obtain financial statements for the Libyan commercial banks; however, the disclosure level in the accounts is rather limited and restricts the possibility of in-depth financial assessments of the banks. Article 38 of the articles of association of the Umma Bank requires the board to prepare, at the end of each financial year, a balance sheet and a profit and loss account, in addition to a report covering the activities of the bank during the financial year. Two auditors appointed by the general assembly audit the bank.

The Bank of Commerce & Development

The Bank of Commerce & Development (BCD) is the only privately owned commercial bank operating in the Libyan market. It started operations in 1996. Since then it has grown quickly, although it holds only a 6 per cent share of commercial banking assets. The BCD is based in Benghazi, although most of its business is done through its branches in Tripoli.

Ahlia

Since the mid-1990s the government has been encouraging the establishment of local regional banks (Ahlia) and several licences have been issued. By mid-1998, the number of regional banks operating in the country reached 38, while the total number of licences granted by the Central Bank stood at 47. These banks are established by local communities with the aim of serving and meeting the requirements of the specific regional locality of the bank. Each of these banks is owned, run and funded by members of its local community. The main private bank is the Bank of Commerce & Development, which was established as a result of changes to laws regulating the economy and banking (in particular, Law no. 1 of 1993 for Banks, Currency and Credit).

Based in Tripoli, the National Banking Corporation is the central authority that coordinates the activities of the regional banks. However, the regional banks remain subject to the supervision of the Central Bank. The corporation is owned collectively by all the regional banks that operate with more than LD500,000. It provides clearing services for the regional banks and conducts international activities on their behalf.

Other banks

Several other banks also exist in Libya; they were established to assist in the development of certain sectors, such as housing, agriculture and manufacturing.

The insurance market

The first attempt to control the insurance market in Libya came in 1959, with the promulgation of Law no. 7. At the time, most commercial activities in the Libyan insurance market were in the hands of foreign companies and their agents in Libya. After the Revolution, Law no. 131 was issued (in 1970) and there was a more concerted attempt by the Libyan government to bring the insurance market under the control of the state. The Ministry of Economy became the government body responsible for issuing valid certificates of insurance practice in the country and for the formation of insurance companies.

Since that time, the most significant legislative developments and other regulatory events taking place in the Libyan insurance market have included:

1. The promulgation of Law no. 156 of 1970, which allows the Government to have a stake in the capital of all the insurance companies that operate in the Libyan insurance market.

2. Decree no. 1 of the Ministry of Economy (1971), which accommodates for the decrease of private shareholders' shares in the capital of the insurance sector.

3. Decree no. 14 of 1971, which allowed the Libyan government to seize the activities of all foreign companies operating in the Libyan insurance market.

4. Law no. 80 of 1971, which allowed the Libyan government to nationalize all insurance companies operating in Libya.

5. A Ministry of Economy Decree of 1971 (no. 52), which limited all insurance activities in Libya to two companies: Libya Insurance and Al-Muktar Insurance Co.
6. In 1981, a further decree provided for the merger of the two companies above into the Libyan Insurance Company, which was the only insurance enterprise allowed to operate in the Libyan market. A decree from the Libyan treasury was later issued to increase the capital of the Libyan National Insurance Company from LD2 million to LD30 million. This company offers the following insurance types: marine cargo, marine hull, aviation, inland transport, fire, burglary, offshore, family protection, motor insurance and life insurance.
7. Since 1999, some deregulation of the insurance market has been taking place. The United Insurance Company was formed and allowed to operate in all lines of insurance activity in the country. It is believed that some private-sector share capital is included in the capital structure of this enterprise.
8. During 1999–2000, legal provision was made for two more (private-sector) insurance companies to enter the Libyan market. The two companies are Al-Hussein Insurance Company and Rabta Insurance Services Company, but neither has yet started commercial activities.

3.2

The Foreign Investment Environment:
Economy, Banking and Priority Sectors

Geoff Duncanson, British Arab Commercial Bank

Introduction

It is now becoming evident that, following the suspension of UN sanctions in 1999 and the sustained recovery in oil prices, Libya is emerging as a market of immense potential and is generating renewed interest among investors. Although the degree of openness of the Libyan market remains comparatively limited, there are a number of encouraging signs that the Government is pursuing a more conciliatory approach towards foreign businesses. Within and outside the mainstay hydrocarbons sector, serious foreign candidates looking to take advantage of what the country has to offer should look closely at Libya sooner rather than later, to ensure the necessary relationships with Libyan partners begin to emerge.

This chapter will be divided into two broad sections. The first will consider the economic policy environment, including the size of the Libyan market and the main policy issues of concern to the development of economic liberalization in the country. This section will also give a brief overview of both the domestic and international banking scene. The second section will give an indication of the key economic sectors in which opportunities are likely to arise and some comments will be made about how an exporter should consider the issue of 'how to get paid'.

Economic policy environment

Libya is not a large economy in world terms. Its population, put at about 5.4 million, is growing quickly and is heavily skewed towards the youth end of the age pyramid – and therefore of interest to suppliers of all types of capital goods, provided these can be paid for. The country is heavily dependent on hydrocarbons and the state plays a highly dominant role in economic affairs. Despite official encouragement for the opening up of the economy to private-sector involvement in recent years, investors remain wary in the absence of clear policy signals. This is not uncommon in closely managed economies, despite the trend towards greater openness.

The trend towards greater openness is set to continue following the end of a long period of economic and political isolation during the 1990s, when UN sanctions were operational. Although the United States remains largely hostile and has not lifted its separate set of sanctions imposed in 1986, these unilateral measures are not as debilitating as the almost eight years of multilateral UN sanctions. On one level, the sanctions imposed discipline on economic management and forced the country to live strictly within its exported means. On another level, however, businessmen were unable to travel abroad easily, the key hydrocarbons sector was starved of investment and spares, and other projects, aimed at widening what is a very narrow economic base, had to be put on hold.

Elsewhere on the policy front, one of the key issues facing not only Libya but all of North Africa is the extent to which each of these countries – and they are all unique and at varying stages of development – joins the European bandwagon. All these markets already conduct the majority of their trade with Europe, but the question is whether or not to join a common market.

The potential risks for Libyan policy-makers are that European traders would overwhelm local businessmen if tariff barriers are removed. On the other hand, the potential reward for Libya would be access to a far larger market and help with market restructuring along the way. Tunisia, Morocco and Egypt are all committed in principle to the so-called 'Barcelona process' – the framework agreement for free trade and greater economic openness for the countries bordering the Mediterranean Sea.

It goes without saying that Libya has many issues to address if it is to come on board. For much of the 1990s, while its neighbours were embarking on structural policy reform of their economies aimed at making the transition to a more conventional market economy first possible and then bearable, Libya was isolated by sanctions. The main issues confronting Libya include privatization, macroeconomic transparency, public sector reform and creating an adequate legal framework able to cater to the foreign investor.

Banking sector

Before 1969, European banks operated branches in Libya. In 1970, these branches were mostly nationalized and renamed under titles reflecting state ownership. The one exception was the National Commercial Bank, which was newly created at this time. The main bank in Libya at present, the Libyan Arab Foreign Bank (LAFB), which specializes in international banking business, was established in 1972. Nine years later, the Libyan Arab Foreign Investment Company was established and also focused its business offshore. But in this case, as its name suggests, the institution is responsible for managing portfolio investments abroad.

Thus, historically, all these financial institutions have one thing in common: they are all owned by the state – although their ancestry, procedures and geographic locations give rise to subtle differences in approach. It can be reasonably expected, however, that a significant degree of their lending activities has either been directed or at least guided by political considerations. Auditing practices and disclosure requirements are not aimed – as they are in the West – at protecting depositors and creditors, who are in any case themselves government entities for the most part. Perhaps because of the high level of state involvement, the banking habit is not well developed in Libya. What this means in practice is that most people have not been persuaded of the benefits of keeping money in banks. Most small-scale transactions are therefore settled in cash, which one can assume is tucked away under mattresses.

One fairly recent development has been the establishment of public/private sector-owned regional banks set up to foster development in their particular localities – examples being the National Bank of Tripoli and the National Bank of Benghazi.

There is one private-sector bank in Libya at present, the Bank of Commerce and Development, which was started in 1996 and is growing rapidly. However, for the most part, entrepreneurs have been discouraged or crowded out of the banking sector, as in other sectors of the economy.

In theory, the future potential of domestic banking in Libya is excellent. This is, after all, a small country with significant wealth. Apart from mobilizing deposits into the banking system, which could then in theory be put to more productive broadening of Libya's economic base, these customers could be sold life insurance, savings products and so forth, which would diversify income sources.

With regard to international operations, none of Libya's domestic banks maintains a branch network abroad. Instead, the government has followed a policy of taking strategic investments in foreign institutions. The British Arab Commercial Bank (BACB), in which the LAFB holds a 25 per cent ownership stake, is a good example of this policy. The LAFB has similar investments (at a greater or lesser level) in banking institutions in, among others, France, Italy, Egypt, Spain, Turkey and the United Arab Emirates. In all cases, the LAFB holds equity in locally regulated commercial banks, often in a consortium with a more familiar institutional investor alongside Libyan and other interests. In the case of the BACB, the LAFB is in a consortium with HSBC, one of the world's largest financial services institutions, having more than 5,000 offices in 82 countries and territories worldwide.

Market potential for exporters considering Libya

In terms of the primary sector, given the pace of population growth, there is a widespread need for infrastructure development: power transmission, telecommunications, transport, schools, hospitals and so forth.

Picking out one or two major sectors, one cannot ignore hydrocarbons, which have transformed the Libyan economy over the past 40 years and remain the country's lifeblood. Not surprisingly, there is a very substantial requirement for goods and services to support the oil infrastructure, which was starved of investment for much of the 1990s.

Second, water is the key long-term resource issue facing North African and Arab markets. Libya's solution to the question of water is unique. Following almost 20 years of construction and between US$25 billion and US$30 billion in expenditure, the Great Man-made River (GMR), a network of huge pipes and reservoirs fed by desert aquifers, is delivering fresh water to the northern coastal towns. Clearly there are substantial spares and operation and maintenance (O&M) works associated with this project. In fact, the GMR was designed to foster greater self-sufficiency in agriculture, always a strategic issue in developing countries and particularly so where water is an issue as it is in Libya. Hence agribusiness is a sector that will give rise to opportunities in the medium term.

Note also that there are strong seasonal demands for certain types of product. For example, live animal shipments are required around the time of key religious festivals, which move forward by approximately 10 days each year, which can scupper even the best-laid marketing plans!

Looking at the secondary sector, as noted earlier, Libya's economic base is very narrow and strictly limited beyond the oil sector. This means virtually all manufactured and semi-manufactured goods need to be imported, which is good news for Western producers whose domestic populations are declining and who are increasingly looking to export markets to drive volume increases. Libya's young, rapidly growing and well-educated population needs refrigerators, cars and computers, and there is great market potential in almost every sector.

Turning to services, as a former administrative centre of the Roman Empire, Libya boasts some of the finest archaeological remains in the world and there is clearly potential in tourism development. Much work needs to be done in terms of infrastructure, building and refurbishing hotels, and in similar fields. However, with its large Mediterranean coastline, Libya has the natural resources to leverage its tourist potential much further. Other consultancy opportunities are to be found in all of the sectors addressed in this chapter.

Furthermore, there are a number of grand projects that are much talked about, such as the trans-Maghreb railway, large-scale smelters, fertilizer factories and so forth. Financing for these investments will, under current circumstances, be on a case-by-case basis and be subject to state allocation of revenues. A more traditional project-financing approach would be to tie the financing of a project to the level and timing of future cash flows.

Perhaps the moves towards greater openness and possible encouragement of foreign equity participation in future projects, or progress towards more open-market deregulation under the EuroMed (Barcelona) processes, will in due course encourage more capital flows to finance development. Certainly, the government has indicated that of the US$35 billion in the development funding it has identified, about US$6 billion is expected to be sourced from the private sector. However, as things stand, it appears that the present state of affairs is likely to persist.

Getting paid for provision of goods and services

The confirmed credit approach is the way in which most exporters achieve secure terms in dealing with the Libyan market. The BACB is able to confirm credits from the market and, despite common perceptions, it should be noted that the Libyan market did not close while UN sanctions were in force. UK trade with Libya alone was of the order of £250 million a year, even at the height of sanctions. This figure is for recorded trade, alluding to the fact that the actual level of goods shipped to Libya was even higher, although some will have gone via entry ports in either the Far East or the Gulf.

BACB is a leading source of support for UK or any world exporters seeking to work with Libya. BACB has been on cover for Libya for over 25 years, and for those enterprises trading regularly with the Arab world such long-standing relationships count for a great deal when dealing with discrepancies or the intricacies of a market where patience is more of a necessity than a virtue.

Conclusion

Although Libya is a relatively small market, it clearly offers considerable potential and, particularly at this time of environmental concerns and high oil prices, Libya's low-sulphur crude is in demand and commanding a healthy premium in the European gasoline markets.

The population is growing strongly and this gives rise to import requirements across all sectors of the economy, which inevitably presents opportunities for exporters in the West. Libya presents itself as a market offering opportunities to committed exporters, notwithstanding long lead times, and the business process is characterized by the inevitable delays and frustrations that arise when dealing with a centrally controlled economy. However, building relationships in Libya today will most likely bear fruit when greater regional autonomy, as a result of the recent administrative changes inside the country, result in faster budgetary allocations to needy sectors.

In the longer term, the market will deepen and grow as private-sector involvement and inward investment are encouraged by the Libyan authorities. In short, this is not a market for carpetbaggers and fair-weather friends, but one for committed players, with the reward you derive ultimately based on the steadfastness of your support and the partners you choose.

3.3

Business Taxation

EWM, Malta

The principal taxes relevant to a foreign company are set out below. With only minor amendments, tax law and tax rates have not changed since their introduction in the early 1970s.

Company income tax (profits tax)

Branches of foreign companies registered under Law no. 65 of 1970 (Company Law) are subject to company income tax on profits, assessed under Law no. 64 of 1973 (Income Tax Law).

Foreign companies registered under Law no. 5 of 1997 (Encouragement of Foreign Capital Investment) are exempt from company income tax on profits for five years, extendable to eight, if those profits are reinvested.

Oil company profits are subject to petroleum tax under Law no. 5 of 1955, but companies that have signed exploration and production-sharing agreements (EPSAs), subsequent to their introduction in 1974, are deemed to have had their liability to petroleum tax settled by the National Oil Corporation of Libya (NOC).

Libyan statute tax law is straightforward and the basis of determination of taxable income, assessment and payment of tax, and the appeal process, set out in Law no. 64 of 1973, resembles tax law in many countries. However, practice differs from theory.

The assessment of company income tax under Law no. 64 is in two stages.

Preliminary assessment

All foreign entities must file a tax return annually with the Libyan tax department within one month of the date of approval of the annual branch accounts (effectively the date of the audit report), and not later than seven months from their year-end. This return should be accompanied by a balance sheet and profit and loss account. Foreign entities exempt or not subject to company income tax should note this on the tax return.

It is accepted practice that 'estimated accounts', or a 'three-line estimate' of income, expenses and profit or loss, will initially suffice, pending submission of final figures as soon as is possible thereafter, but the tax department is becoming increasingly reluctant to accept these submissions and will usually demand that supplementary information be submitted with them.

Head office accounts should also be submitted with the annual tax return.

Based on this submission, in whichever form, the tax department will raise a preliminary assessment on branches subject to company income tax, levying tax on declared profit at scale rates set by the law, plus Jihad tax. No tax is payable at this time if a loss is declared.

As this is, in effect, self-assessment, there is no right of appeal against the preliminary assessment.

Final assessment

At the request of either the branch or the tax department, a 'tax audit' of the branch's books and records will be performed in order to determine the final liability to company income tax for a particular year. It is current practice for the tax department to conduct an audit every other year.

Final accounts, together with a final tax return, must be submitted to the tax department at the commencement of a tax audit if they have not already been submitted.

In extreme cases, the tax department may insist on an annual tax audit, but this is unusual. The five-year statute of limitations is extended to perpetuity for the assessment of company taxes.

The audit by the tax department inspectors is based on the Arabic statutory records of the branch (see Chapter 3.4, Accounting and Audit).

If a loss is declared in the preliminary tax return, and a profit in the final, a penalty of 25 per cent of the tax payable is assessed.

Although company income tax law is based on the usual 'add-back' basis, whereby disallowed expenditure is added back to declared net profits or losses, current practice is that the tax department raises assessments based on a percentage of turnover – the 'deemed profit' basis of assessment. Tax is therefore payable even when losses are declared. Only in exceptional circumstances, where detailed Arabic records have been maintained, will the add-back basis be applied.

The level of deemed profit applied to turnover varies according to the nature of the branch's business activity. This ranges from between 12 and 15 per cent for civil works and contracting, between 15 and 25 per cent for oil service, to between 25 and 35 per cent in the case of design/consulting engineers. Within these broad ranges, each case is reviewed individually, and once the 'preliminary' final assessments are issued, taxpayers have a period of 30 days in which to negotiate an agreed settlement, or to appeal. Thereafter, an appeal process exists through First and Second Appeal Committees, the Court of Appeal and thence to the Supreme Court. Apart from the most exceptional of circumstances, the minimum percentage negotiable is 15.

The ranges noted above could be exceeded if it is found that the branch's records/declarations are lacking or false. Up to 10 per cent may be added to turnover for 'doubt'. Above all, the deemed profit percentage applied to any year will be higher than the profit percentage declared in the annual tax return. Company income tax is payable in four quarterly instalments.

It is possible for foreign companies to limit their branch tax liability by agreement with their employing party to pay any excess over 15 per cent deemed profit, or to reimburse taxes, but this is increasingly difficult to negotiate.

Company income tax exemption is exceptional but may be granted:

- if approved by the General People's Committee (Cabinet) for a particular contract;
- if negotiated under Law no. 8 of 1992, under which tax-exempt contracts may be awarded for certain strategic industries, which are:
  - iron and steel;
  - aluminium;
  - cement and building materials;
  - passenger and light transport vehicles.

Direct contractors to the Great Man-Made River Authority are exempt from company income tax under Law no. 11 of 1983.

Company income tax rates

Table 3.3.1 Company income tax rates

	Libyan dinar	Company income tax (%)
On profits up to	10,000	20
On next	20,000	25
On next	30,000	30
On next	40,000	40
On next	50,000	45
Over	150,000	60

In addition, a further 4 per cent on profits is payable for Jihad tax.

Petroleum tax

Until 1974, foreign oil companies signed 'concession agreements' in accordance with the provisions of Petroleum Law no. 25 of 1955, under which they were entitled to export all oil found within the concession area. Only four such agreements remain extant. A complex formula results in the foreign company receiving 6.5 per cent of the market value of oil as profit.

Since 1974, the Libyan oil authorities (currently the NOC) have entered into EPSAs under which foreign oil companies take a negotiable share of oil production. Any liability to petroleum tax is deemed to have been settled by the NOC within its share.

There is no double taxation agreement between the United Kingdom and Libya, but, by concession, taxes paid on income are allowed as a deduction from any UK liability, subject to the provision of documentation required by the UK Inland Revenue authorities. Other taxes paid are allowed as a deduction, as expenses.

Personal taxes

All Libyan nationals and resident expatriate employees are subject to personal income tax. Expatriates working in Libya are subject to tax from the date of their arrival if they have been in Libya for more than 30 days in any calendar year.

Monthly salary declarations must be filed with the Revenue authorities. All salaries, wages and benefits-in-kind which accrue as a result of working in Libya are liable to Libyan income tax.

At the same time as carrying out the tax audit for company income tax purposes, as noted in the previous sections, the tax inspector will review the branch's records to determine whether there are any salaries or benefits-in-kind paid locally, or which could be deemed to have been paid locally, which have not previously been subjected to personal taxes. A wide range of benefits-in-kind is usually assessed. The additional payroll taxes due on such undeclared salaries and benefits will be assessed on the company, in addition to the company income tax assessment, at a rate of either 15 or 20 per cent (plus 3 per cent Jihad tax). These assessments can be material.

Personal income tax audits of oil and income tax-exempt companies are also conducted at regular intervals.

Personal tax assessments (see Table 3.3.2) are payable within 60 days of receipt, but are subject to negotiation for the 30-day period from the issue of the preliminary assessment (as company income tax above).

Table 3.3.2 Annual rates of personal tax

Income (Libyan dinar)	Personal tax (%)
First 1,800	8
Next 1,200	10
Next 1,800	15
Next 1,800	20
Next 1,800	25
Balance	35

Taxable incomes are also subject to Jihad tax as follows:

- 1% if income does not exceed LD50 per month;
- 2% if income does not exceed LD100 per month;
- 3% on incomes over LD100 per month.

All individuals are granted a personal allowance: LD480 for a single person, LD720 for a married man without children, and LD900 for a married man with children. It is understood that a married woman with taxable income is entitled to the single person's allowance without prejudice to the married allowance granted to the husband. Allowances are apportioned for a period of less than one year.

Foreign income of foreign employees and of their wives and dependants is exempt from Libyan personal tax.

General tax

General tax, or surtax, is a personal tax levied on taxable incomes in excess of LD6,000 per annum, net of income taxes already paid (see Table 3.3.3).

Table 3.3.3 Rates of general tax

Income (Libyan dinar)	General tax (%)
First 6,000 per annum	Exempt
Next 3,000	15
Next 5,000	25
Next 8,000	35
Next 15,000	45
Next 25,000	55
Next 40,000	65
Next 100,000	75
In excess of 200,000	90

The tax is levied on total income earned in a calendar year, less the amount of personal tax paid, and is due by 28 February of the following year. All taxpayers subject to the tax must submit a return of their total income for the year before this date or 80 days before their departure from the country. As a matter of practice, these returns are prepared and submitted by the employer.

General tax is also levied, at a rate of 15 per cent, on a percentage of undeclared payroll benefits identified during the course of a tax audit.

Jihad tax

Jihad tax is payable under Law no. 44 of 1970 and is imposed on taxable salaries, wages and so forth, and on retirement pensions at the rates previously noted.

Jihad tax is imposed on taxable corporate profits at a rate of 4 per cent.

Social security contributions (INAS)

Social security contributions (INAS) are payable in accordance with Law no. 13 of 1980 and pertinent regulations as amended by Law no. 1 of 1991.

Social security contributions are payable by all persons working in Libya. The contributions are computed on gross income, either weekly or monthly, and from 1 June 1991 are as shown in Table 3.3.4.

Table 3.3.4 Social security contributions (%)

	Foreign branch	Libyan-defined entity
Employee's contribution	3.75	3.75
Employer's contribution	11.25	10.5
Contribution from Public Treasury	n/a	0.75
Total	15	15

The social security authorities may insist on the inclusion of an amount in addition to salary to take account of the cost of housing and subsistence, whether such amount is paid to the employee or not.

INAS is payable on the 10th day of the month following the payment of salary. A fine of 5 per cent per annum is made for late payment.

The INAS authorities conduct audits in the same way as the tax department, but at longer intervals of, perhaps, 5 years. The additional

INAS due on undeclared salaries and benefits identified will be assessed on the company at the standard 15 per cent rate plus a late payment penalty of 5 per cent per annum. Again, these assessments can be material.

Stamp duty

Stamp duty is assessed under Law no. 65 of 1973, as amended by Law no. 16 of 1998. Article 2 states that any document to be 'used' in Libya must be registered with the tax department within 60 days of signature. The definition of 'used' is a matter of legal interpretation, but is broad.

Stamp duty of 2 per cent of the total value is payable on registration of a main contract. (The registration of a subcontract is 1 per cent of the contract value.) Any invoices rendered under a registered contract should be stamped by the tax department, signifying that registration duty has been paid on the contract to which the invoice relates. Employing parties will refuse to pay invoices not registered with the tax department. Registration of contracts and invoices can only be effected using the Arabic version.

Stamp duty of 0.5 per cent is withheld from payments made by local government bodies.

Stamp duty of 0.5 per cent is also payable on any official receipt, including receipts for contract registration duties, corporate and personal taxes, etc. According to law, companies should ensure that invoices presented to them for payment bear the relevant registration and stamp duties.

Additional duties may be applicable when conducting business within Libya. There are 44 assessable schedules within the law.

Foreign companies registered under Law no. 5 of 1997 (see above) are exempt stamp duty on contract registration.

Customs duties

Imports into Libya are subject to customs duties at rates that vary from 0 per cent to in excess of 400 per cent, depending on the nature of the import. A detailed schedule of tariffs is published.

Equipment imported into Libya for use in the oil sector is exempt from customs duties under Article 16 of Law no. 25 of 1955 (Petroleum Law).

Capital equipment imported into Libya for use in a project licensed under Law no. 5 of 1997 (Encouragement of Foreign Capital Investment) is exempt from customs duties. Parts and raw materials are exempt for five years.

Temporary importation of equipment is exempt, subject to the payment of a customs deposit, but the requirements surrounding the exemption are stringent, and a breach of temporary import conditions leads to substantial fines and penalties.

3.4

Accounting and Audit

EWM, Malta

Statutory requirements

Business entities operating in Libya are required by law (the Civil Code and Income Tax Law no. 64 of 1973) to maintain a detailed general ledger, general journal and inventory ledger (the 'statutory books'), which should contain every transaction entered into by the entity.

Before use, the statutory books must be stamped as registered with the tax authorities and the Commercial Court. It should be noted that a ledger or journal will not be registered if it already contains accounting entries – in other words, one cannot register existing books of account. Similarly, transactions pre-dating the date that the books are registered will be disallowed.

Practical implications

It is difficult to maintain the detailed records required, in Arabic, but in an effort to comply with the law, foreign companies write up their statutory records on the basis of monthly transaction summaries extracted from their subsidiary books and records.

In addition to compliance with the law, the maintenance of statutory books assumes importance as a result of the audit of the branch's records by the tax department. At the commencement of an audit, the inspector will request production of the statutory books. If these are not available, a perfunctory audit of the English (or other language) books of account will be made and it is likely that a punitive assessment will be raised.

If statutory books have been maintained, even in summary form, the inspector will issue assessments at a more reasonable level. In this connection, it should be stressed that in all instances adequate documentation of expenditure, cross-referenced to summary journals and hence to the statutory books, should be maintained.

Accounting method

Oil companies are subject to the accounting requirements of Petroleum Law no. 25 of 1955, as amended, and the terms of their exploration and production sharing agreements (EPSAs). The law and agreements require the application of 'sound and consistent accounting practices usual in the (modern) petroleum industry'. Other entities normally prepare financial statements on the accruals basis of accounting, but the cash basis is also accepted. There are no Libyan standards as such and there is no standard setting body.

Financial statements

All foreign entities, including oil companies and companies registered under Law no. 5 of 1997 (Encouragement of Foreign Capital Investment), must submit accounts to the tax department within seven months of their year-end. Final accounts should be submitted as soon as is possible if estimated accounts were submitted initially, and within one month of the approval of the accounts by the directors. In addition, accounts should be submitted annually to the Secretariat of Economy, the Investment Promotion Board, and to other relevant authorities, in accordance with the terms of the business licence.

The manager and accountant are legally responsible for the veracity of the accounts.

Accounts must be in Arabic and must include a balance sheet, a profit and loss account, notes to the accounts, and a report signed by a Libyan public accountant. There is no requirement to submit a cash-flow statement and the accounts need not show comparative information. The notes to the accounts are usually perfunctory.

Accounts are usually prepared on a calendar basis, the accounting period of the state, but the choice of year-end may be changed, subject to the approval of the local authorities. An initial accounting period must not exceed 18 months.

Audit requirements

All foreign companies are subject to audit by the tax and social security departments, and may be audited by the Public Control Board (National Audit Office).

Branches of foreign oil companies are also subject to audit by the National Oil Corporation of Libya (NOC).

Foreign companies registered under Law no. 5 of 1997 (see above) are subject to audit by the Investment Promotion Board.

Accounting profession

The accounting and audit profession is governed by the Libyan Union of Accountants and Auditors. Membership of the union is restricted to Libyan nationals and members are designated 'Libyan Public Accountant'. Only a Libyan public accountant may sign an audit report for use in Libya. Admittance to membership requires the holding of a bachelor's degree in accounting or a related discipline, and the undertaking of practical experience.

Accounting positions in all companies, national and foreign, are limited to Libyan nationals with the exception, in practice, of one senior position in foreign entities.

Part Four

Key Industry Sectors

4.1

Libya's Hydrocarbons and Mineral Resources: An Historical Overview

Marat Terterov[1]

Petroleum industry

Since the early 1960s, the petroleum industry has increasingly dominated the whole economy, although in 1984 it provided direct employment for fewer than 10,000 Libyans. The development of the oil industry was remarkable, in terms of both its rapidity and its proliferation. An exceptional combination of circumstances contributed to the development of the petroleum sector. Like Algerian oil, Libyan crude oil, while having a rather high wax content, is lighter and easier to handle than crude from most other petroleum areas. It also has a low sulphur content, which makes it easier on internal combustion engines and less of a pollution contributor than other crude. For this reason, Libyan crude had a receptive market in Europe from the start; furthermore, Libya is one-third closer to European markets than the oil ports of the eastern Mediterranean. When the Suez Canal was closed by the June 1967 war, forcing tankers from Iran, Iraq and the Arabian Peninsula to go around the Cape of Good Hope, the advantages of Libyan petroleum were enhanced. Moreover, the lay of the land itself, which allows the output of the wells to be piped directly and easily to dockside totally over Libya's territory, assured steadiness of supply, which has not necessarily been the case for eastern Mediterranean pipeline outlets. In addition, Libya's petroleum development benefited from the technology and experience acquired by the industry in other parts of the petroleum world during the preceding 50 years. Thus, by 1977, Libya was the seventh largest oil producer in the world. However, Libya's position declined somewhat

[1] This chapter is based on various Internet sources.

in the early 1980s as OPEC production quotas were cut. By 1986, Libya was only the 15th largest producer of crude oil.

For the petroleum industry, the Revolution of 1969 did not represent a rupture of continuity; it did, however, introduce a shift in government attitudes towards the purpose and function of the foreign operating companies in line with its general nationalist-socialist political and socioeconomic orientation. It is therefore useful to visualize Libya's petroleum development in terms of two periods, dividing at 1 September 1969, with the earlier period serving to prepare for the later.

Early exploration and industry development

Active exploration started in 1953 after oil was discovered in neighbouring Algeria. The first well was begun in 1956 in western Fezzan, and the first oil was struck in 1957. Esso (subsequently Exxon) made the first commercial strike in 1959, just as several firms were planning to give up exploration. The first oil flowed by pipeline from Esso's concession at Zaltan to its export facilities at Marsa al Burayqah in 1961. The rush was on, with other companies entering Libya and additional discoveries being made. The original major strikes were in the Sirte Basin, one of the world's largest oil basins, southeast of the Gulf of Sidra; in 1987, this area was still the source of the bulk of Libya's output. In 1969, a major strike was made at Sarir, well to the southeast of the Sirte Basin fields, and minor fields were located in northwestern Tripolitania. New deposits were found in the Ghadames sedimentary basin (400 kilometres southwest of Tripoli) in 1974 and in offshore fields 30 kilometres northwest of Tripoli in 1977.

Further attempts to tap new deposits continued to revolve around Libya's offshore fields during the 1980s. The large Bouri field was brought on stream by the National Oil Corporation of Libya (NOC) and Agip (Azienda Generale Italiana Petroli), a subsidiary of the Italian state oil company consortium, in late 1987. Other offshore exploration ventures were launched following the settlement of maritime boundary disputes with Tunisia in 1982 and Malta in 1983. Libyan access to offshore deposits in these formerly disputed areas was significant because they may contain as much as 7 billion barrels of oil.

Petroleum production in 1985 was still governed by the Petroleum Law of 1955, which was amended in 1961, 1965 and 1971. The Government, through the Ministry of Petroleum, preferred to grant sizeable concessions to a number of different foreign companies. To induce rapid exploitation of deposits, the typical concession contract called for progressive nationalization of Libyan operations run by foreign companies over a span of 10 years, with the Libyan Government's share starting as one-quarter and ending at three-quarters. The Government extracted most of its compensation in the form of product sharing. When early concessions to several large companies by Esso, which was the first to export Libyan crude in 1961, proved to be highly profitable, many independent oil companies from non-communist countries set up similar operations in Libya. In 1969, about 33 companies held concessions. Concessionary terms were somewhat tightened during the 1970s as the post-revolutionary government pursued a more active policy of nationalization. The vehicle for this policy was the revamped state NOC, which, as noted, was formed in 1970 from Lipetco. In July 1970, NOC's jurisdiction was expanded by legislation that nationalized the foreign-owned Esso, Shell and Ente Nazionale Idrocarbuno (ENI) marketing subsidiaries, and a small local company, Petro Libya, and transferred their operations to NOC. These operations included managing companies in the importing, distributing and selling of refined petroleum products at subsidized prices in Libya. In 1971, the companies were merged into a single countrywide marketing enterprise called the Brega Company, which also marketed oil and gas abroad for the Government.

New policy attitudes after the change of political regime

The new government's nationalization campaign commenced in December 1971, when it nationalized the British Petroleum share of the British Petroleum-Bunker Hunt Sarir field in retaliation for the British Government's failure to intervene to prevent Iran from taking possession of three small islands in the Gulf belonging to the United Arab Emirates. It was not until late 1974 that a compensation agreement was reached between British Petroleum and the Libyan Government over the settlement of these nationalized assets. In December 1972, Libya moved against British Petroleum's former partner Bunker Hunt and demanded a 50 per cent participation in its operations. When Bunker Hunt refused, its assets were nationalized in June 1973 and turned over to one of NOC's subsidiaries, as had been done earlier with British Petroleum's assets.

In late 1972, a 50 per cent participation had been agreed upon with the Italian joint company, Agip-ENI, and in early 1973 talks began with the Occidental Petroleum Corporation and with the Oasis group. Occidental, accounting for approximately 15 per cent of total production, was one of the major independent producers. In July 1973, it agreed to NOC's purchase of 51 per cent of its assets. The Oasis group, another major producer, was comprised of the American companies Conoco, Marathon and Amerada Hess. The Oasis group agreed to Libya's 51 per cent participation in August 1973. On 1 September 1973, Libya unilaterally announced that it was taking over 51 per cent of the remaining oil companies, except for a few small operators.

Several foreign oil companies balked at the Libyan proposal but soon found that the Government's policy was firm: agree to Libyan participation or face nationalization. Shell refused to accept Libyan participation, and its operations were nationalized in March 1974. A month earlier, three other reluctant oil companies had been nationalized: Texaco, the California Asiatic Company, and the Libyan-American Oil Company. They finally received compensation for their assets in 1977.

Withdrawal of the Americans

Political events of the 1980s convinced many US-owned companies of the advisability of selling off their Libyan operations. In 1981, Exxon withdrew from Libya, pulling out its long-standing subsidiary operations. Mobil followed suit in 1982 when it withdrew from its operations in the Ras Lanuf system. These withdrawals gave NOC an even greater share in the overall oil industry. Another round of advancing nationalization was made possible in 1986, when US President Ronald Reagan announced on January 7 his intention to require US companies to divest from their operations in Libya. It was unclear at that time, however, whether the five companies involved would sell their shares to NOC (probably at a substantial loss), or merely transfer them to European subsidiaries not affected by the president's sanctions. According to the estimates available in early 1987, NOC's share of the total equity in Libyan petroleum operations then stood at 70 per cent, with two operating subsidiaries and at least a 50 per cent share in each major private concession.

Although NOC had been under nominal control of the Ministry of Petroleum, foreign observers were uncertain what real control the Ministry had over NOC. The Ministry's dissolution in March 1986 produced little comment, which seemed to indicate that NOC was the principal instrument of government policy in the oil sector and controlled about two-thirds of Libya's total oil production. Since 1974, no new concessions have been granted, although the Libyan Government has negotiated production-sharing agreements with existing concession holders to induce them to search for new deposits, particularly in the offshore region bordering Tunisia where the large Bouri field is located. These agreements have called for NOC to receive 81 per cent of production if the discovery is offshore and 85 per cent if it is onshore.

Price policies and pipelines

Libyan price policy has largely been settled in meetings of OPEC, which it joined in 1962. Both the pre-revolutionary and post-revolutionary governments have remained committed to OPEC as an instrument for maximizing their total oil revenues. Petroleum production (almost all of which was exported) declined during the first half of the 1970s, as a result of both the OPEC and Libyan policy of cutting production to influence price. During the late 1970s, production rose slightly, only to fall again in the 1980s when OPEC reduced its members' production quotas in an attempt to halt the oil price slide. In March 1983, Libya accepted its OPEC quota of 1.1 million barrels per day (bpd). This figure was revised downward again in November 1984, when it was set at 990,000 bpd. Libyan oil production in 1986 averaged 1137 thousand bpd, having regained the same production it had in 1981. Generally, Libya has adhered to its OPEC quota.

In 1986, Libyan oil fields were served by a complicated network of oil pipelines leading to the five principal export terminals at Marsa al Burayqah, As Sidra, Ras Lanuf, Marsa al Hariqah and Az Zuwaytinah. The Sidra terminal exported the largest volume of oil, at approximately 30 per cent of the total in 1981. A future sixth terminal was planned at Zuwarah in western Libya. Pipelines to these terminals served more than one company, thus mixing different oil blends that were standardized for export. The share that an individual company received from exports was determined by the amount and quality of the oil that entered the common pipeline. The share of the oil belonging to the NOC was either sold directly on the open market or sold back to its producing partner. Libyan refining capacity increased dramatically in 1985 when the export refinery at Ras Lanuf came on stream with a 220,000-bpd capacity. Other refineries existed at Tobruk (20,000 bpd), Marsa al Burayqah (11,000 bpd), and Az Zawiyah (116,000 bpd), giving Libya an overall refining capacity in 1985 of 367,000 bpd.

Gas industry

Production of natural gas in Libya received a major boost in 1971 when a law was passed requiring the oil companies to store and liquefy the natural gas condensate from their wells, rather than burning it off as many had previously done. However, natural gas production has lagged far behind oil because the high costs of transport and liquefaction have made it a less attractive alternative. A large liquefaction plant was built at Marsa al Burayqah in 1968, but its export performance has been uneven. Approximately 70 per cent of Libya's natural gas production is consumed domestically. Production stood at 12.35 billion cubic metres in 1984, down from 20.38 billion cubic metres in 1980. Total reserves of natural gas were estimated at 600 billion cubic metres in 1985.

Mineral resources

Libya's commercially usable mineral resources – apart from its hydrocarbons – were limited to a large iron ore deposit in the Wadi ash Shati near Sabha in Fezzan, and scattered deposits of gypsum, limestone, cement rock, salt and building stone. There were also small, widely scattered and currently non-commercial deposits of phosphate rock, manganese, barite-celestite, sodium carbonate, sulphur and alum. Although much of the country had been photographed by the petroleum companies and large portions of it had been mapped by the Italians, by UK and US military personnel, and by the US Geological Survey (from 1954 to 1962) in search of water and minerals, the country is so large that in early 1987 much of it still had not been mapped at scales suitable for definitive mineral inventory.

The Wadi ash Shati iron ore deposit is known to be one of the largest in the world. Suitable in considerable part for strip mining, it outcrops in or underlies roughly 80 square kilometres of the valley. According to information in the mid-1980s, none of it was high-grade ore. Preliminary estimates suggest that the amount of 30 to 40 per cent iron-content ore in the deposits totals anywhere between 700 million and 2 billion tonnes. Because of the distances and technical problems involved, profitable exploitation of the deposits would depend on the construction of a proposed rail route to the coast. Development of the deposits would allow Libya self-sufficiency in iron and steel, although probably at costs appreciably above those available on an import basis. In 1974, a state-owned company, the General Iron and Steel Corporation, was formed to exploit the deposits. The Government hoped that the planned iron and steel manufacturing plant at Misratah, completed in 1986, would eventually be able to exploit the Wadi ash Shati deposits. But the commercial viability of using these deposits was not assumed, since initial plans called for the Misratah works to be fed with imported iron ore pellets.

Other scattered iron ore deposits in northwestern Tripolitania and northern Fezzan were apparently insufficient to be commercially exploitable under current conditions. Manganese was known to occur in northwestern Tripolitania and, in combination with the iron ore deposits, at several locations in the Wadi ash Shati. Known deposits, however, were not considered commercially exploitable.

Salt flats, formed by evaporation at lagoonal deposits near the coast and in closed depressions in the desert interior, are widely scattered through the northern part of the country. In some cases, especially along the Gulf of Sidra, they cover large areas. In the 1980s, approximately 11,000 tonnes of salt were produced annually. Evidence of sulphur has been reported at scattered points in the salt flats of the Sirte Basin and in various parts of Fezzan; sulphur occurs in pure form in Fezzan and is associated with sulphur springs in the Sirte Basin.

Sodium carbonate (trona) is formed as a crust at the edges and bottoms of a number of dry lakes in Fezzan. Traditionally, about 100 metric tonnes a year were harvested and sent to market at Sabha. Because sodium carbonate is used in petroleum refining, as well as traditionally in soap making and water refining, production may be increased as part of the Government's development effort in Fezzan.

Because of the Government's interest in social welfare and its financial ability to support it, construction is bound to be a major area of future economic development. Except for wood, the raw materials needed for construction – stone, gravel, clay, limestone, gypsum and cheap fuel – are found in abundant quantities and suitable commercial qualities adjacent to the major population and production centres in both northern Tripolitania and Cyrenaica. In 1986, plans were announced for a new gypsum mine with a planned output of 200,000 to 300,000 tonnes a year. Several thousand tons of gypsum are mined annually and indicated reserves of gypsum total about 200 million tonnes.

4.2

Evolution of Libyan Petroleum Exploration and Production Contracts

Dimitri V Massaras, IHS Energy, Geneva

Introduction

Other chapters have provided an in-depth discussion of the Libyan hydrocarbons sector, giving an historical and contemporary overview of the petroleum industry, as well as examining the regulatory environment.

This chapter will provide a detailed discussion of the evolution of Libyan exploration and production contracts, the most recent leasing activity taking place in the country, and the related negotiations and discussions taking place between the National Oil Corporation of Libya (NOC) and foreign oil companies for exploration and production rights.

The National Oil Corporation of Libya (NOC)

NOC and its upstream exploration and production subsidiaries – Agoco, Sirte, Waha and Zueitina – control the entire upstream petroleum industry, and account for more than 60 per cent of total Libyan hydrocarbons production. NOC also has refining, petrochemical, product distribution and oil field services subsidiaries. The major NOC subsidiaries are shown in Table 4.2.1.

NOC also acts as the Secretariat of Energy and is responsible for granting petroleum rights to foreign oil companies. It also regulates all related activities, which it carries out through a series of exploration and production sharing agreements (EPSAs).

Table 4.2.1 Major NOC subsidiaries

Upstream E & P	Distribution	Services
Arabian Gulf Oil Company (Agoco)	Brega Oil Marketing Co	National Drilling Co
Sirte Oil Company		Arabian Drilling & Workover Co
Waha Oil Company		Joweff
Zueitina Oil Company		North African Geophysical Co
		Arabian Geophysical Exploration Service Co
		National Oil Fields Catering Co
		Arabian Libyan Algerian Geophysical Co

The current EPSA model contract offered by NOC is the exploration and production sharing agreement, Round III (EPSA III), whereby the Libyan Government, through the NOC and its upstream subsidiaries, retains title of exploration acreage and the foreign oil company acts as contractor to NOC.

NOC was established by Law no. 24 of 1970 to replace the Libyan General Petroleum Corporation (Lipetco), founded in 1968 under the supervision of the Ministry of Petroleum. The company is run by the People's Committee of NOC, comprising the company chairman and three senior managers.

Following a large-scale reorganization of the structure of government in 2000, the People's Committee of NOC, which formerly reported to the Secretariat of Energy, now reports direct to the General People's Committee (Cabinet).

Although NOC was directly involved in exploration and production operations between 1974 and 1978, it was reorganized under Decision no. 10 of 1979 and is now a holding company and carries out its activities through more than 30 subsidiaries and joint ventures.

In January 2002, NOC appointed Dr Abdulhafid Al Zlitnei as its new chairman. Dr Zlitnei has been the Secretary (Minister) of Planning, Economy, Commerce and Trade as well as Governor of the Central Bank of Libya. He represents Libya at the OPEC ministerial meetings. He replaced Ahmed Abdul-Karim, who was appointed to manage Oilinvest, NOC's overseas investment arm.

Petroleum Law no. 25 of 1955

Petroleum exploration and production activities are broadly governed by Petroleum Law no. 25 of 1955 and regulations issued under it. Until the late 1960s, a concession system existed with no direct state participation. In 1973, existing regulations were amalgamated, and a decree issued establishing the basis for the award of petroleum rights under EPSAs, in place of concessions.

In August 1979, the General Secretariat of Congress issued Decision no. 10, under which NOC was empowered to enter into EPSAs with foreign oil companies to undertake exploration at their own risk. Such EPSAs remain the basis of licensing today, and are subject to approval of the General People's Committee.

Libya plans to revise the Petroleum Law, and the related model contract. However, government reorganization and the appointment of a new NOC chairman have delayed ratification of the Law, which is now expected to be ratified soon in a much-reduced form, dealing mainly with the downstream refining sector.

The EPSA III contract and the previous practice of negotiating the major fiscal terms of each contract on an *ad hoc* basis will continue. The new 'gas clause', promised by NOC in 2000, has not yet been released in a new model contract. However, contracts negotiated in the current licensing round may be found to contain specific new clauses covering gas exploration and development terms as well as environmental requirements and terms.

Legal, fiscal and contractual terms

Libyan petroleum contracts have evolved over the years from reconnaissance permits in the 1950s to concessions in the 1960s, joint ventures and participation agreements in the 1970s and EPSAs in the 1980s and 1990s.

Reconnaissance permits

Reconnaissance permits were granted in 1953 and 1954 to nine companies. The permits did not require seismic acquisition or drilling. There was no guarantee that an exploration concession would be granted to follow the reconnaissance permits.

Concession contract terms

Petroleum Law no. 25 regulated concession contracts. Esso (ExxonMobil) was the first company to be granted a concession, in November 1955. By 1965, Libya had granted 137 such contracts. Concession contracts required the payment of royalty and taxes based on the official selling price (OSP), which was set by the foreign oil company and came to be a point of discord in later years.

Until the late 1960s the concession system existed with no direct state participation. In 1973, existing regulations were amalgamated and a decree issued establishing the basis for the award of petroleum rights under EPSAs, in place of concessions.

Joint venture contract terms

Libya established its first national oil company (Lipetco) in 1968, following the approval of Law no. 13. The company was authorized to enter into joint venture contracts, the first of which was signed with Elf Aquitaine of France in 1968.

Very few contracts were signed under joint venture contract terms. However, they provided Libya with its first experience of direct petroleum operations. Under joint venture terms, both parties were liable for the payment of royalty, taxes and fees.

EPSA I contract terms

EPSAs were first introduced in Indonesia as a way of compensating foreign oil companies for taking all the exploration risk, and also providing the finance for developing and bringing on-stream the oil and gas fields. They were quickly adopted by most OPEC countries. The Libyan EPSAs do not provide for cost recovery before NOC starts taking its share of produced oil. However, they do provide for NOC to pay all royalty, taxes and fees. All EPSAs are governed by Libyan law.

EPSA I was launched in 1974 and provided for sharing of gross production between the parties. This was followed by EPSA II in 1980–81, which improved the contractual terms in favour of NOC. EPSA III was introduced in 1988 and provided for flexible contract terms, cost recovery, and sharing of remaining production between the parties. An EPSA III model contract was reissued in 1999, containing the same provisions as the original model contract.

Contracts awarded from 1974 were based on the following fiscal terms:

- NOC to provide the exploration acreage, with all exploration expenditure borne by the contractor;
- direct participation by NOC in any commercial development, with expenditure shared by both parties in proportion to the sharing of crude oil production;
- NOC's share of development expenditure to be repaid with interest by the contractor, allocation of a negotiated proportion of gross

production and contractor exemption from royalty, income tax and fees.

Fiscal terms, some of which are negotiable, include: a total of 25 years for exploration and production, carried state participation (minimum 50 per cent), signature bonus, cost recovery ceiling, profit sharing on a sliding scale linked to both production ('B' or 'base factor') and contractor profitability factor ('A factor'), with taxes paid from the state's (NOC) share.

Contracts are negotiated and signed by NOC. However, the General People's Committee must approve each contract, at which point it becomes effective.

EPSA II contract terms

Contracts awarded in the early 1980s were based on the following fiscal terms:

- all exploration expenditure borne by the foreign oil company;
- direct participation by NOC in any commercial development, with development costs carried without repayment;
- allocation of a negotiated proportion of gross production to cover both profit and recovery of the contractor's costs;
- all royalty and income tax liabilities and fees paid by NOC.

Under EPSA II contracts, NOC's share of development expenses was carried by the foreign oil company and repaid over a negotiated time period (5 to 20 years), commencing after an agreed cumulative production level was reached or on a specific anniversary of production export. This repayment was normally with interest, but sometimes without, and sometimes less than 100 per cent of the amount carried. NOC bore its share of operating costs and of further exploration expenses in accordance with its percentage.

EPSA III contract terms

EPSA III is a production-sharing contract between NOC and the contractor, with provision for cost recovery and sharing of remaining petroleum. Under EPSA III contracts, exploration is entirely at the contractor's risk. NOC participates in any commercial discovery, holding an interest of 50 per cent, although a higher level can be negotiated. Royalty and income tax are paid by NOC on the contractor's behalf. The rates are set in the Petroleum Law. The present rates were introduced by the amending Law no. 2 of 1975 and depreciation is fixed by Law no. 3 of 1983.

The NOC pays its working interest share of development costs and a negotiated share of operating expenses. The defined participation percentage is applied to all production and is immediately allocated to NOC, which is not entitled to any production to recover its costs over and above its participation percentage. NOC does not reimburse the contractor for past exploration and appraisal costs. If one of the parties does not pay its share of costs, after 90 days the other party may recover amounts owed from the non-paying party's share of production.

Contracts awarded since the late 1980s have been based on modified fiscal terms and include the following:

- direct participation by NOC in any commercial development (typically 50 to 75 per cent) with payment of a negotiated share of development costs;
- allocation of a negotiated proportion of production for recovery of the contractor's costs and provision of the contractor's profit (indicatively 35 per cent);
- sharing of the remainder of the allocated production after cost recovery ('net crude oil') on the basis of negotiated incremental sliding scales linked to production rates ('B' or 'base factor') and the proportion of cumulative revenue to cumulative expenditure ('A factor').

Other significant contractual terms include the following:

- overall contract duration of 25 years;
- three- to six-year initial exploration period with negotiable extensions;
- no mandatory interim relinquishments;
- work commitments for seismic data acquisition and drilling of exploration and appraisal wells;
- financial commitments for the initial exploration period;
- exemption from rental payments and duties on imported machinery and equipment;
- international arbitration under rules of the International Chamber of Commerce (ICC).

NOC participates from the time of declaration of a commercial discovery and funds 50 per cent of the capital expenditures. All prior expenditures are for the account of the contractor. Operating expenses are shared between NOC and the contractor, usually in the same proportion as the negotiable percentage of crude oil allocated solely to NOC. This percentage usually ranges from 60 to 75 per cent of production. NOC may, in practice, arrange for its share of costs to be financed by the contractor until production commences.

The Secretariat of Energy was abolished in March 2000 and its powers transferred to NOC. Subsequently, NOC presented preliminary information on the new regime, indicating that the EPSA III model will continue to be used, with major terms negotiable/open for bidding and additional provisions to cover the utilization of natural gas.

Recently, it has been reported that the wholesale changes to the licensing and fiscal regime previously anticipated in the new Petroleum Law have been restricted to provisions largely relating to the downstream sector. The promised model contact 'gas clause' has not yet appeared. However, new contracts resulting from the latest licensing round are reported to contain more specific gas provisions.

NOC policy under EPSA III

NOC wants to encourage natural gas field development for both local and export markets. Plans are to utilize gas in the refining and power generation industries in Libya and to export a large portion of the 185,000 barrels per day (bpd) of oil consumed locally. The OPEC quota system limits only production, not exports.

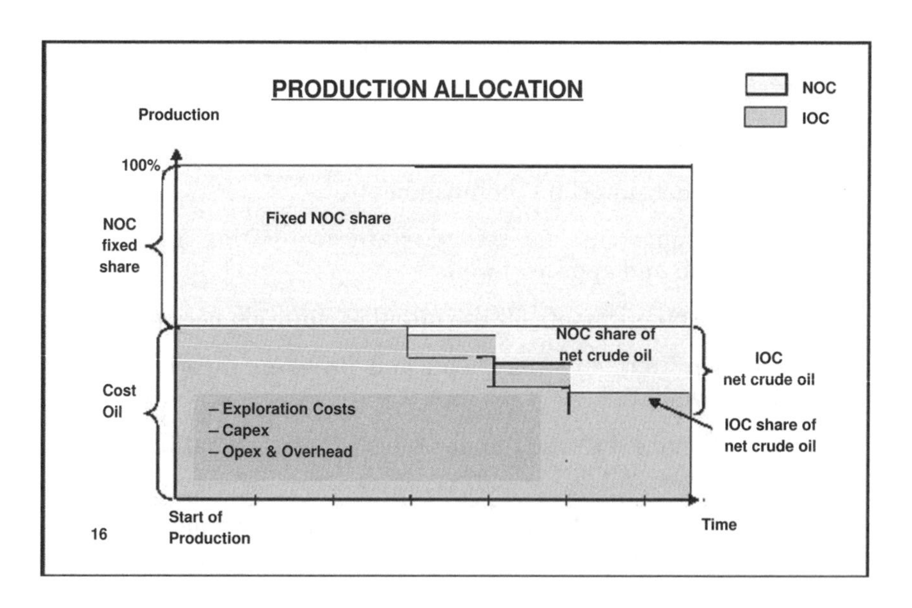

Source: National Oil Corporation (NOC) of Libya

Figure 4.2.1 Production allocation

NOC has revised the 'B' or 'base factor' and the 'A factor' in the fiscal terms of EPSA III. The new 'base factor' for gas is 1.0, and for oil is based on a negotiable sliding scale corresponding to a production rate of 20,000, 50,000, 100,000 and 150,000 bpd of oil. Previously it was based on a sliding scale from 0.10 to 0.95 corresponding to a production rate of 10,000 to 75,000 bpd.

The 'base factor' is a negotiable number and is defined based on the level of production. For example:

Production (bpd)	**'Base factor'**
Up to 20,000	B1
20,001–50,000	B2
50,001–100,000	B3
100,001–150,000	B4
In excess of 150,000	B5

Oil remaining after cost recovery is split between NOC and the contractor according to a formula linked to (a) production rates, and (b) 'R' – or ratio – of the contractor's cumulative revenues over its cumulative costs.

The formula determining the share of this 'profit oil' (also referred to as 'net crude oil' or 'NCO' in the model contract) accruing to the contractor comprises three elements: a 'base factor' calculated according to the rate of production, an 'A factor' worked out according to the ratio of the contractor's cumulative revenues to cumulative costs, and 'net crude oil'. The 'A factor' is also a negotiable number – it is a function of the 'R' or 'ratio', which is defined as the cumulative value of crude oil received by the foreign oil company (second party) over the cumulative petroleum operations expenditures incurred by the second party. For example:

'Ratio' or 'R'	**'A factor'**
≤ 1.5 to 1.0	A1
≥ 1.5 to 1.0 ≤ 3.0 to 1.0	A2
≥ 3.0 to 1.0 ≤ 4.0 to 1.0	A3
More than 4.0	A4

The contractor's share is thus calculated on the basis of: 'base factor' × 'A factor' × 'NCO'. The remaining net crude oil is allocated to NOC.

No income taxes, royalties, rents or other fees are imposed on foreign oil companies' share of production. The foreign oil companies pay for all exploration costs. NOC and the foreign oil companies share the development costs. Operating costs are shared according to equity. For the purpose of determining the value of crude oil, the official selling price (OSP) applicable during the month of production is used.

EPSA IV contract terms

NOC plans to introduce bid rounds in the near future, after the completion contract awards that are currently in negotiation. EPSA IV will be based on the public bidding approach and will introduce more incentives to investors.

Along with the revised EPSA IV terms, NOC will include environmental baseline studies (EBS) and environmental impact assessment (EIA) studies prior to the start of exploration and production activities. The new EPSA agreements will include stipulations for the exploitation of gas and another for remediation of the oil field sites after the completion of oil operations.

Gas clause

A gas clause includes the following:

- extension of the term of the agreement as appropriate (30 years for non-associated gas);
- in the event of a commercial natural gas discovery, disposition of natural gas shall be done jointly to international and local markets;
- gas pricing will be based on a formula including a combination of a 'floor price' and 'take or pay' commitments to ensure economic viability of the development programme;
- the conclusion of a gas sales agreement is required before the development plan can be implemented.

Abandonment

Abandonment expenses will be treated as a petroleum operations cost and shall be recovered. When the 'R' or ratio is equal to or greater than (≥) 1.5, the procedures and cost estimates shall be introduced to the budget. The estimate shall be updated each calendar year. Each party shall bear and finance 50 per cent of the cost. The operator will be responsible for maintaining an interest-bearing escrow account in US dollars or any other freely convertible currency such as the euro.

Current EPSA negotiations

NOC started negotiations with foreign oil companies in January 2001, hoping to sign EPSA contracts by the end of that year. However, it was

May 2003 before the first upstream contracts were signed with OMV/Repsol and with RWE-Dea. NOC has three full-time teams conducting the negotiations in exploration and production blocks, field development/production properties, and downstream refinery and petrochemical projects.

In exploration and production, NOC has been negotiating with about 17 groups of companies or consortia on a similar number of packages, consisting of about 70 open blocks. It started to award the first packages in May 2003.

In the area of field development/production properties, NOC is negotiating on 14 oil-producing fields to be redeveloped. In addition, it is negotiating for the development of four oil discoveries that have not been developed. Some fields have difficult geological structures and stratigraphy, some are near depletion and some need enhanced oil recovery.

The proposals submitted so far include the technology to be used, the incremental output to be achieved and the timing of the proposed programme. NOC is working on a comprehensive model contract for the development and exploitation of certain oil fields. Much work needs to be done in this complicated area before agreements are signed. For example, the Haram oil field, discovered about 20 years ago in the Sirte Basin, is one of the fields included in this category. This field has not been developed because of the low gravity of the oil and the structural and stratigraphic complexity of the reservoir. Four or five proposals have been submitted for the development of the field.

In the downstream refining and petrochemicals area, NOC is negotiating with about 20 companies that were invited to participate on a 50–50 joint venture basis in upgrading and expanding the refinery facilities at Ras Lanuf, Brega and Al Zawiya, as well as building a new 20,000 bpd refinery at Sabha. Proposals include refinery projects as well as the expansion of oil loading facilities at the port of Al Zawiya. Lengthy negotiations will be needed prior to reaching agreement on some projects.

The three teams, working independently, report directly to the NOC board of directors and meet monthly with the NOC board to review progress. The basis of the negotiations is Libya's Petroleum Law and subsequent EPSA amendments, legislation and agreements. The new agreements that NOC has started to sign with foreign oil companies must also be approved by the General People's Committee.

NOC has unveiled details of Libya's long-term plan to attract investment in the petroleum sector. Based on negotiations under way, Libya expects an investment of US$10 billion over the next 10 years; of the total, US$6 billion will be invested in exploration projects, US$1 billion in development projects, and US$3 billion for downstream refining and petrochemical projects.

Bid rounds and acreage offers

Petroleum operations in Libya started in 1955, and have been very active ever since. Between 1955 and 1968, 137 concessions were granted to 42 foreign oil companies. There was a brief period in 1968 and 1969 when joint venture agreements with NOC were in vogue, but since 1969 only EPSAs have been negotiated. There are no longer any active joint venture agreements. EPSAs have been issued in three rounds, of which the first was initiated in 1974, with new terms introduced in 1980–81 (EPSA II) and 1988–2001 (EPSA III).

During the 1980s, licensing activity was administered mainly through licensing rounds that took the form of informal invitations to place bids for acreage. However, during the 1990s, licensing was on a more *ad hoc* basis, with NOC periodically notifying companies of available blocks and inviting expressions of interest. In 1999, NOC resumed more active promotion of exploration and field development opportunities.

Foreign bidding companies

Repsol-OMV

On 27 May 2003, NOC awarded six blocks to the Repsol-OMV consortium. The blocks are located as follows: Block M1 (7,865 sq km) Murzuq Basin; Block S36 (15,000 sq km), Sirte Basin; Block K1 (17,500 sq km), Kufra Basin; Block K2 (17,400 sq km), Kufra Basin; Block O9 (11,000 sq km), offshore Sirte Basin; Block O10 (8,000 sq km), Sirte Basin.

Fiscal terms include an exploration period of six years, with commitments to acquire 6,500 km of new 2D seismic data, drill 12 exploration wells and invest US$90 million. Activities will be operated by Repsol with 60 per cent and OMV holding the remaining 40 per cent. The six blocks together cover 76,765 sq km.

RWE-Dea

On 29 May 2003, NOC awarded six blocks to Germany-based RWE-Dea. The blocks are located as follows: Block C1 (7,000 sq km), Block C9 (5,736 sq km), Cyrenaica Platform; Block S54 (1,731 sq km); Block S57 (2,250 sq km); Block S58 (2,000 sq km), Sirte Basin; Block K2 (11,553 sq km), Kufra Basin.

Fiscal terms and commitments include: five-year exploration period, acquisition of 5,000 km of 2D seismic data, drilling of 10 exploratory wells, investment of US$56 million. The combined area of the six blocks is 30,270 sq km. The agreement also includes a special stipulation for the exploitation of gas and another for remediation of the oil field sites after the completion of the oil operations.

TPAO

Turkiye Petrolleri Anonym Ortakligi (TPAO) was officially awarded an EPSA for Block NC188 (6,558 sq km), Ghadames Basin, and Block NC189, Sirte Basin.

The EPSA for Block NC188 is for a five-year period starting on 22 February 2000. TPAO was awarded Block NC189 at the same time; for both blocks, it has committed to drill a minimum of five exploration wells, acquire new 3D seismic, and reprocess vintage 2D seismic.

Block NC188 is located south-west of Mizdah, and straddles the southern escarpment of the Djebel Nefusah Uplift and extends southwards on to the Hamada Al-Hamra. The northern part of the block lies on the Djebel Nefusah and the southern part on the Hamada, with the southern escarpment of the Djebel Nefusah passing through the block.

Block NC189 is located immediately west of the Waha and Defa fields, at the southern end of the Beda Platform and the Hagfa Trough. It is a large block, roughly square but with two portions, comprising Blocks 59-West Central operated by Waha Oil Company and Block NC107, excluded from Block NC189.

Total

On 18 May 2001, Total (TotalFinaElf) announced that the EPSA for Block NC191 (16,600 sq km), Murzuq Basin, was ratified by the General People's Congress and NOC. TotalFinaElf is the only foreign partner with NOC. The effective date of the EPSA is 26 March 2001. Fiscal terms include the acquisition of 4,000 km of 2D seismic, which was completed in 2003, and the drilling of two exploration wells.

Also on 18 May 2001, Total announced that the EPSA for Block NC192 was ratified by the General People's Congress and NOC. Fiscal terms include the acquisition of 500 km of 2D seismic, and the drilling of one exploration well. Block NC192 (1,200 sq km) is located in the eastern area of the Sirte Basin, about 480 km south of Benghazi.

Petro-Canada

On 29 January 2002, Petro-Canada agreed to acquire the upstream operations of Veba Oil Company from Germany-based parent company E.ON and majority owner British Petroleum for US$2 billion in cash.

Veba Oil, in partnership with NOC, holds exploration and production rights in eight blocks with an area of 25,190 sq km and is the operator of Block 9 (2,017 sq km); Block 10 (2,283 sq km); Block 11 (6,334 sq km), which holds the Zenad-Ghani and Dahra and Hofra oil fields; Block 12 (2,997 sq km), which holds the Amal oil field; Block 13 (3,000 sq km); Block 57 (2,999 sq km); Block 72 (4,999 sq km) and Block NC84A (561 sq km).

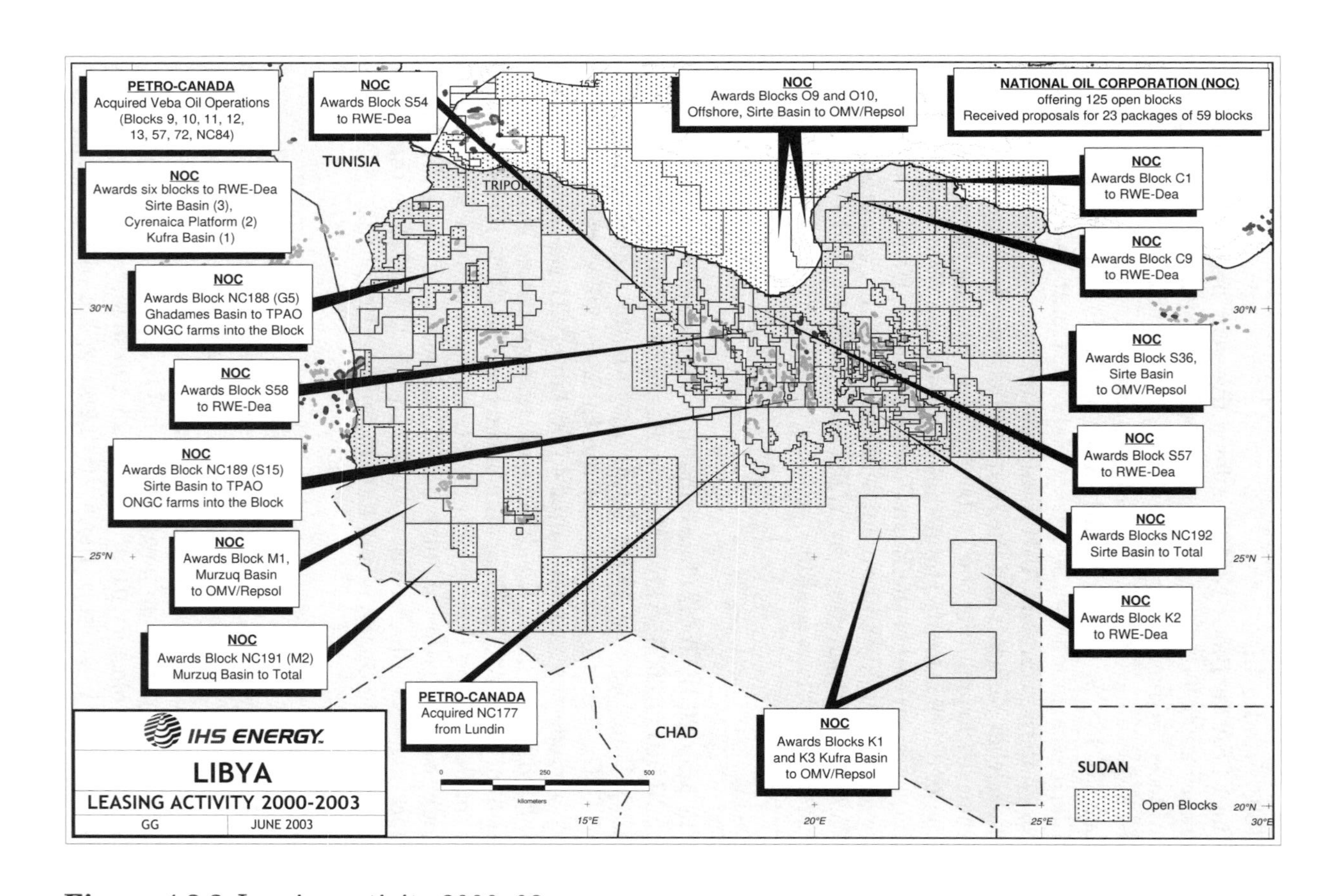

Figure 4.2.2 Leasing activity 2000–03

During December 2002, Veba was producing about 85.2 million bpd (42 million bpd net to Veba) in Libya from 198 wells in 30 oil fields, the largest of which are Amal (32 million bpd) and Zenad–Ghani (35.5 million bpd).

On 21 June 2001, Petro-Canada announced an agreement to purchase 25 per cent of Block NC177 from Lundin Oil Company for US$75 million. The remaining 75 per cent interest is held by NOC. The block contains the Al-Naga North and Al-Naga West oil fields, which are now producing about 7,000 bpd of oil. Petro-Canada remained operator of the block.

4.3

Oil Production, Reserves, Pipelines and Refineries

Dimitri V Massaras, IHS Energy, Geneva

Introduction

The oil industry is the key to the overall economy of Libya and accounts for US$ 12 billion per year from oil and gas exports. Petroleum exploration, production, refining and marketing of oil and natural gas as well as liquefied natural gas (LNG) are the strongest elements in the local economy and account for about 95 per cent of Libya's foreign currency earnings and about 75 per cent of government revenues.

Oil production

During 2002, Libyan oil production was averaging 1.3 million barrels per day (bpd) of oil, only about one-third of the 3.3 million bpd produced in 1970. Libya would like to increase oil production to about 2.0 million bpd.

During 2002, the National Oil Corporation (NOC) and its upstream subsidiary companies Arabian Gulf Oil Company (Agoco), Waha Oil Company (Waha), Sirte Oil Company (Sirte) and Zueitina Oil Company (Zueitina), accounted for some 800,000 bpd (62 per cent) of the country's production. This figure has been declining in the past few years due to difficulties in obtaining spare parts for US-made equipment installed at the Sirte Basin oil fields. Non-US companies have enabled Libya to maintain its current oil production capacity.

ENI/Agip, Wintershall, Petro-Canada (Veba), OMV and Repsol are the foreign oil companies producing oil in Libya. Agip was the dominant foreign producer with operated production of around 180,000 bpd, followed by Repsol with 158,000 bpd, Wintershall with 105,000 bpd and Petro-Canada (Veba) with 82,000 bpd. Total production by the foreign oil companies was about 500,000 bpd or 38 per cent of the total.

Total (TotalFinaElf) and Norsk Hydro (Saga) are comparatively minor producers, with 37,000 bpd from the Mabruk oil fields, Block 17, Sirte Basin. However, this is about to change soon, as Total and partners are now developing the Al-Jurf oil field and other discoveries in Block 137N and 137S, offshore in the Pelagian Basin.

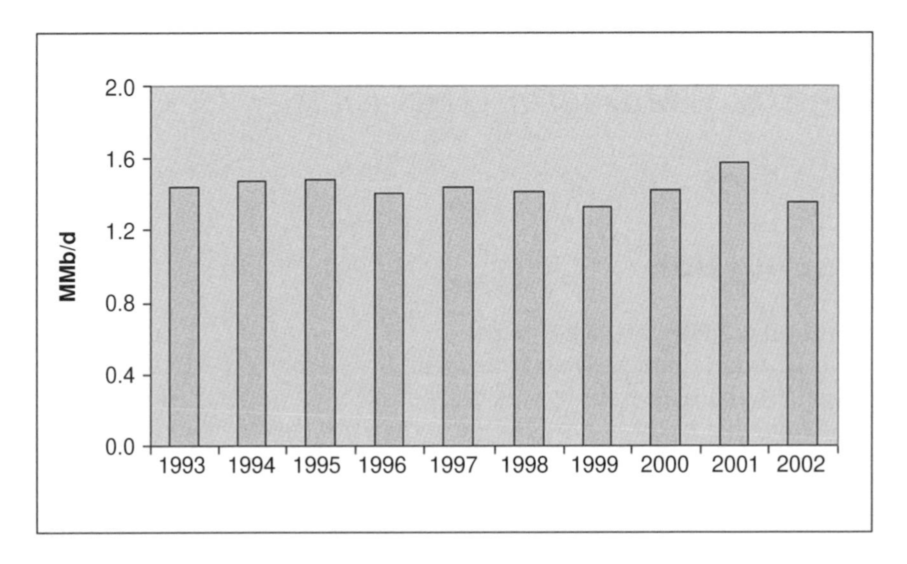

Figure 4.3.1 Oil production in Libya from 1993–2002

Oil reserves

The National Oil Corporation (NOC) has not announced any revisions to Libya's oil reserve estimates since 1999, when it was announced that the oil reserves were 29.5 billion barrels of oil. Accounting for production since then, and also the very few small discoveries made in the past few years, the estimated remaining proven producible oil reserves are now about 27 billion barrels. However, in 2001, OPEC published a reserve estimate of 36 billion barrels for Libya.

Libya's oil reserves are located mainly within three main trends in the Sirte Basin, the western trend (Samah, Beda, Raguba, Dahra-Hofra and Bahi fields), the north trend (Defa, Al-Wafa, Nasser and Hateiba fields) and the east trend (Sarir, Messla, Gialo, Bu Attifel, Intisar, Augila-Nafoora and Amal fields).

Of Libya's existing onshore oil fields, 12 have reserves of 1.0 billion barrels or more, and two have reserves of 0.5 to 1.0 billion barrels. Most oil fields in the Sirte Basin have been producing for about 30 years, with the exception of Murzuq Basin oil fields, which came on stream in 1996. The Sirte Basin oil fields were discovered between 1956 and 1972, and are now undergoing natural decline rates of 7 to 8 per cent a year.

Offshore there is a relatively narrow continental shelf and slope in the Gulf of Sirte and the Mediterranean Sea. The largest offshore field is Bouri, which has proven reserves of 2.0 billion barrels of oil and 2.5 trillion cubic feet of gas. The field was discovered by Agip in 1976 along with 14 large and small gas discoveries in Block NC41.

Oil refineries and refining capacity

Libya has a total of five oil refineries, of which two are relatively large and three are very small (Table 4.3.1). Together the refineries operate at 340,000 bpd or 10 per cent less than total design capacity of about 380,000 bpd. The two larger refineries are located at Ras Lanuf and Zawia. The three small refineries are located at Tobruk, Sarir and Marsa el-Brega.

Table 4.3.1 Refineries and refining capacity of Libya

Refinery	Capacity (bpd)	Start-up
Ras Lanuf	220,000	1965
Zawia	120,000	1974
Tobruk	20,000	1986
Sarir	10,000	1989
Marsa el-Brega	10,000	1965
TOTAL	380,000	

The total refining capacity is nearly twice the 165,000 bpd domestic refined petroleum products requirements, which includes gasoline, kerosene and residual fuel oil. The remaining products are exported.

Libya is Africa's second biggest oil producer, after Nigeria, and the biggest African oil supplier to Europe. It provides a high-quality, sweet crude oil with low sulphur content, has very low production costs and the oil fields are close to the refineries and markets of Europe.

Libya is planning a comprehensive upgrade of its entire refining system, with a particular aim of increasing output of gasoline and other light refined petroleum products such as unleaded gasoline, reformulated gasoline, low-sulphur fuel oil (LSFO) and jet fuel.

The refineries are outdated, unsophisticated and consume a lot of energy in the form of oil, which Libya needs to export (Table 4.3.2). They are not capable of producing products that correspond to the

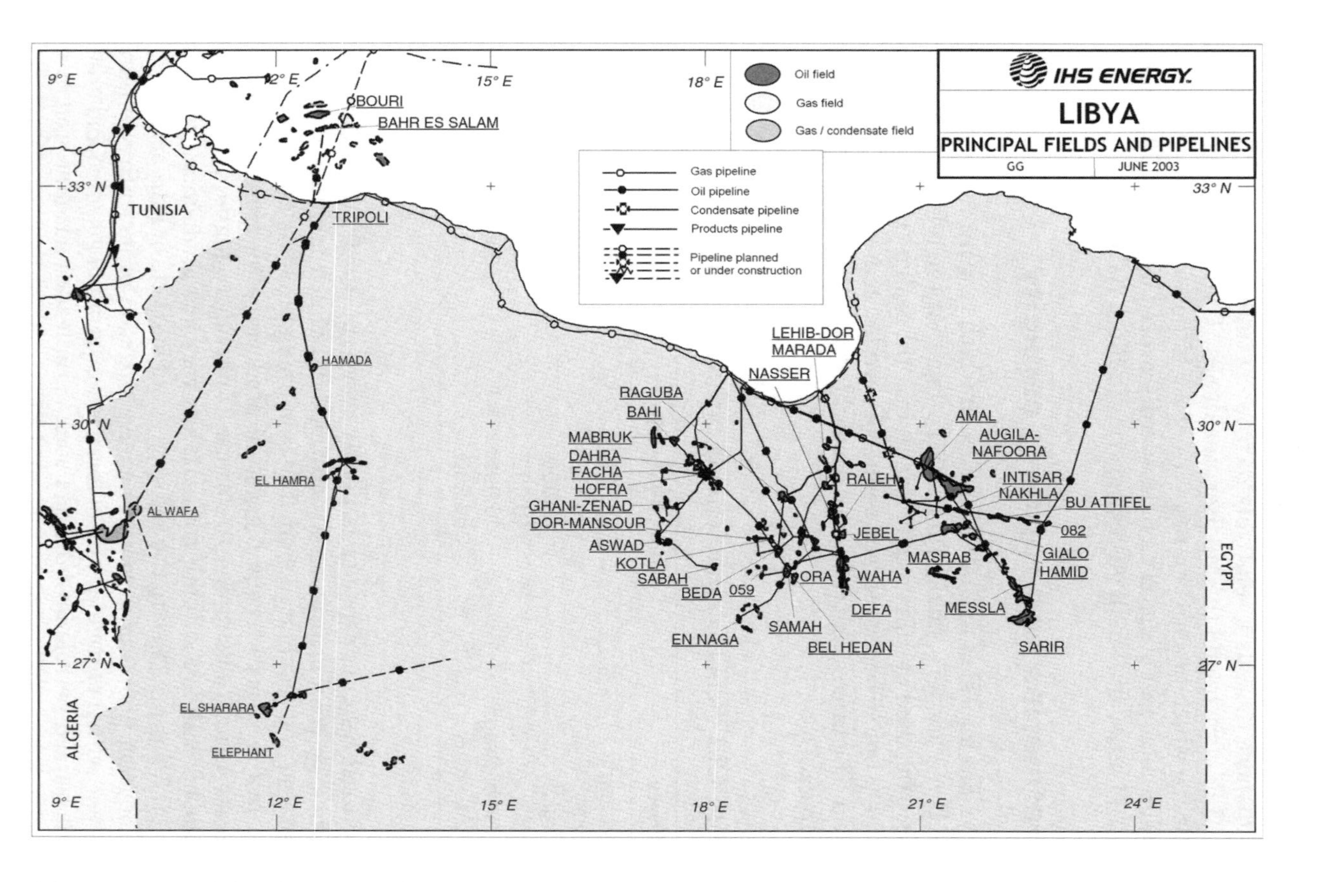

Figure 4.3.2 Libya's principal fields and pipelines

Table 4.3.2 Consumption of refined petroleum products ('000 bpd)

Category	1998	1999	2000	2001	2002
Gasoline	43.9	42.7	42.2	40.3	46.2
Kerosene	10.9	7.4	6.5	7.2	7.5
Distillates	59.5	64.1	59.9	60.7	62.9
Residuals	43.7	39.9	39.6	43.9	39.8
Other	12.8	9.2	8.1	7.7	8.8
TOTAL	170.8	163.3	156.3	159.8	165.2

specifications required by the EU consuming countries, such as unleaded gasoline, reformulated gasoline and LSFO.

Libya's refining sector has been hard hit by UN and US sanctions, which banned Libya from importing refinery equipment. In addition, EU environmental standards have been more stringent since 1996. Libya's refineries have suffered from technological and equipment limitations and are now in serious need of upgrading.

In addition to its domestic refineries, Libya has three refineries in Europe. Oilinvest, the overseas arm of NOC, has a network of refineries in Germany, Italy and Switzerland with the capacity to refine 300,000 bpd.

There are proposals for two new refineries: a small facility at Sabha to refine about 20,000 bpd of crude oil from Repsol's Murzuq Basin oil fields for domestic consumption, and a much larger one in Misurata with the capacity to refine 200,000 bpd of crude oil for export.

Crude oil pipelines and loading terminals

Libya's crude oil and refined products pipeline transportation network is very extensive (Table 4.3.3), and as oil production has declined since the late 1970s, there is sufficient spare capacity available for any new production. The main crude pipelines system in the Sirte Basin all runs to terminals on the Mediterranean coast.

The oil pipeline (724 km, 30 in, 200,000 bpd) from Repsol's Murzuq Basin oil fields to the Zawia refinery and terminal joins the Al-Hamra fields cluster, whose oil is transported by a separate oil pipeline (241 km, 18 in, 100,000 bpd). There appears to be little capacity available on either of these oil pipelines.

Libya exports nine different grades of crude oil through six oil loading terminals and storage facilities (Marsa al-Hariga, Zueitina, Marsa el-Brega, Ras Lanuf, Sidir and Zawia). Plans are under way to expand the oil loading terminal and refinery facilities at Zawia.

Table 4.3.3 Crude oil pipelines

Oil pipeline	Owner/operator	Length miles/km	Diameter inches/cm
Sarir to Tobruk	Arabian Gulf Oil Company (Agoco)	320/515	34/86
Sarir to Messla	Arabian Gulf Oil Company (Agoco)	25/40	30/76
Messla to Amal	Arabian Gulf Oil Company (Agoco)	128/206	42/106
Hamada to Zawia	Arabian Gulf Oil Company (Agoco)	241/388	18/46
Amal to Ras Lanuf	Petro-Canada (Veba)	170/274	30/76
Amal to Ras Lanuf	Petro-Canada (Veba)	170/274	36/91
Tibisti to Asida	Petro-Canada (Veba)	84/135	24/61
Zagout to Sidir	Waha Oil Company	166/267	24/61
Waha to Zagout	Waha Oil Company	27/43	24/61
Waha to Samah	Waha Oil Company	40/64	24/61
South Defa to Waha	Waha Oil Company	25/40	30/76
Gialo to Waha	Waha Oil Company	94/191	30/76
Zagout to Samah	Waha Oil Company	22/35	24/61
Samah to Dohra	Waha Oil Company	114/183	32/81
Dohra to Bahi	Waha Oil Company	43/69	30/76
Bahi to Sidir	Waha Oil Company	44/71	30/76
Nasser to Brega	Waha Oil Company	107/172	36/91
Rebuga to 110km mrkr	Waha Oil Company	55/88	20/50
91.5km mrkr to Brega	Waha Oil Company	57/92	16/40
Bu Attifel to Intisar	Agip Oil company (NOC)	83/133	30/76
Bu Attifel to Intisar	Agip Oil company (NOC)	83/133	10/25
Remal to Bu Attifel	Agip Oil company (NOC)	47/76	12/30
Intisar 103 to Zueitina Terminal	Zueitina Oil Company	137/220	40/101
Intisar 103 to Zueitina Terminal	Zueitina Oil Company	137/220	20/50
Zella to Hofra	Zueitina Oil Company	70/112	20/50
Murzuq to Zawia	Repsol Oil Operations	452/728	30/76

4.4

Petroleum Geology of Libya

Dimitri V Massaras, IHS Energy, Geneva

Introduction

There are six sedimentary basins in Libya, four of which have proven petroleum systems. These are, in order of importance, Sirte, Murzuq, Ghadames, Pelagian, Cyrenaica and Kufra. The Sirte Basin extends offshore and the Pelagian Basin is located entirely offshore.

Sirte Basin

The Sirte Basin is an aborted Cretaceous rift system, which started development as Africa separated from South America, and the Tethys Sea – the predecessor to the Mediterranean Sea – started to close. The age and type of the sediments are similar to the contemporaneous aborted rifts of the Central African Rift System extending from Nigeria to Sudan.

The Sirte Basin is a moderately mature basin in spite of recoverable reserves in the range of 45–50 billion barrels of oil and 30–40 trillion cubic feet of gas discovered so far. Nearly 90 per cent of Libya's oil reserves and 53 per cent of gas reserves are located in the Sirte Basin.

Since the first Petroleum Law was enacted in 1955, the Sirte Basin has been a very active petroleum province. Between 1955 and 1968, 37 concessions were granted to 13 companies. In the 1960s, several revisions of the Petroleum Law were decreed. In 1971, political changes occurred in Libya and a junta, led by Colonel Muammar Qadhafi, came to power. The government acquired majority interests in all concessions and nationalized the assets held by BP, Hunt and Amoseas (now ChevronTexaco).

Exploration started in 1955, when the first geophysical survey was conducted. In 1958, the first wildcats were drilled by foreign companies,

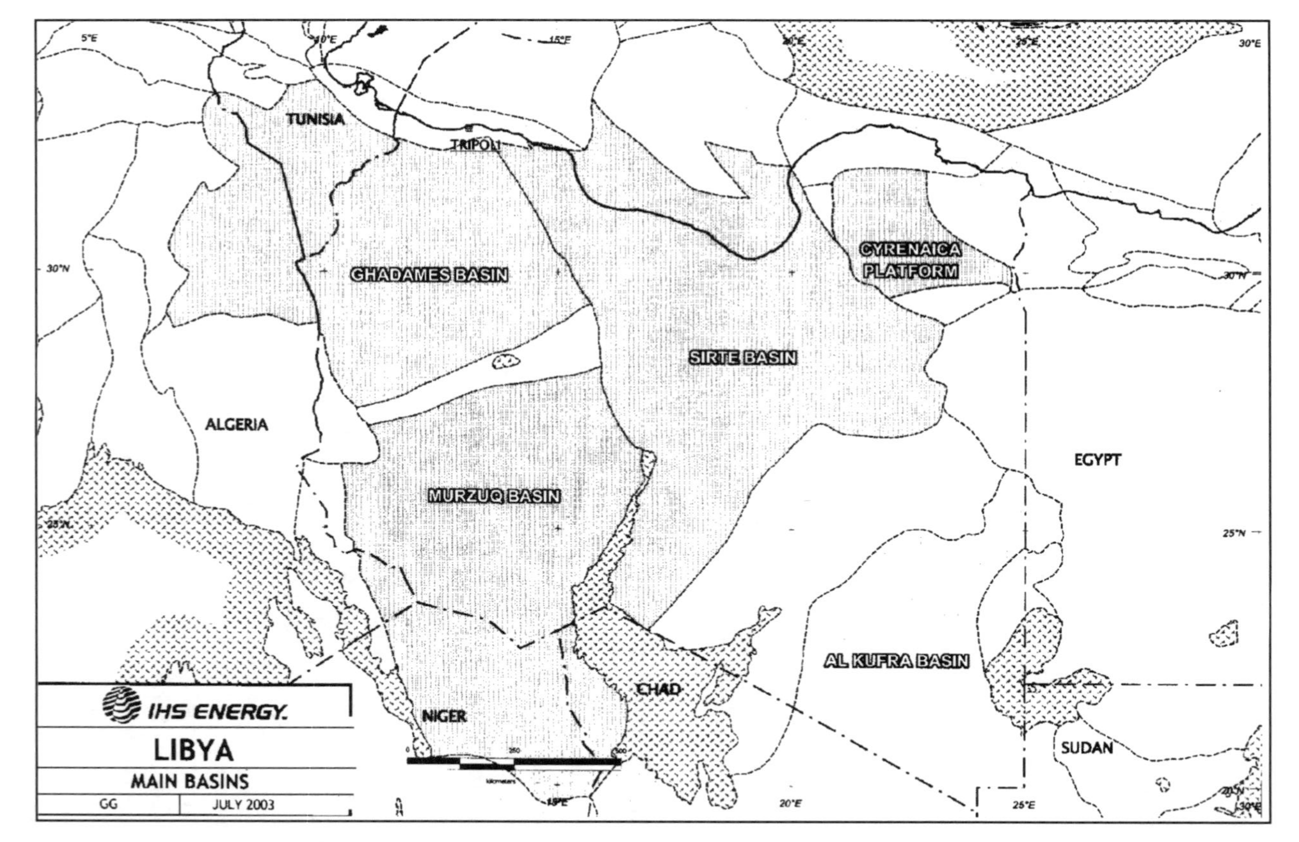

Figure 4.4.1 Libya's main basins

resulting in four discoveries, of which three were giant and one small. From then to 1969, the number of new field wildcats (NFWs) increased rapidly.

About 700 NFWs were drilled and a total of 106 discoveries were made, including 16 giant and super-giant fields (Amal, Beda, Nasser, Waha North, Waha South, Defa, Gialo, Sarir, Augila-Nafoora, Bu Attifel and Intisar). These were the most successful years for discovered reserves. Almost 90 per cent of the Sirte Basin reserves were found in the first 10 years of exploration during the 1960s.

In the 1970s and 1980s, exploration declined due to the nationalization programme and US sanctions, and averaged only 20 to 22 NFWs a year and about 56 discoveries in each decade. The finding rate was 12 million barrels/NFW, compared to 62 million barrels/NFW in the previous period. With the exception of the Messla and Al-Sarah giant fields, other discoveries were relatively small in size.

New-field wildcat drilling in the 1990s declined, ranging from about 15 NFWs a year in the first half to eight a year in the second half of the decade. A total of 42 discoveries were made, all of medium to small size.

The most successful operators were Oasis Oil Company – a consortium of Amerada Hess, ConocoPhillips and Marathon – which found some 27 per cent of the basin's total reserves, followed by Esso (Exxon), Mobil (now ExxonMobil) and BP.

In the offshore areas the first seismic data acquisition started in 1960, which led to the first drilling in 1963. Two gas discoveries were made by Arco (now part of BP) in 1967 and 1968 with reserves estimated to be 800 billion cubic feet of gas. In 1993, Lasmo (now part of Agip) acquired 2,800 kilometres of 2D seismic in blocks NC173/1 and NC173/2.

Murzuq Basin

The Murzuq Basin's geological structure and stratigraphy are very similar to the Ghadames Basin adjacent to the north. During the Paleozoic period, the two basins were connected and formed a single basin. The same Silurian shales were deposited in the low areas of the eroded Ordovician substratum and constitute both rich source and reservoir rocks.

The Devonian play is not yet developed in the Murzuq Basin, as nowhere does it appear to have reached maturity. Also, Devonian shales distribution is patchier, given the more marginal position of the area on the Gondwana continent. Hercynian movements at the end of the Paleozoic cut the Murzuq Basin from its neighbouring basins, and Mesozoic sedimentation was reduced to about 1,000 metres of continental deposits from nearby eroding topographic highs.

The outline of the Murzuq Basin is that of an elongated triangle with a broad apex pointing south-south-east and extending for some 100 kilometres into northern Niger. The relatively small portion that extends into Niger is called the Djado Basin. The Paleozoic sequences of the Murzuq Basin outcrop in the African cratonic area. In geological terms, there is little to distinguish this southern area from the main part of the Murzuq Basin.

The western limit of the Murzuq Basin is defined by the Hoggar Massif; eastern and western flanks of the basin converge southwards and the Paleozoic is expressed at the surface in the form of cuestas of Devonian and Silurian rocks.

The main tectonic episodes involved in creating the structural framework of the Murzuq Basin are: the Proterozoic to Early Paleozoic Pan-African orogeny, the Middle Paleozoic Caledonian orogeny and the Late Paleozoic Hercynian orogeny.

Ghadames Basin

The Ghadames Basin (Berkine Basin in Algeria) is an early Mesozoic sag basin on top of the Gondwana Paleozoic Basin extending from North Africa to Saudi Arabia, with its sequences of shales, including rich Silurian and Devonian source-rocks, and clastics grading from continental in the Cambrian to various marine settings from the Ordovician to Carboniferous. The plays of the Ghadames Basin are very similar to those encountered in the Algerian basins.

The history of the Berkine and Ghadames basins differs slightly, as the Berkine has experienced somewhat more subsidence during the Mesozoic in Algeria. As a result, prospective zones in the Berkine are Devonian and Triassic (TAGI and TAGS) reservoirs, while the Devonian and Silurian sandstones are more the focus of attention in the Ghadames Basin.

Pelagian Basin

The Pelagian Basin is a Cenozoic pull-apart basin, separated from the Djefara Basin by the Sabratha-Cyrenaica wrenching zone, which has up to 3,500 metres of vertical displacement at the top of the Paleozoic level. The Pelagian Basin includes all Libya's offshore production, in particular the largest Mediterranean petroleum accumulation, the Bouri oil, gas and condensate field. Agip's West Libya Gas Development Project covers the Block NC41 gas accumulations. The other ongoing project is Total's (TotalFinaElf) development project located in Block 137N with the Farwa FPSO.

Kufra Basin

The Kufra Basin covers about 500,000 square kilometres of Libya, Sudan, Chad and Egypt. About 75 per cent of the basin is located on Libyan territory. The total basin fill reaches 4,500 metres of Paleozoic sediments, with a thin veneer of Permian to Mesozoic continental sediments.

The basin is not explored, and only two exploration wells have been drilled by Agip. A-1-NC43 was drilled to the total depth of 3,019 metres in 1978 and B-1-NC43 was drilled to a total depth of 4,164 metres in 1980. The wells did not encounter hydrocarbons. The basin is considered non-prospective because of lack of source rocks at depth and good extensive seal rocks.

The name Kufra is derived from the Kufra Oasis, located in the north-central area of the elongated depression. The name is applied to both the topographic feature and the zone of tectonic subsidence which underlies it.

Exploration activity in the Kufra Basin will increase in the near future. In May 2003, the National Oil Corporation (NOC) of Libya awarded three new exploration blocks in the Kufra Basin. Block K1 (16,804 sq km) and Block K3 (19,582 sq km) were awarded to the Repsol-OMV consortium with commitments to drill two exploration wells and acquire 1,500 kilometres of 2D seismic. Block K2 (11,553 sq km) was awarded to RWE-Dea.

Cyrenaica Basin (Platform)

The Cyrenaica Basin or Platform covers most of the northeast portion of Libya and includes two domains separated by the east–west-oriented Cyrenaica fault, an essentially Upper Jurassic–Lower Cretaceous marine depocentre to the north of a Jurassic hinge line inverted during the Alpine orogeny in Miocene times, and a more continental and much thinner Mesozoic sequence underlain by an eroded Paleozoic sequence where Silurian source rocks locally sub-crop the Hercynian unconformity.

The Cyrenaica Platform is comparable to the Western Desert Basin of Egypt. Very little petroleum has been discovered so far, in spite of the 100 wildcats drilled between 1956 and 1974.

The Cyrenaica area is regarded as high risk and low reward until more of the exploration failures, risks and uncertainties can be understood. Most of the exploration was carried out more than 20 to 25 years ago, before the advent of 3D seismic.

4.5

Natural Gas Production, Reserves and Pipelines

Dimitri V Massaras, IHS Energy, Geneva

Natural gas production

Natural gas production is very limited, given the country's great potential. Expansion of natural gas production remains a high priority for Libya, which has plans to use natural gas instead of oil for domestic consumption. This would make more crude oil available for export and at the same time reduce air pollution in the large cities of Tripoli and Benghazi. In addition, there are plans to increase gas exports to the EU starting in 2005. Major gas-producing fields include Attahadi, Hateiba, Zelten, Sahl and Assumud.

In 2002, the estimated average natural gas production rate was about 1.0 billion cubic feet a day (bcf/d) or 367 billion cubic feet a year (bcf/y) (Table 4.5.1).

Table 4.5.1 Natural gas production and use in Libya from 1998 to 2002 (bcf/y)

Category	1998	1999	2000	2001	2002
Marketed	222	183	204	218	219
Flared	64	46	49	48	49
Re-injected	134	74	89.7	86	86.5
Shrinkage	21	21	12.3	12	12.5
TOTAL	441	324	355	364	367

Gas exploitation is in its infancy in Libya, with only six fields of the Sirte Basin feeding the Marsa el-Brega LNG plant built in 1970 by Esso (ExxonMobil). At present, about 219 bcf (60 per cent) of natural gas per year is marketed, about 86 bcf/y (23 per cent) is re-injected into oil reservoirs for pressure maintenance, and about 49 bcf (13 per cent) is flared (down from 80 per cent in 1970). Libya also produces a small amount of liquefied petroleum gas (LPG), most of which is consumed by domestic refineries.

Natural gas reserves

Libya's proven natural gas reserves are estimated by the NOC to be 46.4 trillion cubic feet (tcf), of which 34.5 tcf (75 per cent) is free gas and 11.5 tcf (25 per cent) is associated gas in oil reservoirs. Only 10 tcf (21.5 per cent) of the total proven reserves are considered developed and 16 tcf (34 per cent) are considered underdeveloped. The remaining 20 tcf is undeveloped.

The gas potential of Libya is unexplored and unexploited. Proven plus probable (P+P) gas reserves are considerably larger, possibly 90 to 115 tcf.

The coastal gas transmission system between Tripoli and Benghazi transports 73 bcf (20 per cent) of gas to local consumers as follows: electric power generation 61 per cent, steel mills 31 per cent, cement plants 5 per cent, refineries 2 per cent, other 1 per cent.

Natural gas is found in the Sirte Basin, which holds about 55 per cent of the discovered reserves, the Ghadames Basin (Al-Wafa gas and condensate field) and the Pelagian Basin (Block NC41 fields cluster) holding 45 per cent of the discovered gas reserves.

Natural gas demand

Natural gas demand is expected to increase to 2.0 bcf/d day by 2004 and 3.0 bcf/d by 2006. Gas demand is expected to decrease after 2010, as some oil fields will stop producing oil. Natural gas is used for power generation in the Sahara Desert and it is injected into oil reservoirs for pressure maintenance.

To expand its gas production, marketing and distribution, Libya is looking to foreign participation and investment. In recent years large new discoveries have been made in the Ghadames Basin, offshore in Block NC41, Pelagian Basin, and in the Sirte Basin.

A number of projects are under way to develop the gas potential of Libya, including the Attahadi Field Development Project, Faragh Field Development Project and the West Libya Gas Development Project.

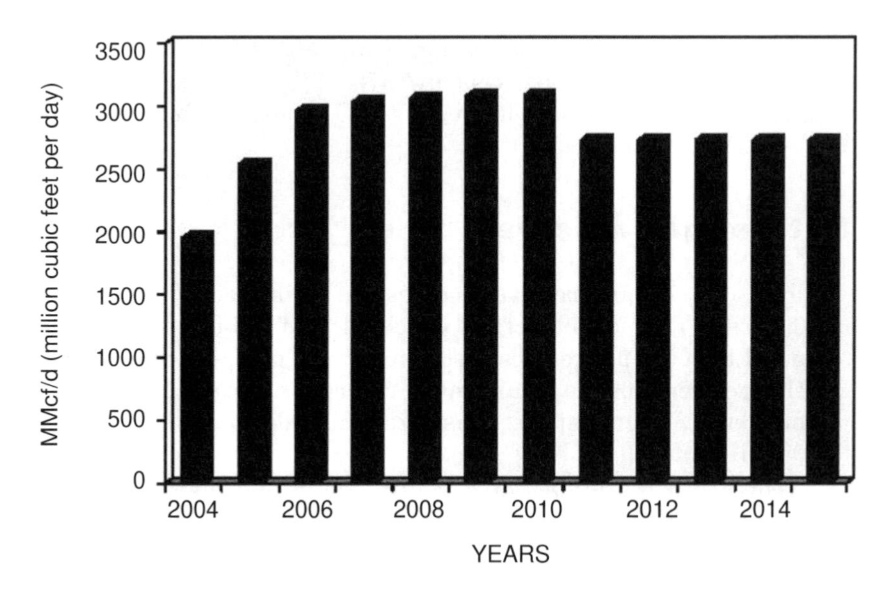

Data source: Sirte Oil Company

Figure 4.5.1 Projected gas demand in Libya

Attahadi Field Development Project (AFDP)

The AFDP, Block 6, Zelten Platform, Sirte Basin, is under development and is expected to produce 270 million cf/d gas when it comes on stream in late 2003. The project includes a field processing facility and a 30-inch gas pipeline to connect with the north–south trunk gas pipelines (30-inch and 36-inch) to the east of the field.

The gas pipeline will be installed to transport the gas 90 kilometres to the east for delivery to the gas processing facilities at Marsa el-Brega on the Mediterranean coast.

Hyundai Engineering & Construction Company of South Korea was awarded a US$247 million turnkey contract from Sirte Oil Company to build the gas processing plant and related facilities. The plant will be able to handle 350 million cf/d. Hyundai commenced construction in September 1999 and plans to complete the project in late 2003.

The Attahadi gas field was discovered in 1964 by Esso and is located 17 kilometres south-south-west of the giant Hateiba gas field, which is also operated by Sirte Oil Company.

Attahadi's recoverable reserves are estimated at 10 trillion cf of gas and 200 million barrels of condensate below 2,750 metres in the

Cenomanian sandstones of the Bahi Formation and the Ordovician to Cambrian sandstones and quartzites of the Gargaf Group.

Development drilling has been under way since 1987, with some 45 exploratory appraisal and development wells drilled to date.

Block 6 (25,223 sq km) was awarded to Esso Libya in December 1955. It has been managed by Sirte Oil Company since 1981, when Esso (ExxonMobil) left Libya.

Faragh Field Development Project (FFDP)

The FFDP, Block 59SE, Sirte Basin it is to be completed in two phases. Phase I, which is under construction, will be completed in late 2003 and involves the installation of facilities and pipelines to produce 30,000 barrels a day (bpd) of oil and 40 million cf/d of gas. Phase II, which is in the engineering stage, will be completed in 2005 and involves the installation of additional field processing facilities to produce an additional 210 million cf/d of gas for a total of 250 million cf/d.

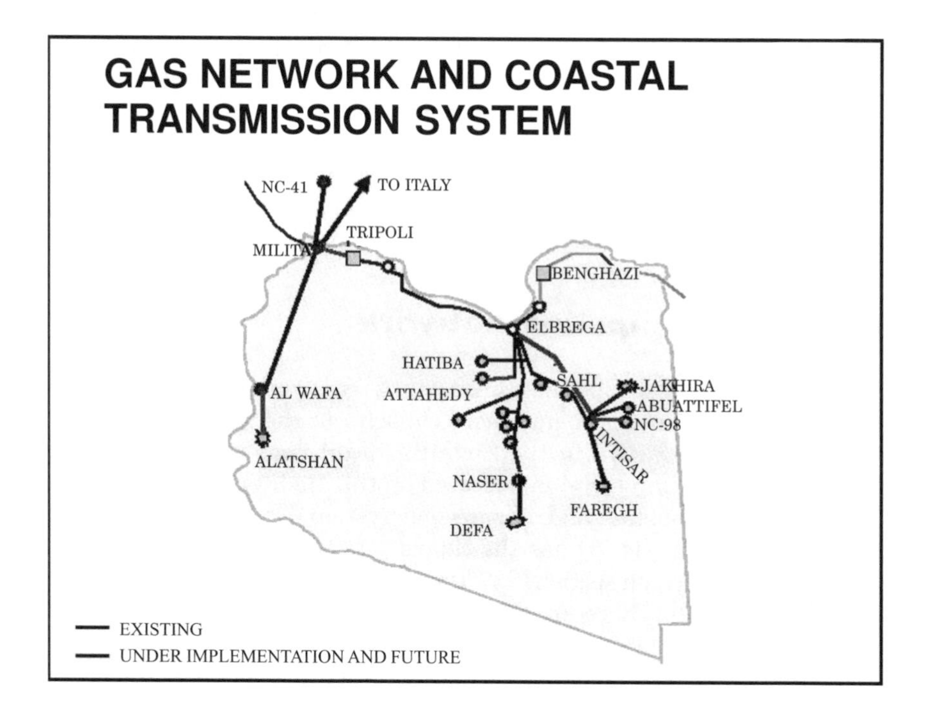

Map Source: Sirte Oil Company

Figure 4.5.2 Gas network and coastal transmission system

West Libya Gas Development Project (WLGDP)

The WLGDP, now under construction by Agip and NOC, will account for a very substantial increase in natural gas production in Libya starting in 2005.

Overall, the WLGDP calls for Libya to export 290 bcf/y (8 bcm/y) of natural gas from a central processing facility (CPF) at Melitah, near Tripoli, to Italy and France over a 24-year period. First production is expected in 2005 and will be exported via a 2,000-kilometre pipeline system from the Al-Wafa and Bar Es-Salam fields to Italy and France. The underwater section of the pipeline will be 550 kilometres long and will be called Greenstream.

In June 2002, Agip affiliate Saipem was awarded a contract worth US$550 million to build and install the Sabratha drilling and production platform at the Bar Es-Salam field, Block NC41, offshore, Pelagian Basin. The overall estimated cost of the project is US$5.5 billion.

In February 2002, US$1.0 billion worth of engineering, procurement and construction contracts (EPIC) were awarded to a consortium led by JGC, Sofregaz and Technimont. The consortium will work on oil and natural gas processing plant and other infrastructure at the Al-Wafa field in the Sahara Desert and the coastal gas and condensate processing plant near Melitah on the Mediterranean coast.

Edison Gas of Italy has contracted to take about half of the gas production, or 140 bcf/y, and has plans to use it for power generation in Italy. In addition, Energia Gas and Gaz de France have each committed to taking around 70 bcf/y.

Natural gas pipeline network

Libya's natural gas pipeline transportation network (Table 4.5.2) is very extensive, with plans to add more capacity in the next few years. The main pipeline system in the Sirte Basin all runs to factories, power plants and loading terminals located on the Mediterranean coast.

There is a coastal gas transmission system. The Brega to Benghazi section (257 km, 34 in) has the capacity to transport 250 million cf/d. The Brega to Tripoli section (787 km, 34 in) has the capacity to transport 500 million cf/d. There are three compression stations at Brega, Sidra and Weshkah.

The coastal gas transmission system has the capacity to transport 500 million cf/d and has feeder lines to the petrochemical plants at Ras Lanuf, fertilizer plant at Brega and the steel complex at Misurata.

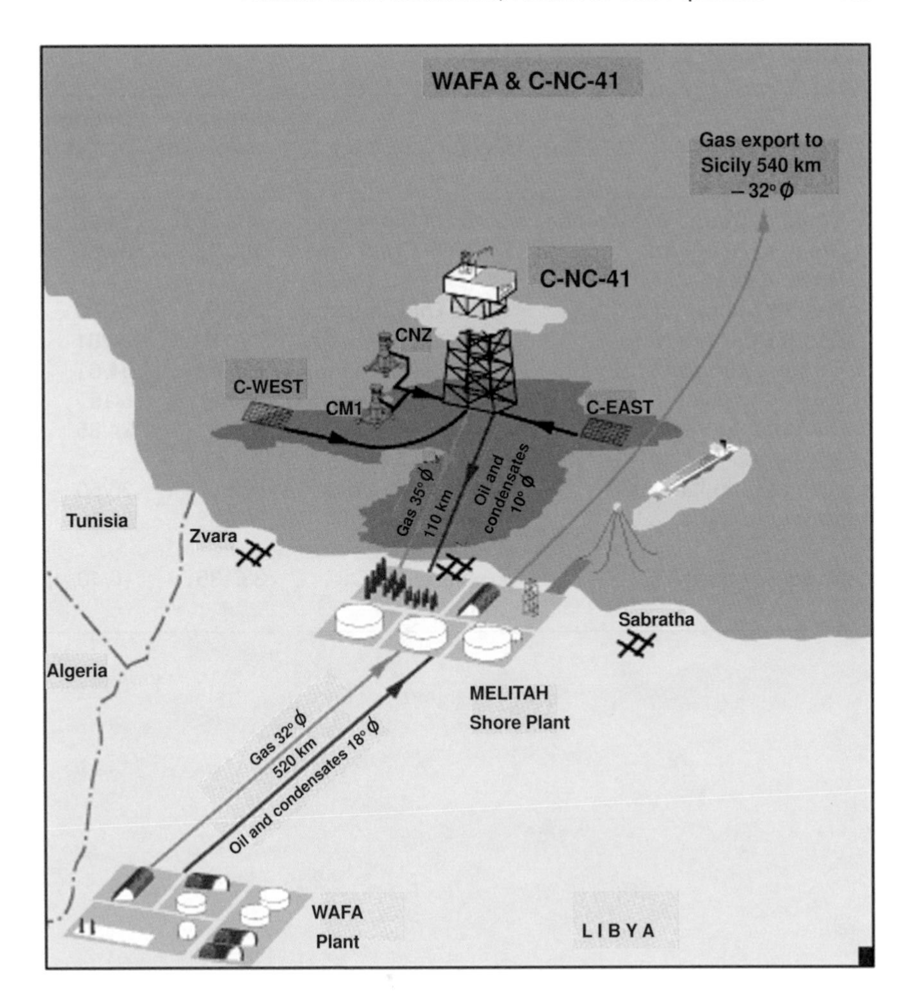

Source: Agip Oil Company

Figure 4.5.3 Conceptual plan of the West Libya Gas Development Project

Table 4.5.2 Natural gas pipelines

Gas pipeline	Owner/operator	Length miles/km	Diameter inches/cm
Brega to Tripoli (coastal line)	Sirte Oil Company	489/787	34/86
Brega to Benghazi (coastal line)	Sirte Oil Company	160/257	34/86
Bahi to Dohra	Waha Oil Company	30/48	12/30
South Dohra to Nasser	Waha Oil Company	73/117	24/61
Faragh to Intisar 103A	Waha Oil Company	68/109	24/61
Masrab to Gialo	Waha Oil Company	25/40	6/15
Bu Attifel to Intisar 103A	Agip Oil company (NOC)	85/137	34/86
Jakhira to Intisar 103A	Wintershall Libya	53/85	20/50
Messla to Sarir	Arabian Gulf Oil Company	83/135	20/50
Messla to Sarir	Arabian Gulf Oil Company	83/135	16/40

4.6

The Power Sector

MEC International

Introduction

Libya's electricity sector is run by the state-owned General Electricity Company (GECOL). The country has been self-sufficient in energy since the 1960s, with no imports or exports of electricity. 14.8GWh of electricity was produced in 1999, entirely from fossil fuels, and mainly in oil- rather than gas-fired power stations. Per capita consumption of electricity is higher than that of any other African country. Libya currently has an electric power production capacity of about 4.5 gigawatts. Projects have been planned to develop other gas-fired facilities, though most appear to have stalled.

Capacity expanded fast during the 1990s, with two new 720-megawatt plants constructed at Zuwara and Zuwaitina. Plans to utilize natural gas include an 800-megawatt power plant in Zuwara, a 1,400-megawatt power plant to be located on the coast between Benghazi and Tripoli, and a 1,200-megawatt combined power and desalination complex in Sirt (bidders include Alstom, ABB, Siemens and Deutsche Babcock). However, a 1995 plan for Siemens to build a 450-megawatt gas-fired power plant in Sabha, 300 miles south of Tripoli, appears to have stalled. GECOL's biggest current project is to expand Libya's network of power substations, which are concentrated mainly in Benghazi, Sabha and Tripoli. There are also plans to exploit transmission lines for telecommunications.

Government plans for development of the sector

GECOL's chairman, Umran Abu Kraa, recently said that plans for 2002–2006 and 2006–2011 were being prepared. He also said that there was a major project in hand to reorganize GECOL. In addition, he did not expect BOT (Build-operate-transfer) contracts in the first five-year plan, though they were possible in the second.

GECOL expected demand from its one million customers to reach 2,650 megawatts in 2001, with capacity expected to double by 2010 and again by 2020. The company plans to add 5,000 megawatts in generating capacity by 2010. It estimates investment needs for the next 20 years as follows:

- new power stations: US$3.265 billion before 2010, and a further possible US$2.5 billion before 2020;
- a new 1,500km, 400 kV grid (reinforcing the existing 220 kV and 66 kV systems): US$1.5 billion before 2010, plus a further US$300–500 million by 2020;
- upgrading and reinforcing the national distribution networks: US$950 million before 2010, plus a further US$500 million to 1 billion by 2020;
- US$220 million for national, regional and distribution control centres.

Investment needs therefore amount to US$5.935 billion by 2010, and possibly as much as US$10 billion in total by 2020.

GECOL plans to link Libya's grid to Egypt and Europe. Libya and Tunisia are already working on a 225 kV grid linking the two countries, due to be completed in early 2001. In recent months, GECOL has hinted at the possibility of allowing private investment in Libya's power generation and distribution. The country's power sector requires substantial investment, and GECOL is looking at alternatives to public financing, but it remains unlikely that Libya will undertake any large-scale power privatization or allow independent power projects anytime soon. Abu Kraa is keen to foster foreign electricity sector contacts and supported a visit by the UK Energy Council in November 2000.

Research and development were needed for wind energy, Abu Kraa said, and two farms of 50-megawatt capacity are planned. There are also plans for combined solar-fuel generation. Libya's available solar energy is 3.5×10^9 GWh per year, and wind speed in some locations is 6.7 metres per second – suitable for a wind farm, according to GECOL. Research in wind generation has been underway for 20 years, but with little result. On the subject of environmental considerations, Abu Kraa said that gas generation would be widely used because of low emissions.

The major new element in GECOL's latest plans is desalination, which is forecast to double in capacity in the next five years. There are plans for new capacity of 600,000 cubic metres per day in a number of desalination plants across the country from Zuwara to Tobruk to be in production by 2006. The Tripoli plant will have a capacity of 250,000 cubic metres per day. Invitations have been sent to consultants and construction companies and a response is awaited. When asked, Abu Kraa dismissed the idea of handing over desalination to the local governorates (Shaabiyat), which he said would not be technically competent. The desalination plants supply drinking water, as the water from the Great Man-made River (GMR) was for agricultural use. A member of the Great Man-made River Authority told a business delegation from the United Kingdom that the cost of a cubic metre of water from the river was 23 US cents, compared with 60 cents for desalinated water. It was clear that there was rivalry between the GMR and GECOL.

4.7

The Great Man-made River Project

Salem El-Maiar, Libyan Water Researcher

This chapter is based on PhD research, GMRA, Internet sources and interviews with senior Libyan officials.

Introduction

Throughout the Middle East and North Africa (MENA), the urgency of the quest for water is assuming ever-larger proportions. Water resources are scarce and often unreliable, while demand is rising fast. The reason for this is simple: the highest average rate of population growth, urbanization and industrialization, expensive agriculture and the pressing need for food security and self-sufficiency are all raising consumption at an alarming rate.

In common with other countries of the MENA region, Libya has always suffered a shortage of water and has historically relied on artesian supplies and on shallow wells in local aquifers. As its population has grown over the past three decades, there has been an increasing settlement of the country's Mediterranean coastline, where shallow aquifers have been near the surface and settled farming has developed on rich agricultural land. In general, rainfall is scanty and erratic. At best, annual rainfall does not exceed 250 millimetres in the Green and the Western mountains, and evaporation rates are too high.

Demand for water along the coastal belt and in the main cities it supports has increased, with the result that water levels in the local aquifers have fallen and the quality of the water has progressively diminished. Salinity is increasing at an 'alarming' annual rate, according to the General Water Authority (GWA). Resulting water shortages are a threat not only to the well-being of the population, but also to environmental, agricultural and industrial development.

To reverse this progressive decline, a reliable source of fresh water was needed for the heavily populated coastal strip, which extends from Tobruk in the east, through Benghazi, to Tripoli in the west.

History

Early in the 1960s, during oil exploration deep in the southern Libyan desert, vast reservoirs of high-quality water were discovered. Subsequent investigations have proved the reserves available, and defined the limits of a number of potentially vast aquifers. The water held in these aquifers was laid down during the European Ice Ages, between 14,000 and 38,000 years ago, when Libya had a temperate climate and torrential rainfall.

Four major underground basins were located during exploratory drillings. In the south-east, the Kufra Basin covers an area of 350,000 square kilometres and has an estimated groundwater storage capacity of 20,000 cubic kilometres in the Libyan sector, distributed through an aquifer layer over 2,000 metres deep. The basin extends beyond the southern border of the country to the north of Kufra, then swings north-east over the border with Egypt. South of Tazerbo, the basin connects with the Sirte Basin, which underlies the Sarir Calanscio gravel plain to the Mediterranean. The fresh-water aquifer in the Sarir Basin is some 600 metres deep and is estimated to hold more than 10,000 cubic kilometres of water.

South of Jebel Fezzan, the Murzuq Basin extends from Qaraf Arch in the north to beyond Libya's south-western borders. The total area of this basin is estimated to be 450,000 square kilometres, with an upper aquifer thickness of around 800 metres and an estimated storage capacity of 4,800 cubic kilometres. North of Jebel Fezzan, the Hamada Basin extends from the Qaraf Arch and Jebel Sawda to the coast; capacity has yet to be estimated.

During the 1970s some of these desert aquifers were developed and used locally for irrigation projects, but it was realized it would not be easy either to develop the infrastructure that would be required or to attract farmers from the well-developed coastal areas to the remote and inhospitable desert region. Thus, the idea of bringing the desert water to the coastal belt where the water was needed was conceived and the notion of a river, a man-made river, was born.

In October 1983, the Great Man-made River Authority (GMRA) was created, as an independent ministry, and invested with the responsibility of taking water from the aquifers in the south and conveying it to the coast by the most economic and practical means.

Alternatives were studied. It was determined at this time that for every Libyan Dinar invested the water output would be:

Pipeline from Europe	0.74 cubic metres
Desalination	0.79 cubic metres
Transportation by ship	1.05 cubic metres
GMR	14.7 cubic metres

Source: Great Man-made River Authority

Phases of the project

From the outset, studies were made to determine the most practical and cost-effective way of carrying these immense quantities of water to the centres of population. It was agreed that the work should be phased.

Phase I

This phase, known as SS/TB, cost US$5.2 billion and extends for nearly 1,600 kilometres. It is designed to convey 2 million cubic metres of water a day, provided from a total 234 wells at Sarir and Tazerbo. The contract was awarded to South Korea's Dong Ah Consortium (DAC) as contractor, and Brown & Root of Houston, Texas, as consultant. Water from the well-fields is initially delivered to a 4 million cubic metre holding reservoir at Ajdabiya, then to end reservoirs at Benghazi and Sirte.

Phase II

Phase II cost US$7.4 billion, is 2,115 kilometres long, and has a design capacity of 2.5 million cubic metres of water a day. The contract was awarded in 1986 to the same team, but Brown & Root's UK branch carried out the consultancy work, following the US air strikes on Tripoli and Benghazi. The well fields, comprising more than 500 wells, are east and north-east of Jebel Hasouna.

Phases I and II are already supplying potable water to the main cities of Tripoli and Benghazi, as well as to population centres along the pipeline routes.

Phase III

This 390-kilometre phase, costing US$6 billion, connects Sirte and Sedada. It is also designed to augment a link between Kufra and Tazerbo that should supplement phase I with 1.6 million cubic metres a day. This phase is near completion and being implemented almost entirely by Libyan staff.

Phase IV

The final stage of the project consists of two separate water supply systems. The first – about 700 kilometres long – will take water from Ghadames to Zawara and Zawia. The second, of roughly 500 kilometres, is to supply the city of Tobruk from Al-Jaghboub. These two supply systems are at the preliminary geo-technical study and investigation stage. When they go ahead, they will offer major opportunities for foreign investment, participation and technical cooperation.

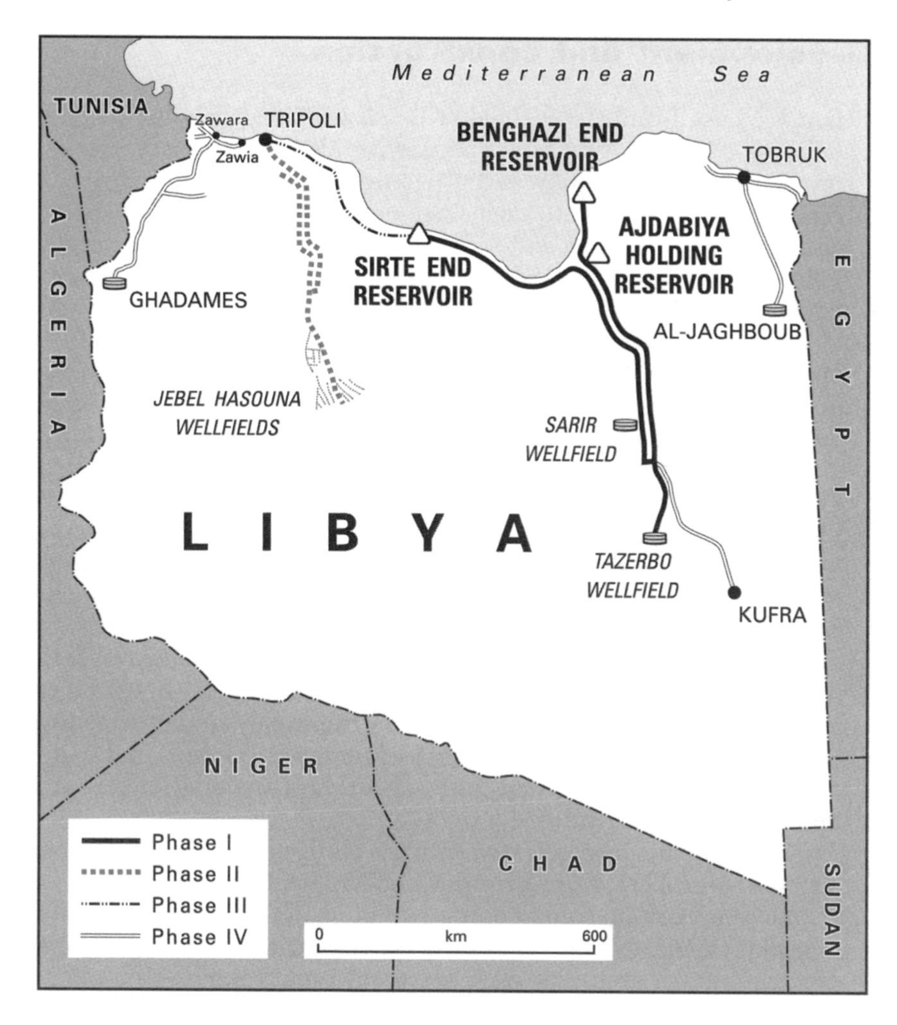

Figure 4.7.1 The four phases of the project

Once completed and fully operational, the GMR should deliver well over 6 million cubic metres of water a day from 1,350 production wells, via 600,000 pipes covering a distance of more than 4,400 kilometres. Geologists and hydrologists say the rate of extraction from the four basins will provide several hundred years of potential production and is designed to avoid excessive reduction in water levels. This will keep pumping costs to a minimum and ensure that well-fields remain productive over a longer period. The equipment used in the project has a design life of 50 years, but this could be extended indefinitely by a rolling replacement and refurbishment programme.

Development and construction

DAC's Phase I contract, valued at US$5.2 billion, included designing, building and operating pipe plants with all the necessary aggregate production, water supply and other infrastructure. In addition, the company was required to undertake detailed design and construction of the conveyance lines and Ajdabiya holding reservoir, to design and build support facilities, offices, workshops, stores and personnel accommodation, and to install certain owner-supplied items into their works.

Phase I was completed in September 1993 and the responsibility for operating the SS/TB system, providing all relevant operating manuals and procedures, and for training the authority's staff to take over operations was passed to GMRA in September 1994.

Further contracts have since been let. A consortium of Dong Ah and Japan's C Itoh and Company was awarded the US$65 million contract for the design, construction and initial operation of a 90 megawatt gas turbine generator power plant at Sarir. EB Engineering of Norway won a contract valued at US$75 million to design and install a permanent communication and control system (PCCS). Turkish contractors STFA and ENKA built end reservoirs at Sirte and Benghazi, to Brown & Root designs, for US$85 million and US$65 million respectively. Contracts totalling US$74 million were also let for the supply, and in some cases, installation, of a variety of items, including well pumps and motors, associated transformers and control gear, line and end control valves and reservoir sluice gates.

Other contractors associated with the GMR project include Siemens, Ameron, Marubeni, Price Brothers and Nippon Koei UK.

The construction, equipment, installation and commissioning of the pipe plants, one at Brega and one at Sarir, continued through 1985 and 1986 and these processes were all major undertakings. The plant at Brega consists of two parallel fabrication lines, each nearly a kilometre long, with extensive welding and fitting shops for the fabrication of embedded steelwork from imported coils of sheet steel and from steel sections.

The contractor had to locate and develop suitable sources of concrete aggregates and build the necessary aggregate crushing, screening and washing plants.

'The World's Largest Civil Engineering Project'

- The aquifers that feed the GMR hold 120,000 cubic kilometres of water, a volume equal to two-thirds of the Black Sea.
- The 5 million tonnes of cement used in making the pipes is enough to build a road linking the city of Sirt in northern Libya to Mumbai (Bombay) in India.
- The pipe transporters have travelled a distance equivalent to the Sun and back.
- The total depth of all the water wells drilled is over 70 times the height of Mt Everest.
- The pre-stressed steel wire used in making the pipes would circle the Earth 280 times.
- The amount of aggregates used would build 20 pyramids the size of the Great Pyramid at Giza, Egypt.
- The 1,500 wells pump 6.5 million cubic metres of water a day, enough to provide over 1,000 litres of water daily to each Libyan citizen.
- The pipeline is 4,400 kilometres long and extends over an area roughly equivalent to Western Europe.

Source: Great Man-made River Authority

Wells were sunk at Jalu, 250 kilometres from the Brega plant, when the aquifer there had been found to hold water of a suitable quality for concrete. A pipeline was laid from the Jalu well-field to the Brega plant, where the water was also used for domestic and other purposes. Accommodation for the workforce, and for GMRA and Brown & Root staff, was constructed; this was fully self-contained, with medical and catering services, as well as extensive recreational facilities. Diesel generators were installed to meet the considerable power demand; other facilities included water treatment and sewage disposal.

A similar facility was built at Sarir, with three parallel pipe fabrication lines and all facilities. The third line was specifically geared to the production of the smaller-diameter pipes – down to 600 millimetres – required in the well-fields.

The first pipes were manufactured at the two plants in mid-summer 1986. After an initial running-in period, the design output of 44 pipes a day from each line – a total of 220 units a day – was regularly achieved and frequently exceeded.

The pipeline was designed as a pre-cast concrete cylindrical pipe (PCCP) structure. A PCCP consists of a cylinder of sheet steel formed from steel coil with socket and spigot ends, and intermediate stiffeners fabricated at the plant and hydraulically tested. These are then fitted into steel moulds and concreted, with the concrete forming both an internal lining and an external core.

The steel moulds are removed and the concrete is steam cured to achieve a working strength at an early stage. After curing, the pipe core is placed on a vertical rotating table and spirally wrapped with high-tensile wire ranging in diameter from 4.88 millimetres to 7.25 millimetres. The ends of this wire are locked off into embedded anchor plates. Finally, the exterior of the pipe is protected with a sprayed mortar coating and is again steam cured.

Chemical action within the pipe concrete provides considerable corrosion protection to all the embedded steel, but where the ground in which the pipeline is buried is particularly aggressive, additional protection is provided by the spray application of a protective coating.

The two pipe manufacturing plants have been completely operated by Libyan staff for more than five years.

Allocation policy

It was originally planned to allocate more than 85 per cent of the water supplied by Phase I for agricultural development, bringing significant social benefits. By allocating the lion's share to agriculture, the hope was to achieve food self-sufficiency and economic independence. Of the remainder, about 12 per cent was allocated for municipal use and 3 per cent for industry (see Table 4.7.1).

Table 4.7.1 Allocation of phases

Phase	Municipal	Agricultural	Industrial	Total
Phase I	410,170	1,506,030	83,800	2,000,000
Phase II	1,316,090	1,175,660	8,250	2,500,000
Phase III	253,000	1,427,000	0	1,680,000
Total	1,979,260 (32%)	4,108,960 (66%)	92,050 (2%)	6,280,000 (100%)

Source: Great Man-made River Authority (2002)

Naturally, demand for water will always occur as a direct result of population growth, urbanization and improvement in the standard of living. Owing to the heavy demand for domestic usage, it was decided recently to readjust the allocation policy and increase the municipal sector to 32 per cent and reduce the agricultural sector to 66 per cent (see Table 4.7.1).

Conclusion

The GMR is narrowing the gap between water supply and water demand – and doing so with remarkably few problems, given its size and complexity. There have been some pipe corrosion problems, but these were solved by Libyan engineers and have led to the establishment of a Technical Corrosion Centre and a Libyan Corrosion Society that will benefit not only the present generation of Libyan engineers, but also those to come in future. The GMR has been hailed by international experts as an innovative project that utilizes the latest technology in engineering, hydrology and materials sciences. By bringing water from the south to the people living on the coast it has made a strategic contribution towards improved conditions for the Libyan population. The GMR certainly gives Libya a breathing space to develop new technologies and a sound integrated water resource allocation and management policy.

4.8

Agriculture

The General Authority of Agriculture, Animal and Marine Wealth, and MEC International

Despite the dominance of Libya's oil industry, agriculture remains the main occupation of the Libyan people. All farming activity is closely dependent on rainfall, however, which is often erratic, and irrigation is problematic. Agriculture accounts for approximately 5–7 per cent of GDP but employs approximately one-fifth of the work force. Harvests of barley, the main staple, fluctuate from year to year, and Libya is not agriculturally self-sufficient. In addition to barley, wheat, tobacco and olives are grown in the north; dates and figs are grown on the oases; and grapes are cultivated on the mountain slopes. Other primary food crops include maize, potatoes and sugar beet. The primary meat products are beef and veal, chicken, camel and lamb. The government sponsors land reclamation and hydroponic agriculture and has sold expropriated land to peasants at subsidized prices. It also provides credits for seed, fertilizers and machinery, and has greatly expanded the land under irrigation. Libya imports approximately 75 per cent of its food requirements.

After a number of years of low rainfall, the water table has fallen dramatically, and diesel and electric pumps are overworked in lifting underground water resources from greater depths. Seawater is drawn into large aquifers near Tripoli, with the result that water for both agricultural purposes and human consumption is becoming increasingly salty. Only a small fraction of Libya's land receives adequate rainfall to support agriculture without assistance from underground wells or from seawater. The Great Man-made River (GMR) project was begun in 1984 with the objective of carrying water in a large diameter pipeline from well-fields in the south to the northern coast, including Tripoli, Benghazi and Sirt. With the advent of the GMR, eastern provinces are projected to increase agricultural output. The scheme, which is expected to take 25 years to complete, has had little noticeable effect so far on the overall shortage, partly due to its high operational costs.

Most of Libya's arable and pasture land is to be found in Tripolitania, and here approximately 22 per cent of the working population was engaged in agriculture before the GMR began. Only about 1 per cent of the country's land is cultivated, with about 8 per cent in use as pasture. Principal crops are tomatoes, citrus fruits, barley, wheat, potatoes, olives, figs, apricots and dates. Libya's best dates, the 'deglet nur', come from the southwest. Sheep and goat rearing is an important activity in the north. Cattle have been imported from the United Kingdom.

Fodder is the most important single field crop, as large amounts are needed to sustain Libya's livestock. Mutton is greatly prized and sheep are kept by most farmers. Libya has 5.6 million sheep, 1.3 million goats, 140,000 cattle, 160,000 camels and 60 million poultry. Some semi-nomadic shepherding of sheep and goats takes place in traditional areas of pasture land. However, this 'family herding' practice is becoming a thing of the past. Land tenure has changed dramatically over the past century. The original system was one of tribal land ownership, but with Italian colonization much of the land became state controlled and, between 1951 and 1961, gradually became absorbed by the government of the independent state of Libya. The human rights decrees of 1977, however, have meant a gradual reassertion of private rights with regard to land, and small farmers are once more allowed private ownership of land and other property.

The fishing industry is currently small, but possesses considerable potential, with small quantities of fish being exported to Malta, Greece and Tunisia. There is a tuna cannery at Zanzur, and sardine canneries exist at Zuwara and Khums. Offshore fisheries and sponge beds are exploited by Greek, Italian and Maltese vessels. The most valuable agricultural exports are fish, sheepskins, dry onions, nuts and fresh vegetables. Agricultural exports in 1998 were worth US$78 million, while the value of agricultural imports was US$1.1 billion.

Libya purchased 50,500 tonnes of US durum wheat in December 2000. It had arranged to buy 20,000 tonnes in August 1999, when the Clinton Administration eased sanctions against the country, but US industry officials have said that the year's durum purchase fell through and was never exported to Libya. Libya imports about 1.4 million tonnes of wheat annually, including 400,000 tonnes of durum wheat, according to US grain industry estimates. Canada has been a major supplier of durum for Libya since the United States imposed sanctions on the country in the late 1980s. A spokeswoman for US Wheat Associates said that new investment in mills in Libya would lead to it becoming a 1.5 million-tonne wheat market in less than three years. In September 2000, Libya purchased 26,100 tonnes of US corn for the first time since the 1985–86 marketing year. In late 1999, Libya and Zambia negotiated an agreement whereby Libya would supply Zambia with crude oil and other petroleum products, while Zambia would grant Libya the use of 50,000 hectares of farmland.

Table 4.8.1 Libya's production of primary crops (tonnes)

Product	1995	1996	1997	1998	1999
Bananas	0	0	0	0	0
Barley	23,000	28,200	42,100	65,000	75,000
Cocoa beans	0	0	0	0	0
Coconuts	0	0	0	0	0
Coffee, green	0	0	0	0	0
Maize	400	400	430	450	455
Potatoes	198,320	206,000	205,000	206,000	209,000
Rice, paddy	0	0	0	0	0
Soybeans	0	0	0	0	0
Sugar beets	0	0	0	0	0
Sugar cane	0	0	0	0	0
Wheat	117,000	124,000	156,400	165,000	168,000
Total production	338,720	358,600	403,930	436,450	452,455
Growth rate (%)	–	5.9	12.6	8.1	3.7

Source: UN Food and Agricultural Organization

4.9

Libya's Tourism Potential

Jonathan Wallace

An unspoilt destination

Africa's fourth largest country is the Mediterranean's finest, unspoilt destination for tourists. Libya has more than 1,700 kilometres of virgin beaches and the finest and best-preserved cities of the ancient world in the entire region. The desert embraces oases of breathtaking beauty, galleries of prehistoric rock art and medieval towns still thriving. Moreover, the people are hospitable, charming and (without any doubt) the least bothersome to visitors of any North African country.

There are 13 World Heritage sites in Libya, all of them breathtaking and many little known outside the country. The leading ones are:

- **Leptis Magna:** 90 kilometres west of Tripoli, the most outstanding archaeological settlement in Libya. The city was abandoned to the desert after the Arab invasion in the seventh century and never built over. For this reason its preservation and grandeur are without parallel and finer than any similar sites in Italy itself or elsewhere in the Mediterranean basin. Leptis (also known as Lepcis) was one of the oldest Phoenician towns in North Africa, and then became an important trading centre under Roman rule, thanks to its location and as the birthplace of the Emperor Septimus Severus. Its extensive infrastructure is still visible, although only a third of the huge site has been excavated. A full day is needed to see what has been revealed of the city, which includes Roman baths, complete streets, a market-place, temples, a port and lighthouse, and an amphitheatre.

- **Sabratha:** 70 kilometres west of Tripoli, an early Phoenician settlement dating from the sixth century BC, buried under the ruins of the Roman town built between AD 138 and AD 180 and partly submerged beneath the sea. The ancient town was excavated in the 1920s and 1930s, revealing its original streets, houses and public squares, and a large Roman amphitheatre.

- **Cyrene:** 200 kilometres east of Benghazi, founded around the middle of the seventh century BC by Greek immigrants and built on a plateau 621 metres above sea level. Without doubt one of the highlights for any visitor to Libya. Cyrene gradually developed into a kingdom, which later submitted to Alexander the Great and then Ptolemaic rule. It reached its peak of development in the third and second centuries BC, later being revitalised under Roman rule. Cyrene's fine architecture reflects all these periods.
- **Apollonia:** 15 kilometres north of Cyrene, Apollonia was built as a port for that city. Named Apollonia during the Hellenistic period, it continued to be used in the Byzantine era, some of the port eventually becoming submerged because of changing sea levels. The amphitheatre, baths and walls of the original town can still be seen, along with some fine Byzantine remains, including five churches.
- **Ptolemais:** a Hellenistic city that served as the port of ancient Barce, but with origins dating back to the sixth or seventh century BC. A number of significant buildings can be seen at the site, such as the first century BC 'Palace of Columns', an Arch of Constantine and a large Hellenistic mausoleum. Many late-Roman buildings have still to be fully excavated.
- **Ghadames:** an old oasis town in the desert, 640 kilometres southwest of Tripoli. Blessed with good springs, the town was historically one of the most important settlements in the region and is one of Libya's leading World Heritage sites. Occupied by the Romans and Byzantines, and with evidence of prehistoric habitation, Ghadames is still a bustling centre, drawing the enigmatic Tuareg from the surrounding desert.
- **Germa, Ghirza and Fezzan:** ancient Libyan towns of the early Libyan tribes such as the Garamantes, who resisted and then coexisted with Roman occupation, prospering through trade from Africa with the Romans.
- **Tripoli:** Libya's leading city. It is cosmopolitan, friendly and has fine displays of architecture as relics from its long history of multicultural occupation. The Medina and Souq alone will take half a day to explore. The museum contains some fine pieces, taking the visitor through the city's long history, from Roman statuary to Muammar Qadhafi's blue Volkswagen Beetle, which he drove when masterminding the overthrow of the Idris monarchy and the expulsion of British and American occupying forces.

Libya's negative image must be changed

Libya is far from ready to welcome tourists in any number. Visas are difficult and time-consuming to obtain, even for the business visitor. The country has a negative image abroad after many years of biased reporting and political demonization. Its name evokes images of terrorists, and a violent antipathy to all Westerners. Nothing could be further from the truth, except, perhaps, for the description of the economy. And this is changing, although as with all else in Libya, it is changing slowly. As yet the government has done nothing to promote a more realistic image abroad. Much public relations work is needed to show potential travellers the real delights awaiting them.

Planning for development

Sanctions and decades of self-imposed isolation have blocked any development designed to meet the standards and needs of any but the hardiest visitor. Development of basic facilities is badly needed if Libya is to become a destination for the modern tourist. However, tourists do visit – and they are arriving in increasing numbers. It is not uncommon to see groups of earnest Japanese being escorted around the museum in Tripoli, while intrepid north Europeans (especially Germans) explore the desert in off-road vehicles and even on motorcycles.

Looking to capitalize on the economic benefits a vibrant tourist industry can offer, Libya is preparing a US$2,000–3,000 million investment programme to attract thousands of foreign visitors. Tourism was identified as a priority sector in the country's US$35,000 million, five-year development plan announced in December 2000. The indications are that political rhetoric is starting to translate into a coherent policy for the sector's promotion. If managed and developed correctly, the industry could prove a significant alternative source of revenue for an economy largely dependent on oil.

Neighbouring Egypt has shown what can be achieved: its 5 million tourists a year bring in more than US$4,000 million to the local economy.

'Our first priority is to establish a strong tourism infrastructure and the associated services required in collaboration with local, Arab and foreign investors', Fathi el-Musrati, president of the Tourism Investment & Promotion Board (TIPB), told a major travel market conference in Dubai. The TIPB says nine sites have been ring-fenced for development under its master plan for tourism. 'We want to provide investment opportunities for a wide variety of activities and not just conventional tourism', says Aymen Seif Ennasir, director of the TIPB's planning committee. 'These will include ecological, religious, health and sports adventure tourism projects.'

Nine sites for development

The TIPB is offering nine greenfield sites to international investors:

- **Bzimah oasis:** Located in the south-west, 160 kilometres north-west of Kufra, the oasis offers a range of opportunities for tourism development. The TIPB is targeting the Bzimah lake as a centre for the area's industry. Developers have been invited to submit proposals for a tourism village on the lake shore that will include spa facilities, accommodation and other amenities. The lake, seven kilometres from north to west, has a high salinity and mineral content, making it ideal for health tourism. There are hot springs at Umm Larbah, on the western shores of the lake. The area is also ringed by the Bzimah mountain range, where the TIPB plans to establish a nature reserve and exploit the possibilities for ecological and adventure tourism. However, access to the area is limited. The nearest airport is at Kufra.
- **Zallaf and Ubari:** East of Bzimah, the Zallaf and Ubari deserts incorporate the four giant lakes of Gabrawn, Umm Almaa, Mafu and Mandara. The lakes have three times the level of salinity found in seawater and the TIPB is planning to offer basic tourism services from prefabricated desert camps. In a second phase of development, the TIPB intends to establish a permanent tourist village at Ubari. The nearest airport is at Sabha.
- **Allud valley:** The valley is 206 kilometres south-east of Misurata and is strewn with ruins dating from the Roman period up to the Italian colonial occupation. The area is also served by artesian wells, where the TIPB plans to develop spa and health resorts, including tourist services, hotel accommodation and restaurants.
- **Surman national park:** This densely forested park lies 50 kilometres west of Tripoli and is within easy reach of the spectacular archaeological ruins of Sabratha, which boasts one of the largest Roman amphitheatres in North Africa. The TIPB is planning to establish tourist villages at both Surman and Sabratha.
- **Al-Kouf national park:** In the Green Mountain region of north-east Libya, the park is near the ancient city of Pentopolis and close to the beaches stretching between Benghazi and Derna. The TIPB plans to develop hotels and tourist facilities in the local towns of Al-Byda and Al-Marj.
- **St Mark's valley:** The birthplace of the Christian apostle St Mark, the valley is in the Green Mountain area. The TIPB plans to establish tourist resorts on the nearby beaches of Ras al-Halal. Facilities are expected to include a health therapy and water sports centre, tourist accommodation and restaurants.

- **Ras al-Tin:** The delightful beach is 55 kilometres west of Derna port and close to the war cemeteries at Tobruk. The TIPB is planning to develop a leisure tourism complex at Ras al-Tin.
- **Al-Twebya:** Al-Twebya beach, famous for its palm trees, is 25 kilometres outside Al-Khoms. Al-Twebya is also within driving distance of the unspoilt ancient Roman city of Leptis Magna. The TIPB is planning to develop a beach resort to cater for leisure, cultural and sports tourism.
- **Silin:** In the Al-Mergheb region, 100 kilometres east of Tripoli, Silin beach is the first site to be developed by the TIPB. Italian tour operator Valtur has an agreement to develop a 600-room leisure complex near the beach and the Roman ruins at Villa Silin. The site is also close to beaches in the Al-Khoms and Al-Twebya areas.

The five-star Corinthia hotel leads the way

Libya has about 6,000 hotel beds at present. The TIPB plans to provide more than 60,000 more over five years. Maltese hotel operator and developer the Corinthia Group was one of the first off the mark. The company has invested US$125 million in building Libya's first five-star hotel, in Tripoli, with 300 rooms, a business centre and a 10,000-square-metre commercial centre. The Bab Al-Africa Corinthia has two towers – the taller, at 28 storeys, opened in March 2003. The building has already become an icon for the city. 'It has been specifically designed to blend modernity into Tripoli's traditional architecture', says Mark Gaucci, the hotel's public relations executive. 'This will be one of North Africa's most luxurious hotels.' It will have to be: the one-night rack rate for a single room is US$280. At the older four-star Al-Kabir and Al-Mahari hotels on the corniche, a double room costs less than US $100 a night.

The project was financed through private equity and a Libyan Arab Foreign Bank loan. The government has also lent its support, providing a suitable site for the project, exemption from duty on imported construction materials and a seven-year tax break on the hotel's operation. Corinthia intends to target business customers stopping in Tripoli but also wants to attract the tourist trade from mainland Europe, which the company says will be the main source of its revenue in future.

'When we develop one hotel we also look to open two or possibly three more properties', says Corinthia Group chairman Alfred Pisani. 'Corinthia now plans over the next five to six years to develop at least three more 300-room hotels, at a cost of US$80 million each, in Benghazi, Sirte and Sabratha. These hotels will focus on the tourist market, which has a massive potential for growth in Libya. It is virgin country for tourism, and what is more important, it is easily accessible from Europe.'

In Tripoli, Corinthia is being closely followed by Switzerland's Moevenpick hotel chain, which the TIPB says is negotiating a US$40 million deal with the municipality to develop a hotel complex in the city centre.

On the coast, Italian tour operator Valtur has also been quick to establish a market presence, signing a US$50 million contract to develop a site near the Roman ruins of Villa Silin. The planned 145-hectare beach complex will include more than 400 bungalow chalets, with an 18-hole golf course covering 60 hectares.

Twenty-three airlines provide services

The country's airports were reopened for European business following the suspension of sanctions in 1999. Twenty-three international carriers are currently running services for mainly business customers. European airlines are looking to expand their services as demand increases. 'British Airways (BA) currently operates three flights a week serving mostly business clients, with a 70 per cent load factor and very little tourist business', says Charlie Gassoub, BA's Libya manager. 'However, we are following the tourism sector and what the government is doing very closely.'

In a world of shrinking opportunities, Libya's embryonic tourist industry presents a chance that is too good to miss. Many have already started investing in Libya and many more are keeping a close eye on developments.

Providing the government's re-assimilation into the international fold goes smoothly, and its appetite to attract foreign visitors and invest in the industry's infrastructure continues, the next five years promises to be a busy and interesting time.

4.10

Telecommunications

MEC International

Government attitude to investment in telecommunications

Telecommunications are stated to be a priority within the Government's investment programme. New government machinery to promote telecommunications development has been set up, but plans are still fluid and few details have yet been made public. At present, tele-density is approximately 10 per cent, but the Government is seeking to boost this to 27 per cent by 2015 and 37 per cent by 2020. This will require estimated investment of US$10 billion over the 2000–20 period. Foreign investors will be asked to provide up to 50 per cent of the total, although there are as yet no signs that the sector will be liberalized or the national telephone company offered for full or partial privatization.

The Government is aware of the importance of communications and IT in the new world order. The mobile network became operational in 1996 and mobile telephones (at exorbitant prices) are already everywhere, and in a population 50 per cent of which is said to be aged below 20, the younger generation are rapidly getting connected, not least because of the poor state of land lines. Many are already avid Internet users. Private, government and offshore investment will increasingly head into the communications and IT sectors. Telecommunications access to Libya is already difficult because of growing pressure on a limited number of lines. Meanwhile, Tripoli is committed to building a national backbone network to connect banks, universities and other public sources to the Internet. At present, five nodes with a total of 150,000 subscribers have been constructed, and with continued free access to information, these subscriber numbers are set to increase.

Foreign players

The foreign companies most visible in the market are Alcatel and Ericsson. These companies are providing the infrastructure for the existing local mobile operator, Al-Madar. It is believed that the Libyan fixed-line provider GPTC is itself maintaining equipment that was delivered several decades ago; telecommunications switchgear was installed by Ericsson more than 20 years ago. They and others are currently awaiting a request to tender for its upgrade. There is not believed to be any current, notable presence from overseas firms in GPTC.

Possible entrants

The question of future companies entering the market is key.

To develop the infrastructure, Libya's telecommunications authorities are looking for overseas partners. Candidates would be major telecommunications companies such as BT and France Telecom, but an alternative (such as Orascom, an Egyptian company with licences across Africa) might be considered. LTT (Libya Telecom and Technologies) are running a competition for a prime contractor such as Siemens, Alcatel or Ericsson to deliver a turnkey mobile network solution, but are probably out of their depth. A telecommunications consultant may eventually be engaged, but at present the view seems to be that a prime contractor will provide the complete solution.

Great Man-made River (GMR)

The pipelines of the Great Man-made River (GMR) are buried and thus population settlements are unlikely to develop along the line itself. The main IT opportunity therefore is for a digital telemetry system to replace the existing analogue technologies. There is, however, a need, both practical and political, for telecommunications even in some of the remotest parts of Libya. In the electrification programme, 1,500 kilometres of existing line are to be upgraded, and links are planned with Egypt, the Maghreb and Europe. The new transmission lines will be exploited for telecommunications and a separate company may be developed. At the end of 2000, the GMR project awarded a telecoms contract with a value of US$27 million. Other contracts are expected to be passed for tender in the next couple of years, including one worth around US$40 million.

Government investment plans

In 1990, the GPTC laid out a plan for the development of telecommunications in Libya covering the period 1993–2020, with the following aims:

- adoption of modern digital technology and the replacement of old technology;
- fully automatic telecommunications services;
- reduction of waiting lists;
- improved connectivity, and services to remote areas;
- tele-density of 10 per cent by 2000 and 37 per cent by 2020;
- provision of data transmissions such as the Internet;
- provision of GSM services;
- necessary organization and finance in place to execute medium- and long-term plans.

Libya is also involved in the Thurya satellite communications project with a net contribution of US$25 million, the ICO satellite project (for mobile communications) with a net contribution of US$4 million, and the African Satellite Project (RASCOM) which is valued at more than US$400 million. Libya will participate in the last project in a way that will allow it to maximize benefits to its services and operations and its role in decision-making.

The budget for the plan in 2000–2020 is set out in Table 4.10.1. It is split between systems expenditure (subscriber equipment, cable networks, exchanges and carrier networks) and construction and auxiliary services expenditure (buildings, service centres, transportation, training, consultancy and technical support).

Finance for the plan will come from government subsidy, foreign partners' investment, commercial borrowing and GPTC's revenue.

Table 4.10.1 Telecommunications budget, 2000–2020 (US$ million)

	2000–2010	2011–2020	Total
Systems expenditure			
Subscriber equipment	1,376.71	2,207.79	3,584.50
Cable networks	2,390.57	1,989.07	4,379.64
Exchanges	903.25	1,320.43	2,223.68
Carrier networks	1,497.57	1,085.07	2,582.64
Construction & auxiliary services	1,335.04	1,359.25	2,694.29
Total	7,503.14	7,961.61	15,464.75

The media

The Libyan Government has teamed up with the Tunisian Government to bring a new satellite TV channel to the Maghreb region. The channel will be based in Tunis and will focus on news coverage. It appears that this new satellite channel is a form of response to Qatari TV's al-Jazira, which is popular in the region. Libyan television programmes are mostly in Arabic but there is a 30-minute news broadcast each evening in both English and French. It is also possible to watch the occasional sports programme. However, the officially encouraged spread of satellite dishes means that audiences for Libyan TV are greatly reduced.

Russia has expressed its readiness to assist in the development of a multi-role civilian satellite, Libsat. Newspapers and periodicals are published by Jamahiriya News Agency, the Press Service and trade unions. The main newspaper is Al-Fajr Al-Jahid. The official Libyan news agency is Jana. In radio, the Socialist People's Libyan Arab Jamahiriya Broadcasting Corporation broadcasts in Arabic and English from Tripoli and Benghazi. Some foreign newspapers are available.

4.11

Transport Infrastructure

MEC International and the Libyan General Authority for Transport and Communications

Introduction

It is expected that the international transport market will witness huge developments during the next decade, compelling many countries to reconsider their policies for transport and adopt trends for achieving the objectives envisaged to serve their interests and those of other parties. Taking into consideration Libya's central geographic location in the African continent, its proximity to the shores of southern Europe, and its convenient location to many enclave countries not having access to the sea, it should be apparent that Libya is best placed to serve as the perfect transport corridor linking the Arab east and the Arab west, on the one hand, and West African countries and the Middle Eastern region on the other. This means that from the perspective of transport, Libya is located in the crossing point of the two large corridors for trade and transport: the side or lateral corridors along the North African coast and the vertical corridors extending from the Mediterranean Basin to the Gulf of Guinea through Chad. As a result of this geo-transportational significance, the Libyan authorities have given due attention during the past 25 years to the development of infrastructure in the transport sector, aiming at recreating the basic necessities for the transport industry and to enable it to provide a link between North and South, and East and West, thus becoming a main crossing point for transport traffic/movement in a large part of the African continent.

Investment in Tripoli's infrastructure

The Secretary (Chairman) of Tripoli Shaabiya (Governorate), Izz al-Din Hinshiri, has commented that the basis of business partnership must be clear from the beginning and established on a solid foundation. Libya had ambitious plans in the next five-year plan, which were focused on improving basic infrastructure in areas such as ports, communications, roads, schools, hospitals and human resources. The Shaabiya would be responsible for handling many of these projects, to the value of LD5 billion. It would focus on roads, sewage treatment plants, construction of housing, agricultural projects, manufacturing and strategic projects such as the metro (light railway), harbour development, the airport and two desalination plants. With regard to the Tripoli metro, there were in fact two major projects: first the metro, and second the underground. The priority was the metro, and this was at the stage of bidding for finance and technology. Libya was quite prepared to consider a BOT project but it was not clear if the correct legal framework was in position. Libya was seeking transfer of technology, said Izz al-Din Hinshiri, and joint ventures with local companies in the construction industry. Foreign companies would be well advised to talk to the Sha'biyat, and contact could be made through the Union of Chambers of Commerce via the Chairman, Abdulrahman Shater. The Sha'biyat was seeking long-term partnerships, not fair-weather friends. There was also scope for technology training and the training of human resources. The overall impression gained by the meeting was that the Shaabiyat were an important new dimension in the development of Libyan infrastructure, and foreign companies would be well advised to keep in touch with them.

Roads

Libya's vehicle ownership is the highest in Africa, with 209 vehicles (with four or more wheels) per 1,000 population in 1996 (compare South Korea 226, Saudi Arabia 166, United States 769). Sixty-eight per cent of those are passenger cars, with the other 32 per cent being commercial vehicles. Libya has very few motorcycles, perhaps only a few thousand. The country is also one of the cheapest places in Africa to buy fuel at the pumps: in 1998, super gasoline was US$0.22 per litre (compare Egypt 29 cents per litre, Algeria 31 cents per litre, Morocco 79 cents per litre, Chad 70 cents per litre, Tunisia 60 cents per litre), while diesel was only slightly less competitive at US$0.17 (compare Nigeria 10 cents per litre, Egypt 12 cents per litre, Algeria 16 cents per litre, Morocco 47 cents per litre, Chad 61 cents per litre, Tunisia 33 cents per litre).

Libya has an extensive network of around 25,000 kilometres of tarmac roads, and most major towns and villages are already accessible by car. However, the construction of a 1,400-kilometre road linking the country with Chad and Niger is a priority. Other plans include the construction of an east–west trans-Libyan motorway, 50 kilometres inland from the coast, linking Libya to Tunisia and Egypt, and spending around US$375 million on developing the road transportation fleet for goods and passengers on the Chad–Niger route.

Rail

Libya has had no rail network in operation since 1965, but there are plans to build a new 3,170-kilometre 1.435 metre (standard gauge) track, leading to contracts worth about US$4 billion alone; the total cost of the railway is estimated at US$10 billion. The Libyan Railways Authority issued tender documents in 1998 to lay the track along the coast from the Tunisian border to Tripoli and Misratah, then inland to Sabha. Design work and some preparatory earthmoving are in hand, but no major work has begun. Other plans made jointly with Egypt would establish a rail line from Sollum, Egypt, to Tobruk, with completion originally set for mid-1994; Libya signed contracts with Bahne of Egypt and Jez Sistemas Ferroviarios in 1998 for the supply of crossings and point work. Tripoli is to have a light railway, initially 60 kilometres, and again design work has begun; this will be a turnkey contract and will be under the authority of the Tripoli Shaabiya.

The Chairman of Libya's national rail company, the Railway Executive Board, Muhammad Abd al-Samad, stated that the railway project was extremely valuable because of Libya's position as a central transport link. He referred to links between Morocco and Europe through Spain, to sea transport, and to Libya's links with Africa. He stated that Libya was a crossroads for trade, that RAPCO would benefit greatly from cooperation with foreign companies and was looking for all kinds of cooperation, including BOT, and that the modernization project had been marketed to companies worldwide. The Chinese have started work on the Tripoli/Tunisian border section. An economic study of the railway has been carried out by a French company.

Feasibility studies are in progress, or required, for many aspects of the railway, including signalling systems, power etc. Much of what is needed will be manufactured locally, but there is a need for rolling stock, and the rails will be imported. The locomotives will be diesel-electric. The outline budget is US$10 billion. A budget of US$400 million has been set aside for studies, some of which (perhaps half) has already been spent. General approval has been given for the whole project, but there is some confusion as to whether the budget has been agreed, or will be agreed by stages. There will be free zones, most likely in Misratah and Sirt. BOT is envisaged, possibly with a Libyan partner, but it is not yet clear whether a supplier of rolling stock, for example, would actually operate the system; the Railway Executive Board was flexible. The timescale is not firm, but five years might be envisaged for the Tunisian border/Sirt section. According to the chairman, agreement had already been reached with the Tunisians about the link-up.

The network's specifications are as follows:

Length of network:	3,170 kilometres	Wagons:	8,642
No. of stations:	96	Earth works:	115,000,000 cu.m
No. of culverts:	1,205	Concrete works:	1,960,000 tonnes
No. of locomotives:	244	Steel:	261,000 tonnes
Rails:	370,000 tonnes	Aggregates:	2,500,000 m^3
Concrete sleepers:	6,800,000 pcs	Cement:	800,000 tonnes
Ballast:	11,600,000 m^3	Fastenings:	27,200,000 pcs
Design speed:	160 km/h	Maximum gradient:	0.6%
Operation speed:	120–140 km/h (passenger)	Min. horizontal radius:	1,600 metres
		Min. vertical curvature:	10,000 metres
	80–100 km/h (freight)	Formation width:	7.2 metres
Axle load:	22 tonnes	Rail type:	54:60 kg/m
Track type:	Single line	Switches & turnouts:	UIC
Gauge:	1435 mm		
Fastenings system:	Elastic		

Table 4.11.1 Expected investment for the railway network project

Description		%	Cost (US$ million)
1	Studies, design and technical assistance	4	400
2	Earthworks	16.4	1,640
3	Roads and bridges	18.6	1,860
4	Stations and buildings	12	1,200
5	Track works	22.8	2,280
6	Signalling and telecommunications	11.2	1,120
7	Rolling stock and workshop	15	1,500
	Total	100	10,000

Source: Railway Executive Board

Table 4.11.2 Railway investment timetable (US$ million)

	Year 1	Year 2	Year 3	Year 4	Year 5
Studies, design/tech assistance	100	75	75	75	75
Earthworks	500	380	380	380	0
Bridges works	558	434	434	434	0
Building works	144	264	264	264	264
Track works	684	399	399	399	399
Signalling & telecommunications	336	196	196	196	196
Rolling stock	225	105	390	390	390
Total	2,547	1,853	2,138	2,138	1,324

Source: Railway Executive Board

Water transport

Libya has no inland waterways. It has ports at Misratah, Khums, Benghazi, Darna, Marsa al Brega, Ras Lanuf, Tobruk, Zuwara and Tripoli (which was established as a free port in 1999). Government plans involve upgrading the country's ports. The Government states that its current commercial port capacity is more than 13.4 million tonnes annually.

In 1999, Libya's merchant marine consisted of 27 ships of 1,000 GRT or more (nine cargo, one chemical tanker, three liquefied gas tankers, six crude oil tankers, four ro-ro ferries and four short-sea passenger ships). Libya plans to increase its share of marine transportation by adding or replacing around 36 vessels capable of carrying oil products, crude oil, goods, containers, gas and petrochemicals, at a cost of US$1.2 billion over 10 years.

Aviation

In civil aviation, there are important work programmes underway in Tripoli and Benghazi, as well as the extension of the airport of Sirt. The country has approximately 142 airports and airfields, 59 of which have paved runways. The airports and the civil aircraft fleet are in disarray after sanctions imposed a ban on flights to and from Libya and led to the suspension of operations by Libyan Arab Airlines (LAA), its national carrier. Libya's current plans involve strengthening the airport infrastructure and developing the navigation assistance system and air control, at a cost of approximately US$1 billion. The air transportation fleet will also be expanded by adding 25 new passenger aircraft, at a cost of US$3 billion over five years. BAe Systems and others have been in negotiation with Libya about providing new aircraft, training staff and reconstructing airports. The LAA was earlier rumoured to have decided to buy 24 airbuses.

The LAA currently wet leases some aircraft for its European route (a wet lease means that the plane is leased but maintenance etc of the craft remains the duty of the plane's owners). Officials at BAe say the Libyans still need to make a full plan of action with their civil aviation industry. The LAA believes that it has lost US$3 billion as a result of sanctions.

In the field of military aircraft, a Russian aircraft manufacturer is hoping to sell Libya several advanced MiG-31 fighter-bombers. Russia, a major supplier of military and civil hardware to Libya during the Soviet era, may also overhaul Libya's current fleet of almost 90 MiG-25 planes.

In October 2000, a Moroccan company signed an agreement to extend and modernize Sirt International Airport although work has not yet begun. The agreement includes the construction of a departure lounge and a control tower. It also guarantees meteorological services, lighting the tarmac and building a terminal. The agreement, which was signed by the Secretary of the People's Committee of the General Authority for Transport and Communications and by Ahmed Biyaz, Director-General of the National Bureau of Airports in Morocco, commits the company to train Libyan engineers to manage these services.

Alitalia, Lufthansa, British Airways and KLM now offer regular flights between Libya and Europe.

Part Five

Appendices

Appendix 1

Agents and Import Restrictions

Agents

From 1 January 2003, Libya tried to introduce new legislation covering the role and requirements relating to commercial agencies (including commission agents and distributors). To date, however, this has not yet taken effect. But it is only a matter of time. In summary, the new law will mean that foreign companies selling certain products to Libya will need to employ a registered Libyan agent to be able to do so. The agent must be Libyan. Registered agents will be restricted to the number of agency agreements they are able to undertake, and will be required to demonstrate the ability to offer immediate service and spares backup to the products in their range. The new law can be said to be consumer protection in its orientation. When dealing with the National Oil Corporation or other oil-related companies it is not advisable to use an agent.

Products affected

The list of products affected is as follows:

Agricultural machines

Agricultural materials, supplies and related equipment

All kinds of cars, boats, planes and related spares

Beauty materials

Building supplies

Child care supplies

Cleaning materials

Clothes

Electrical and home appliances

Electrical materials and equipment

Electronic appliances for various uses

Fishing machinery and supplies

Food products

Fresh fruits

Furniture and accessories, including wood for production

Light agricultural equipment

Machines, equipment and other photocopier supplies

Meat and livestock

Medical equipment and supplies, including laboratories, tools and testing equipment and related spares and supplies

Motorcycles

Office supplies and equipment

Precious metals

Road and quarry equipment and spares

Scales and measurement supplies

School and office stationary

Shoes and leather products

Supplies for bakeries and confectioners

Textiles

Tobacco, matches, lighters and accessories, and liquid gas

Toys and sports goods

Transportation and communication services.

Watches, their spare parts and accessories

Workshop supplies.

Goods that are currently subject to state monopoly, eg bulk food commodities under the National Supply Company (NASCO), etc, are *not* covered by commercial agency law.

Companies that supply the Libyan oil and gas industry via Umm Al Jawaby in London or Medoil in Dusseldorf should be largely unaffected by this new legislation. These organisations will be able to continue their procurement and training services on behalf of NOC companies without any change of status. However, listed products sold directly in-country to Libyan oil companies will be caught by the new law.

Foreign companies registered in Libya will be able to continue to provide their services according to their current registration provision and business licence – there is no need to engage additional Libyan partners or agents.

Import controls

Prohibited items include all alcohol products as well as the import of obscene literature, pork, pork products and any kind of related products. All goods made in Israel are prohibited for import. The import of dogs and cats necessitates two veterinary health certificates and a rabies inoculation card. The embargo on UK consumer goods was lifted in December 2001 and there is no requirement for import licences.

Prohibited products

Commodities on the November 2002 prohibited import list are:

Alcoholic beverages

'Arabic sitting rooms'

Bicarbonates of all types

Bleach

Buses of a capacity of 30 passengers or more. Trucks and towing heads designed for civil use, capacity of 15 to 40 tonnes with an axle, bi-axle or tri-axle towing mechanism which are 10 years old or more

Cassette recording tapes

Date syrup

Dog and cat food

Eggs and egg powder intended for consumption

Fresh fruits (citrus, grapes, figs, apricots, watermelons, peaches, pomegranates) 'except when in season'

Fresh, frozen and dried vegetables intended for consumption, except for dried legumes

Frozen fish except for tuna slices intended for manufacture

Hand brooms used with sticks

Liquid pasteurised milk

Mineral and spring water except for sparkling water

Olive oil

Paper napkins except for table napkins, pocket napkins and toilet paper

Pet animals, birds and fish except for those intended for rearing

Plastic covering used in green houses and for other purposes

Plastic piping made from PVC (flexible)

Ploughs and small agricultural equipment (rakes, axles, shovels)

Polygonal iron sheets

Pork products and any related products

Poultry live and dead except for those intended for raising

Preserved meats and food prepared from them

Regular telephone units and telephone devices of a capacity of not less than 60 internal lines

School notebooks

Second-hand vehicles and tyres except for those stipulated in the second part of Article 16

Traditional dress-wear for men and women

Wooden beams and concrete

Yachts that are 75 horse power and 10 metres long intended for more than six people and for pleasure.

Appendix 2

Law No. 5 For Year 1426 (1997) Concerning Encouragement of Foreign Capital Investment:

Issued by The General People's Congress

In implementation of the decisions of the Basic People's Congresses in their Second Regular Session for the year 1425 which have been formulated by the General Convention of the Basic People's Congresses and the People's Committees, Trade Unions, Federations and Professional Organizations (The General People's Congress) in its regular session from 25 to 30 of Shawal corresponding to 4 to 9 Arrabi 1426, and Being cognizant of:

The Declaration of the People's Authority

The Magna Green Document on Human Rights in the era of the Masses

Law No. 20 for the year 1991 concerning the Consolidation of freedom

The Commercial Law and its amendments

Law No. 37 for the year 1968 for the Investment of Foreign Capitals

Income Tax Law No. 64 for the year 1973

Customs Law No. 67 for the year 1973

Law No. 1 for the year 1993 concerning Banks, Currency and Credit

Law No. 1 for the year 1425 concerning the working system of the People's Congress And Committees.

The following law is promulgated:

Article (1)

The aim of this law is to attract investment of foreign capital in investment projects within the framework of the general policy of the State and for the objectives of economical and social development and in particular:

- Transfer of modern technology.
- Training the Libyan technical personnel.
- Diversification of income resources.
- Contribution to the development of the national products so as to help in their entry into the international markets.
- Realization of a locale development.

Article (2)

This law shall apply to the investment of the foreign capital held by Libyans and the Nationals of Arab and Foreign States in investment projects.

Article (3)

In the application of this law, unless the context otherwise requires, the following words and phrases shall have the meanings assigned opposite each:

1. Jamahiriya means The Great Socialist People's Libyan Arab Jamahiriya.
2. The law means the law of Foreign Capitals Investment Encouragement.
3. The Secretary means The Secretary of the General People's Committee for Planning, Economy and Commerce.
4. Authority means Libyan Foreign Investment Board.
5. The Executive Regulation means The Regulation issued for the implementation of the provisions of this law.
6. The Foreign Capital means the total financial value brought into the Great Jamahiriya whether owned by Libyans or foreigners in order to undertake an investment activity.
7. Project means any economic enterprise established in accordance with this law The result of its work is the production of goods for end or intermediate consumption, or investment goods, or the export

or provision of service, or any other enterprise approved as such by the General People's Committee.

8. Investor means any natural or judicial entity national or non-national, investing in accordance with the provisions of this law.

Article (4)

This law regulates the investment of foreign capital brought into the Jamahyria in any of the following forms:

- Convertible foreign currencies or substitutes thereof brought through official Banking methods.
- Machinery, equipment, tools, spare parts and the raw materials needed for the investment project.
- Transport means that are not locally available.
- Intangible rights; such as patents, licences, trade marks and commercial names needed for the investment project or operation thereof.
- Reinvested part of the profits and return of the project. The Executive Regulation shall regulate the manner for the evaluation of the in-kind portions used in the formation of the capital designated for investment in the Jamahiriya.

Article (5)

There shall be established an Authority to be known as 'Libyan Foreign Investment Board' having its own independent juridical personality, under the jurisdiction of the General People's Committee for Planning, Economy and Commerce. The Authority shall be established by a decision from the General People's Committee upon a proposition by the secretary stating the Authority's legal domicile, its secretary and members of its management committee.

The Executive Regulation shall regulate the meetings of the Authority and the administrative procedures required for establishing the Project.

Article (6)

The Authority shall work for the encouragement of foreign capital investment and promotion for the investment projects by various means; in particular shall:

1. Study and propose plans to organize foreign investment and supervise foreign investments in the country.
2. Receive the applications for foreign capital investments to determine whether they satisfy the legal requirements, and the feasibility study

for the project and then submit its recommendations to the Secretary accordingly.

3. Gather and publish information and conduct economic studies relevant to the potentials of investments in the projects that contribute to the economic development of the country.
4. Take proper actions to attract foreign capitals and promote the chances of investment through various means.
5. Recommend exemptions, facilities or other benefits for the projects that are considered important for the development of the national economy, or recommend the renewal of the exemptions and benefits as provided for in the law for further periods of time. It shall submit its recommendations to the relevant authority.
6. Consider without prejudice to the right of the investor to petition and litigate complains, petitions or disputes lodged by the investors resulting from the application of this law.
7. Study and review periodically the investment legislations, propose improvement thereof and submit same to the concerned authority.
8. Perform any other functions assigned to it by the General People's Committee.

Article (7)

The project is required to realize all or some of the following:

- Production of goods for export or contribution to the increase of export of such goods or substitute imports of goods in total or in part.
- Make available positions of employment for Libyan manpower, train and enable some to gain technical experience and know-how. The Executive Regulation shall set the conditions and terms of employment of Libyan manpower.
- Use of modern technology or a trade mark or technical expertise.
- Provision of a service needed by the national economy or contribute to the enhancement or development of such service.
- Strengthen the bonds and integration of the existing economic activities and projects or reduce the cost of production or contribute in making available materials and supplies for their operations.
- Make use or help in making use of local raw materials.
- Contribute to the growth and development of the remote or underdeveloped areas.

Article (8)

Investment is permissible in the following areas:

Industry

Health

Tourism

Services

Agriculture

And any other area determined by a decision from the General People's Committee according to a proposal from the Secretary.

Article (9)

The permit for foreign capital investments shall be granted by the Authority after the issuance of the Secretary's decision approving the investment.

Article (10)

Projects established within the framework of this law shall enjoy the following benefits:

A. An exemption for machinery, tools and equipment required for execution of the project, from all custom duties and taxes, and taxes of the same impact.

B. An exemption for equipment, spare parts and primary materials required for the operation of the project, from all custom duties and custom taxes imposed on imports as well as other taxes of the same impact for a period of five years.

C. Exemption of the project from the income taxes on its activities for a period of five years as from the date of commencement of production or of work, depending on the nature of the project. This period shall be extendable by an additional duration of three years by a decision from the General People's Committee upon a request of the same by the Secretary. Profits of the project will enjoy these exemptions if reinvested. The investor shall be entitled to carry the losses of this project within the years of exemption to the subsequent years.

D. Goods directed for export shall be exempted from excise taxes and from the fees and taxes imposed on exports when they are exported.

E. The project shall be exempted from the stamp duty tax imposed on commercial documents and bills used.

Exemptions mentioned in paras A, B and D of this Article do not include the fees imposed in consideration of services such as harbour, storage and handling dues.

Article (11)

Equipment, machinery, facilities, spare parts and primary material imported for the purpose of the project may neither be disposed of through sale or abandoned without the approval of the Authority and after payment of custom duties and taxes imposed on importation thereof; nor be used for purposes other than those licensed thereof.

Article (12)

The investor shall have the right to:

A. Re-export invested capital in the following cases:

- End of the project's period.
- Liquidation of the project.
- Sale of the project in whole or in part.
- Elapse of a period of not less than five years as of the issuance of the investment permits.

B. Re-transfer the foreign capital abroad in same form in which it was first brought in after the elapse of a period of six months as of its importation in cases where difficulties or circumstances out of the investor's control prevent its investment.

C. It is permissible to transfer annually the net of the distributed profits realized by the project and interest thereof.

D. The investor has the right to employ foreigners whenever the national substitute is not available:

- The foreign employees who come from abroad have the right to transfer abroad a percentage of their salaries and wages and any other benefits or rewards given to them within the framework of the project.
- Conditions and terms regarding the implementation of this Article shall be set by the Executive Regulation.

Article (13)

The project shall not be subject to registration at the commercial register nor at the register of the Importers and Exporters; the Executive Regulation will set the procedures of the registrations at the Authority.

Article (14)

A project established in the local development areas or a project which contributes to food security or a project which uses installation and means conducive to save energy or water or contributes to the protection of environment, will enjoy the exemption mentioned in paras B) and C) of Article (10) of this Law for an additional period by a decision from the General People's Committee upon a proposal from the Secretary. The Executive Regulation will set the terms and conditions according to which the project could be considered as achieving these goals.

Article (15)

Notwithstanding ownership laws in force, the investor shall be entitled to hold title for land use. The investor may also lease such land, construct buildings thereon and be entitled to own any property or lease thereof required for establishment or operation of the project; all as per the terms and conditions set in the Executive Regulation.

Article (16)

The investor shall have the right to open for his project an account in convertible currencies at a commercial bank or at the Libyan Arab Foreign Bank.

Article (17)

Ownership of the project may be transferred in whole or in part to another investor with the approval of the Authority; the new owner will replace its predecessor in all rights, undertakings and obligations arising therefrom in accordance with the provisions of this law and other legislations in force. The Executive Regulation shall set the terms and conditions for the transfer of ownership.

Article (18)

In case it is proven that the investor has violated any provisions of this law or the Executive Regulation; the Authority shall issue a warning to the investor to rectify the violations within a period of time specified therein. In case of failure by the investor to adhere thereto, the Secretary, upon a recommendation by the Authority, may:

Deprive the project from some of the benefits provided for this law.

Oblige the investor to pay double the exemptions granted to him.

Article (19)

The permit of the project may be withdrawn or the project finally liquidated in the following cases:

- Failure to start or complete the project in accordance with the terms and conditions set by the Executive Regulation.
- Violation of the general provisions of this law and Executive Regulation.
- Repetition of violations.

All in accordance with the procedures specified by the Executive Regulation.

Article (20)

The investor shall be entitled to petition in writing against any decision affecting him as per Article (18) or Article (19) of this law, or against any disputes arising because of the implementation of the provisions of this law within thirty days as of the date of notifying him by a delivery guaranteed letter; the Executive Regulation shall specify the proper authority to which petitions should be submitted and processes of petition.

Article (21)

The investor should:

- Maintain regular books and records for the project.
- Prepare an annual budget and profit and loss account audited by a chartered accountant as per the conditions set forth in the Commercial law.

Article (22)

The employees of the Authority designated by a decision from the secretary shall have the power of the judicial officers to control the enforcement of this law and to unveil and record the violations and refer same to the competent authority; for this purpose the said employees shall be entitled to inspect the projects and check the books and records relevant to their activities.

Article (23)

The project may not be nationalized, dispossessed, seized, expropriated, received, reserved, frozen, or subjected to actions of the same impact except by force of law or court decision and against an immediate and just compensation provided that such actions are taken indiscriminately; the compensation will be calculated on the basis of the fair market value of the project in the time of action taken. The value of the compensation in convertible currencies may be transferred within a period not exceeding one year and according to the rate of exchange prevailing at the time of transfer.

Article (24)

Any dispute arising between the foreign investor and the State, due to the investor's act or to actions taken by the State, shall be referred to a court having jurisdiction in the Jamahiriya except where there is a bilateral agreement between the Jamahiriya and the State to which the investor belongs or where a multilateral agreement to which the Jamahiriya and the State to which the investor belongs are parties that provide for relevant reconciliation or arbitration, or there is a special agreement between the investor and the State containing provisions in regard to an arbitration clause.

Article (25)

Foreign investments in existence on the date of issuance of this Law shall enjoy the privileges and exemptions provided for herein.

Article (26)

Provisions of this law shall not apply to foreign capital invested or to be invested in petroleum projects as per the provisions law number 25 of 1995, as amended.

Article (27)

The Executive Regulation to this law will be issued by a decision from the General People's Committee upon a proposal from the Secretary.

Article (28)

Law number 37 of 1968 regarding investment of foreign capitals in Libya is hereby repealed and so are any other provisions that may contradict the provisions of this law.

Article (29)

This law shall be published in the Official Gazette and in the different media and be effective as of its publication in the Official Gazette.

Appendix 3

Facts about Libya[1]

History

Until the second half of the 20th century, Libya was cursed by its geography, which put it in the path of the invading empires of Europe and the Middle East. As a result, Libya has too often been an unwilling outpost of a far-distant capital.

Libya's three regions – Tripolitania (north-western Libya), Cyrenaica (north-east and south-east) and the Fezzan (south-west) – rarely formed a single entity.

Prehistory

Two distinct races appeared in North Africa between about 15,000 and 10,000 BC – the Oranian and then the Capsian – although the origins of both are virtually unknown.

The integration of the Oranians and the Capsians with indigenous peoples resulted in the spread of Neolithic (New Stone Age) culture and the introduction of farming techniques. The earliest evidence of lasting or semipermanent settlements in Libya dates from this time (8000 BC). Rock paintings in the Jebel Acacus and Wadi Methkandoush areas in Libya (as well as in the Tassili Mountains in Algeria) are the greatest source of knowledge about this time of abundant wildlife, rainfall and vegetation.

It is from these Neolithic peoples that the Berbers (the indigenous peoples of North Africa) are thought to be descended. Taking into consideration regional variations and the lack of hard evidence, they appear to have been predominantly nomadic pastoralists, although they continued to hunt and occasionally farm. By the time of contact with the first of the outside civilisations to arrive from the east, the Phoenicians, these local tribes were already well established.

The Phoenicians in Tripolitania (1000–201 BC)

The Phoenician empire, with its origins and base in the Levantine ports of Tyre, Sidon and Byblos (all in modern-day Lebanon), were a seafaring

[1] This Appendix is reproduced with permission, with minor amendments, from *Libya* (2000) published by Lonely Planet Publications

people renowned for their trading activities. By the 12th century BC, Phoenician traders were active throughout the Mediterranean, arriving regularly on the Libyan coast by 1000 BC.

After around 700 BC, their need for permanent settlements to facilitate their trade in gold, silver, raw metals, ivory and even apes and peacocks saw them establish the colonies of Lebdah (Leptis), Oea (Tripoli) and Sabratha. Other ports were later built at Macomades-Euphranta (near modern Sirt) and Charax (Medinat Sultan). Each was a small but essential link in a chain of safe ports stretching from the Levant to Spain. The strategic importance of the Libyan coast was not the only reason for Phoenician interest in Libya – the ports also provided a base for Phoenician merchants to trade with the Berber tribes of the interior, with whom they signed treaties of cooperation.

Phoenician civilisation in North Africa came to be called 'Punic', a derivation of both the Latin *Punicus* and Greek *Phoinix*. The colonies were governed from the city of Carthage (in modern Tunisia), a city whose dominance of North Africa represented the pinnacle of Punic civilisation.

Carthage was founded in 814 BC. Long politically dependent on the mother culture in Tyre, Carthage eventually emerged as an independent, commercial empire. By 517 BC, the powerful city-state was the leading city of North Africa and by the 4th century BC, Carthage controlled the North African coast from Tripolitania to the Atlantic.

Ultimately, ongoing tension with the nascent Roman Empire weakened Carthage and spelled the death-knell for Carthaginian rule. In what was to become a recurring theme in Libyan history, the Carthaginian empire governed Tripolitania from afar. There were few material benefits for Libya's indigenous inhabitants, yet the province was not spared the devastation caused by the Punic Wars with Rome (264–241 BC, 218–201 BC and 149–146 BC). The wars reduced Carthage to a small, vulnerable African state. It was razed by the Romans in 146 BC, the site symbolically sprinkled with salt and damned forever. Tripolitania was left to fend for itself.

The Garamantian Empire of the Fezzan (900 BC–AD 500)

The ancient historian Herodotus (5th century BC), in one of the earliest written references to Libya, spoke of the Garamantes people who lived 'in the part of Libya where wild beasts are found'. As part of the first indigenous empire of significance in Libya, the Garamantes have become a people of legend, seen alternately as a wild, warlike and ungovernable nomadic people or a sophisticated, urban community which made the desert bloom. There is undoubtedly a kernel of truth in both assessments.

The Garamantes may have descended in part from the Neolithic peoples of the region, although there is little doubt that some migrated from the oases to the east, carrying with them a knowledge of cultivation. The community, a loosely connected confederation of tribes, was centred on Garama (now Germa) in the Wadi al-Hayat in the Fezzan. Archaeologists have found evidence to suggest that these cities were more than mere desert outposts. Rather, they were thriving urban centres with markets and forums for public entertainment.

In spite of the competing claims about the nature of Garamantian society, most historians agree that the Garamantes were one of the most advanced and forward-thinking peoples of their time. They are attributed with introducing writing, horses, wheeled transport and, finally, camels to the Sahara. Due to its location in the central Sahara, the Garamantian civilisation exercised significant control over the ancient caravan routes across the desert with strong links to Egypt and sub-Saharan Africa. Salt (a means of preserving meat and other foods) was exchanged for gold and slaves in a lucrative trade. The Garamantes also led successful raids on the cities of the coast, including Lebdah.

Most remarkably of all, the Garamantes empire thrived because of its agricultural prowess, even though they lived far from recognised water sources. Herodotus spoke of the Garamantes as 'a very numerous tribe of people who spread soil over the salt to sow their seed in'. Archaeologists have discovered the remains of hundreds of underground channels. These channels, known as *foggara*, enabled a boom in farming activity in the oases of the wadi. Ultimately, however, this innovative approach to scarce water resources, an approach adopted nearly 2,500 years later by the modern Libyan state, sowed the seeds of the Garamantian decline. By AD 500 the last of the Garamantes people had either died or abandoned Garama, as underground water supplies dried up as a result of overexploitation.

The Greeks in Cyrenaica (631–75 BC)

Legend has it that the inhabitants of the Greek island of Thera were ordered by the oracle of Delphi to migrate to North Africa. In 631 BC, they established the city of Cyrene. Within 200 years, during the period of great Hellenic colonisation, the Greeks had established four more cities – Barce (Al- Marj), Tocra, Ptolemais (Tolmeita) and Apollonia (the port for Cyrene). These semi-autonomous city-states came to be known as the Pentapolis (Five Cities). North Africa became so significant that by around 500 BC the Greeks divided the world into three parts – Asia, Europe and Libya.

In 331 BC, the armies of Alexander the Great made a triumphant entrance to Cyrenaica from Egypt, though the great man himself stopped at the border after the Cyrenaicans greeted him with promises of loyalty. Upon his death in 323 BC, Alexander's empire was divided among his Macedonian generals. Egypt, along with Cyrene, went to Ptolemy. Again, the cities of the Pentapolis retained a significant degree of autonomy, although Greek influence was limited to the coastal areas, with minimal penetration of the Berber hinterland.

Despite significant political turmoil throughout the years of the Pentapolis, Cyrene, in particular, flourished. In the economic sphere, the fertile slopes of the Jebel Akhdar provided Greece with valuable grain, wine, wool, livestock and a herb from the silphium plant, which was unique to Cyrenaica. Cyrene also became one of the Greek world's premier intellectual and artistic centres, producing and exporting some of the finest scholars of the age. The city was famed for its medical school, its learned academics and for being home to some of the finest examples of Hellenistic architecture anywhere in the world. The Cyrenians also developed a school of philosophy with a doctrine of moral cheerfulness that defined happiness as the sum of human pleasures. Such a philosophy was undoubtedly made easier by the temperate and altogether pleasant climate.

The halcyon days of Greek rule could not last for ever. With Greek influence on the wane, the last Greek ruler, Ptolemy Apion, finally bequeathed Cyrenaica to Rome.

Roman period

After the final defeat of Carthage in the Punic Wars, the Romans assigned Tripolitania to their ally, the Berber king of Numidia. In 46 BC, Julius Caesar deposed the final Numidian king, Juba I, who had sided with Pompey, a general in the Roman army and rival of Caesar in the Civil Wars of Rome. Tripolitania was thereafter incorporated into the new province of Africa Nova (later called Africa Proconsularis). In the east, Cyrenaica was formally annexed as part of the Roman Empire in 75 BC.

Communications between Tripolitania and Cyrenaica were hampered by rebellions along the southern coast of the Gulf of Sirt, although, by the end of the 1st century AD, Rome had completed the pacification of Sirtica and the two provinces were united under one administration.

The era that followed was one of Libya's finest. The Pax Romana saw Tripolitania and Cyrenaica become prosperous Roman provinces, part of a cosmopolitan and sophisticated state with a common language, legal system and identity. Many of the towns along the coast enjoyed the full range of urban amenities for which Roman cities were famous – a forum, markets, amphitheatres and baths. Traders and artisans flocked to the Libyan coast from throughout the empire. Tripolitania was a major source of olive oil for Roman merchants and also operated as an entrepot for gold and slaves brought to the coast by Berbers and the Garamantians. Cyrenaica was equally prized, as it had been under Greek rule, as a source of wine, silphium and horses.

A Libyan even became emperor of the Roman Empire. Septimus Severus (who ruled between AD 193 and 211) was known as the 'Grim African'. It was under his tutelage that Leptis Magna was transformed into an important cultural and commercial centre second only to Rome.

The thinly populated territory of Libya enabled the Romans to maintain control with little more than a locally recruited legion of 5,500 men. The Roman army succeeded in penetrating the Saharan provinces of the Fezzan, yet made no attempt to wield administrative power (they had decided that it was not worth the effort).

Despite the relative peace that accompanied Roman rule, the region was not immune to the political instability beyond its borders. In AD 115, a Jewish revolt among settlers from Palestine began and was not quelled until AD 118, after Jewish insurgents had laid waste to Cyrene and destroyed much of Cyrenaica.

In AD 300, the Roman emperor Diocletian separated Cyrenaica from the province of Crete, dividing the region into Upper and Lower Libya – the first time the name 'Libya' was used as an administrative designation. By the 4th century AD, however, Rome was in decline and the fate of the Libyan colonies was sealed by a massive earthquake in AD 365 from which Roman influence in Africa never recovered.

Vandals & Byzantines

In AD 429, a rebellious Roman official invited the Vandals, a Germanic tribe, to Libya in an attempt to gain leverage with the authorities in Rome. The Vandals, with as many as 80,000 settlers in tow, quickly set about conquering Libya, a feat they achieved in 431 under their leader Genseric (Gaeseric). Faced with little choice, the Romans recognised the Vandal ascendancy as long as Libya's civil administration remained, nominally at least, in Roman hands. In 455, the Vandals sacked Rome. The last vestiges of Roman prosperity in Libya quickly evaporated and the Vandals, more adept at pillage and overseas conquests than in administering their colonies, fortified themselves in armed camps. The outlying areas fell once again under the rule of tribal chieftains.

In 533, the Byzantine army general Belisarius captured Libya for the emperor Justinian. Byzantine control was limited to the cities of the coast, Berber rebellions in the hinterland reduced the area to anarchy and the potential prosperity of the provinces was squandered. Byzantine rule was deeply unpopular, not least because taxes were increased dramatically in order to pay for the colony's military upkeep, while the cities were left to decay.

The coming of Islam

With tenuous Byzantine control over Libya restricted to a few poorly defended coastal strongholds, the Arab horsemen who first crossed into Cyrenaica in 642 encountered little resistance. Under Amr ibn al-As, the armies of Islam conquered Cyrenaica. By 643 Tripoli had also succumbed. It was not until 663, when Uqba bin Nafi invaded the Fezzan, however, that Berber resistance in Libya was overcome. By 712 the entire region from Andalucía to the Levant came under the purview of the Ummayad caliph of Damascus.

Despite the rapid success enjoyed by the forces of Islam in religious and military terms, the social character of Libya remained overwhelmingly Berber. While largely accepting the arrival of the new religion, the Berber tribes resisted the Arabization of the region. Although Arab rule flourished in coastal areas, the enmity between the Berbers (who saw their rulers as arrogant and brutal) and the Arabs (who scorned the Berbers as barbarians) ensured that rebellions plagued much of Libya's hinterland.

In 750 the Abbasid dynasty overthrew the Ummayad caliph and shifted the capital to Baghdad, with emirs retaining nominal control over the Libyan coast on behalf of the far-distant caliph. In 800 Caliph Harun ar-Rashid appointed Ibrahim ibn al-Aghlabid as his governor. The Aghlabid dynasty effectively became independent of the Baghdad caliphs, who nevertheless retained ultimate spiritual authority. The Aghlabid emirs took their custodianship of Libya seriously, repairing Roman irrigation systems, restoring order and bringing a measure of prosperity to the region.

In the last decade of the 9th century, the Ismailis (a branch of Shiism) launched an assault on the strongholds of the Sunni Aghlabids. The movement's spiritual leader, Grandmaster Ubaidalla Said of Syria, was installed as the imam of much of North Africa, including Tripolitania. The Berbers of Libya, always happy to thumb their noses at the orthodox Sunni aristocracy, accepted the imam as the Mahdi (Promised One).

The Shiite Fatimid dynasty conquered Egypt in 972 and set up the caliphate in Cairo. The difficulty of maintaining control over Libya plagued the Fatimids, as it had almost every authority before them. At the beginning of the 11th century, Bulukkin ibn Ziri was installed as the Fatimid governor, but he quickly returned Libya to orthodox Sunnism and swore allegiance to the Abbasid caliphs of Baghdad.

The Fatimid anger at what they considered an act of gross betrayal would profoundly alter the fabric of Libyan society. Two tribes from the Arabian Peninsula – the Bani Hilal and the Bani Salim (or Bani Sulaim) – were co-opted into migrating to the Maghreb. The Bani Salim settled in Libya, particularly in Cyrenaica, while the Bani Hilal (who numbered as many as 200,000 families) spread across North Africa. The destruction of Cyrene and Tripoli by this unstoppable mass migration was symptomatic of arguably the most effective conquest Libya had seen. The Berber tribespeople were displaced from their traditional lands, their farmland converted to pasture and the new settlers finally cemented the cultural and linguistic Arabization of the region.

In 1158, the supporters of the Almohad dynasty arrived in Tripolitania from Morocco and established their authority. An Almohad viceroy, Muhammad bin Abu Hafs, ruled Libya from 1207 to 1221 and established the Hafsid dynasty, which outlived the Almohads. The Hafsids ruled Tripolitania for nearly 300 years. There was significant trade with the city-states of Europe and the Hafsid rulers encouraged art, literature and architecture, and gave scholarship priority.

Meanwhile, in the Fezzan in the 13th century, King Danama of Kanem (near Lake Chad) annexed territories as far north as the Al-Jufra oases. His Toubou viceroy founded the autonomous Bani Nasr dynasty, which ruled the Fezzan until the 14th century. They were followed by the theocratic kingdoms of Kharijite sectarians, including the Bani Khattab in the Fezzan. In the early 16th century, the Libyan Sahara fell under the sway of Muhammad al-Fazi from Morocco who, early in the 16th century, founded the Awlad Suleiman dynasty in Murzuq.

Ottoman rule

By the start of the 15th century, the Libyan coast had little central authority and its harbours were havens for unchecked bands of pirates. Hapsburg Spain occupied Tripoli in 1510, but the Spaniards were more concerned with controlling the port than with the inconveniences of administering a colony. Charles V entrusted the territory to the Knights of St John of Malta in 1524. Fourteen years later, Tripoli was reconquered by a pirate king called Khair ad-Din (known more evocatively as Barbarossa, or Red Beard). It was then that the coast became renowned as the Barbary Coast.

When the Ottomans arrived to occupy Tripoli in 1551, they saw little reason to reign in the pirates, preferring to profit from the booty. The French, Dutch and British navies all bombarded Tripoli to warn off further robbery on the high seas, but the Turks saw the pirates as a second column in their battle for naval supremacy. As long as they continued to control the ports of Algiers, Tripoli and Tunis, the Turks were happy to turn a blind eye to the anarchy there.

Under the Ottomans, the Maghreb was divided into three provinces, or regencies: Algiers, Tripoli and Tunis. After 1565, administrative authority in Tripoli was vested in a pasha appointed by the sultan in Constantinople. The sultan provided the pasha with a corps of janissaries (professional soldiers committed to a life of military service). This corps was in turn divided into a number of companies under the command of a junior officer with the title of bey (literally 'maternal uncle'). The janissaries quickly became the dominant force in Ottoman Libya. As self-governing military guilds answerable only to their own laws and protected by a divan (a council of senior officers who advised the pasha), the janissaries soon reduced the pasha to a largely ceremonial role. The sultan, whose forces were stretched to the limits in this vast empire, was in no position to argue.

In 1711, Ahmed Karamanli, an Ottoman cavalry officer and son of a Turkish officer and Libyan woman, seized power and founded a dynasty which would last 124 years. Again, while the Ottomans wielded ultimate authority from afar, power was vested in a local leader acting well beyond his original brief. The founder of the Karamanli dynasty was described by British explorer Hugh Clapperton as 'a cruel and unprincipled tyrant'.

One of the primary preoccupations of the Karamanli dynasty was an attempt to bring the Fezzan (and hence trans-Saharan trade routes) under its control. The sultans of the Awlad Suleiman based in Murzuq resisted the Ottoman army. Periods of stability were due more to expedience than any mutual feelings of brotherhood – they tolerated the presence of each other unless their interests directly clashed. In 1810 the Ottomans dispatched troops to Ghadames to regain control and, soon after, the Ottomans overthrew the Awlad Suleiman by killing the last of its sultans, Ahmed, and re-annexed the Fezzan.

On the coast, Western powers followed the American lead and refused to pay any further protection money to the Karamanli-controlled pirates. England and France began to ask for the repayment of debts incurred by the Karamanli regime. Tripoli's economy collapsed and Yusuf Karamanli – who had fought and won a civil war against his father and brother in 1795 and always made a point of defying his Ottoman overlords – tried to make up the financial shortfall by increasing taxes. Rebellions broke out across Libya and the countryside soon descended into civil war. Yusuf finally succumbed to the pressure and abdicated in favour of his son Ali in 1835. When Ali asked the Ottoman sultan Mohammed II for assistance in repelling a European takeover of Tripoli, the Ottomans took the opportunity to rein in their troublesome offspring and brought the rule of the Karamanli dynasty to a close. With full Ottoman authority restored, the Turks once again relegated Libya to the status of a neglected outpost of a decaying empire.

Less than a decade after the hated Ottoman authority was resumed, the indigenous Sanusi Movement, led by Islamic cleric Sayyid Mohammed Ali as-Sanusi, called on the Cyrenaican countryside to resist Ottoman rule. The Grand Sanusi established his headquarters in the oasis town of Al-Jaghboub, while his *ikhwan* (followers) set up *zawiyas* (religious colleges or monasteries) across North Africa and brought some stability to regions not known for their submission to central authority. In line with the express instruction of the Grand Sanusi, their gains were made largely without coercion.

The highpoint of Sanusi influence was to come in the 1880s under the Grand Sanusi's son, Mohammed al-Mahdi, who was a skilled administrator and a charismatic orator. With 146 lodges spanning the length and breadth of the Sahara, Mohammed al-Mahdi moved the Sanusi capital to Al-Kufra. Harsh Ottoman rule only fuelled the appeal of the Sanusi Movement's call to repel foreign occupation. Remarkably, Mohammed al- Mahdi succeeded where so many had failed before him, securing the enduring loyalty of the Berber tribes of Cyrenaica.

Over a 75-year period the Ottoman Turks provided 33 governors – not one of them distinguished themselves enough to be remembered by history.

Italian occupation

With Ottoman control tenuous at best, the Italian government saw an opportunity to join, albeit belatedly, the scramble for African colonies. On 3 October 1911, the Italians attacked Tripoli, claiming somewhat disingenuously to be liberating Libya from Ottoman rule. The Libyan population was unimpressed and refused to accept yet another occupying force. A major revolt against the Italians followed, with battles near Tripoli, Misrata, Benghazi and Derna.

The Ottoman sultan had more important concerns and ceded Libya to the Italians by signing the 1912 Treaty of Lausanne. Tripolitania was largely under Italian control by 1914, but both Cyrenaica and the Fezzan were home to rebellions led by the Sanusis. Throughout WWI, with the Turks and Germans supplying arms to the Sanusi rebels, the Italians in Cyrenaica could lay claim to controlling only a few ports. Meanwhile, Libyan notables began agitating for self-rule.

The Italian government failed to heed the unrest of a people tired of foreign occupation. In 1921 the government appointed Governor Giuseppe Volpi. The following year, Mussolini announced the *Riconquista* of 'Libya' (a name not used as an administrative entity since Roman times). Marshal Pietro Badoglio, who commanded the Italian army under Volpi, waged a punitive 'pacification' campaign. Badoglio was succeeded in the field by Marshal Rodolfo Graziani. Graziani only accepted the commission from Mussolini on the condition that he was allowed to crush Libyan resistance unencumbered by the inconvenient restraints imposed by Italian and international law. Mussolini reportedly agreed immediately and Graziani intensified the oppression.

The Libyans rebelled, with the strongest voices of dissent coming from Cyrenaica. Omar al-Mukhtar, a Sanusi sheikh, became the leader of the uprising.

After a much-disputed truce in 1929 descended into claim and counter-claim, Italy's Libya policy reached new depths of brutality. A barbed-wire fence was built from the Mediterranean to the oasis of Al-Jaghboub to sever supply lines critical to the resistance's survival. Soon afterwards, the colonial administration began the wholesale deportation of the people of the Jebel Akhdar to deny the rebels the support of the local population. The forced migration of more than 100,000 people ended in concentration camps in Suluq (south of Benghazi) and Al-'Aghela (west of Ajdabiya), where tens of thousands died in squalid conditions. It is estimated that the number of Libyans who died – killed either directly (military campaigns) or indirectly (starvation and disease) – could be a minimum of 80,000 or even up to half of the Cyrenaican population. Up to 95 per cent of the local livestock was also killed. That this was no accident is demonstrated by the Italian determination to win 'even if the entire population of Cyrenaica has to perish'. After Al-Mukhtar's capture, the rebellion petered out. The wholesale massacring of civilians fleeing Al-Kufra was the final outrage of a ruthless occupation.

By 1934 Italian control extended into the Fezzan, and in 1937 Mussolini cynically declared himself the 'Protector of Islam', in the process appointing compliant and conservative Sunni clerics. In 1938–39 Mussolini sought to fully colonise Libya, introducing 30,000 Italian settlers, which brought their numbers to more than 100,000 (proportionally more than French settlers in neighbouring Algeria). These settlers were shipped primarily to Sahel al-Jefara (Jefara Plain) in Tripolitania and the Jebel Akhdar in Cyrenaica, and given land from which the indigenous inhabitants had been forcibly removed. Throughout almost three decades of Italian occupation, a quarter of Libya's population died.

In July 1999 the Italian government offered a formal apology to Libya. The next year reports circulated that Italy had agreed to pay US$260 million as compensation for the occupation.

WWII & the road to independence

Just when the Italians had beaten the Libyan resistance into submission, WWII broke out and Libya once again became a major theatre for somebody else's war. From 1940 until late 1942, the Italians and Germans, led by Lieutenant-General Erwin Rommel, waged a devastating war for the territory between Benghazi and El-Alamein (Egypt), with much of the fighting centred on Tobruk. In October 1942 General Montgomery's army broke through the German defences at El-Alamein. In November the Allied forces retook Cyrenaica; by January 1943 Tripoli was in British hands and by February the last German and Italian soldiers were driven from Libya.

The British administered Tripolitania and Cyrenaica from 1943. The initial military presence became a caretaker administration while the victorious powers decided what to do with Libya. In the meantime, the French were, with British acquiescence, occupying the Fezzan, with their headquarters at Sebha. Ghat was attached to the French military region of Algeria, while Ghadames was subject to French control in southern Tunisia.

The country was hardly a lucrative prospect for potential occupiers: Libya was impoverished and had become renowned for its fierce resistance to colonial rule. The Libyan countryside and infrastructure had been totally devastated – it was estimated that at the end of WWII there were 11 million unexploded mines on or under Libyan soil – and prevailing education levels presented a damning indictment of Italy's colonial neglect.

The Four Powers Commission, comprising France, the UK, USSR and USA, was set up to decide Libya's fate. After the customary squabbling and distrust among the Great Powers, it emerged that Sayyid Idris as-Sanusi (the grandson of the Grand Sanusi) had received promises of independence from the British in return for Sanusi support during WWII. Among Libyans, who found themselves finally being listened to, the notion of independence quickly gathered momentum. Libyan nationalists raced against the clock to prevent France from detaching the Fezzan from the provinces of Cyrenaica and Tripolitania. The United Nations General Assembly approved the formation of an independent state in November 1949, by 53 votes to one (Ethiopia) with five (Soviet bloc) abstentions, which paved the way for Libyan independence.

Tripolitanian representatives pushed for a unitary, centralised state, while the leaders of the Fezzan and Cyrenaica, fearful of being overwhelmed by a more populous and economically powerful Tripolitania, argued strongly for a federal state. The latter option was chosen as the most effective means of preserving Libyan unity. Members of the first National Assembly were appointed by the Mufti of Tripolitania, Emir of Cyrenaica and the Chief of the Fezzan.

On 24 December 1951 the independent United Kingdom of Libya, with King Idris as its monarch, was finally, and unanimously, proclaimed by the National Assembly.

Post-independence period (1951–69)

The Libya of the 1950s was largely preoccupied with building state institutions and rebuilding its shattered economy. In 1952 the first elections for the National Assembly were won by conservatives. The only party of note at the time, the National Congress Party of Tripolitania, opposed the dilution of Tripolitania's influence in a federal system and agitated for a unitary state. The party was quickly outlawed.

In 1953, the Libyan government signed a treaty with the British government which allowed Britain to maintain military bases on Libyan soil for 20 years in return for annual aid of around UK£1 million. The following year, a similar agreement was signed with the Americans who agreed to pay US$40 million over the same period. Libya also forged links across the Mediterranean, signing a friendship pact with France in 1955 and a trade agreement with Italy in 1957.

In June 1959 an oilfield was discovered at Zelten in Cyrenaica. By early 1960, 35 wells had been sunk nationwide and international oil companies clamoured to obtain exploration rights in Libya. Over the decade which followed, Libya was transformed from an economic backwater into one of the world's fastest-growing economies. Private wealth and urban migration increased, creating social upheaval with which the political process was ill-equipped to deal.

From 1960 to 1963, a succession of Libyan governments ruled and then fell; all struggled to adjust to the new and radically different reality of being the custodians of an oil-rich state. In March 1963, a new cabinet was formed under the progressive leadership of Dr Mohi ad-Din Fekini. The federal system was abolished and Libya was proclaimed a unitary state. Officially, this was to increase the efficiencies of the new economy. However, the move fostered unease in Cyrenaica and the Fezzan with Tripolitanian dominance. A bicameral parliamentary system was introduced, with an upper house consisting of 24 senators appointed by the king; the executive power of the three regional administrative councils was handed over to a council of ministers. In a move which outraged the conservative religious establishment, women were granted the vote.

Dr Fekini's reforms did not bring stability and he resigned less than a year after taking office. He was replaced as prime minister by Mohammed Muntasser, whose preoccupation was less with electoral reform than with championing Arab resistance to imperialism (at the time, the charismatic Gamal Abdel Nasser was at the height of his popularity in neighbouring Egypt and his anti-imperialist, Arab nationalism won great support in Libya). Muntasser announced that his government did not intend to renew the military bases agreements with the UK and US governments. The British largely accepted the decision and by March 1966 had withdrawn most of its forces. The Americans held out and their Wheelus Air Base remained the largest in the world outside the US.

After the crushing defeat suffered by the Arab armies in the June 1967 war against Israel, there was widespread unrest in Libya, especially in Tripoli and Benghazi. After attacks on Western embassies and Libya's Jewish population, Libyans soon turned their anger towards their own government, which was accused of failing to send assistance against Israel and being half-hearted in its commitment to the Arab cause. The government and monarchy were caught unawares by this paradigmatic shift in the political landscape and their inability to respond effectively saw their popularity spiral downwards. Their days were numbered.

September coup

On 1 September 1969, an obscure group of military personnel seized power in Libya. Their planning was exemplary. They waited until all senior military figures were in the country and King Idris was in Turkey receiving medical treatment, thereby denying the government a figurehead around which to rally. They reportedly even postponed their coup by a day to avoid a clash with a concert by the popular Egyptian singer Umm Kolthum. There was little opposition to the coup and very few deaths. Among the Libyan population, there was considerable curiosity, as few people knew anything about the shadowy Revolutionary Command Council (RCC) which claimed responsibility. It was not until almost a week later that a young colonel by the name of Muammar Qadhafi emerged as the country's charismatic leader.

Gadaffi's Libya

The revolutionary ripples of the coup soon began to transform almost every corner of Libyan society.

Riding on a wave of anti-imperialist anger, the new leader made his first priorities the closing of British and American military bases, the expansion of the Libyan armed forces, the exile or arrest of senior officers with connections to the monarchy and the closure of all newspapers, churches and political parties. In the mosques, Sanusi clerics were replaced by compliant religious scholars. Banks were nationalized and foreign oil companies were threatened with nationalisation. All assets in Libya belonging to Italians and non-resident Jews were expropriated and close to 30,000 Italian settlers were deported. The rounding-up of political opponents saw Libya gain the unenviable prize of having the highest prison population in the world per head of population.

On the plus side, the Revolutionary Command Council injected massive new funds into agriculture and long-overdue development programmes, and there was an accompanying rise in the standard of living of ordinary Libyans. Ambitious social reforms were also implemented to redress the entrenched inequalities present under the monarchy.

In the mid-1970s, Qadhafi became the self-appointed visionary of the revolution when he retreated to the desert for a period of reflection and writing. What emerged was his Third Universal Theory, spelled out in *The Green Book* (see Appendix 4). While his much-touted alternative to capitalism and communism has always been characterised by confusing implementation in the economic sphere, his political reforms endure. In 1976, the General People's Congress replaced an earlier parliamentary body (the Arab Socialist Union). It had the express aim of political participation by all Libyans rather than a representative system. His dream of 'committees everywhere' soon became a reality. In yet another stamp of his vision on Libyan society, he renamed the country the Socialist People's Libyan Arab Jamahiriya (SPLAJ); *jamahiriya* has no direct translation but is generally taken to mean 'a state of the masses'. This was formalised on 2 March 1977.

The new government's secular reforms involved walking a fine line between its revolutionary programme and placating conservative Islamic critics of the regime's liberalising streak. Qadhafi's unique style of leadership and revolutionary ideals have ensured that assassination and coup attempts have been regular features of the Libyan political landscape from the mid-1970s until the most recent reports of unrest in 1998. While some of this instability derives from disagreements within the revolutionary leadership over the direction of the revolution, the greatest threat has increasingly come from militant Islamic groups.

Some of the less-savoury institutions of revolutionary Libya have been the Revolutionary Committees, which were at the height of their powers in the mid-1980s. Officially set up as conduits for raising political consciousness, they quickly evolved into the zealous guardians of the revolution and the enforcers of revolutionary orthodoxy. Their membership consisted increasingly of members of the Al-Qaddhafa tribe. They were the inspiration for the assassination squads set out to liquidate opposition Libyans living in exile. Assassinations were carried out in Athens, Bonn, London, Milan and Rome, among other cities of Europe.

The activities of these groups reached their nadir in 1984, when members of the revolutionary committees took over the Libyan People's Bureau in London. In April, with Libyan exiles protesting outside, a shot was fired from inside the embassy killing WPC Yvonne Fletcher. After a 10-day siege by the British authorities, the diplomats were allowed to return to Libya but the British government severed diplomatic relations with Tripoli. With the US having done likewise in 1981, Libya's status as a pariah state was confirmed.

In 1986, the US accused Libya of involvement in Palestinian attacks at Rome and Vienna's airports in December 1985 in which 20 people were killed; Qadhafi had labelled the attacks as heroic and the assailants were reportedly travelling on Libyan passports. In an act of considerable provocation and without the sanction of the UN, the US Sixth Fleet conducted military exercises off the Libyan coast with a number of skirmishes resulting. With typical restraint, then US President Ronald Reagan labelled the Libyan leader as 'the most dangerous man in the world'. The spiral into conflict was inevitable.

On 5 April, a bomb went off in a Berlin nightclub frequented by US soldiers, killing two and injuring more than 200. Convinced of Libyan involvement, the US, using aircraft based in the UK and aircraft carriers in the Mediterranean, fired missiles into Tripoli and Benghazi on 15 April. The targets were officially the Aziziyah barracks (Qadhafi's residence in Tripoli) and military installations, but residential areas were also hit. Up to 100 people were killed in Tripoli and around 30 in Benghazi. Two of Qadhafi's sons were injured and his adopted daughter, Hanna, was killed. A defiant Qadhafi renamed his country the Great SPLAJ.

Libya was also under siege on other fronts, with a debilitating war with neighbouring Chad. A 1935 protocol between France and Italy granted 111,370 square kilometres of modern Chadian territory, including the uranium-rich Aouzou Strip, to the Libyans, although all other treaties granted the area to Chad. Libya's support for armed opposition movements inside Chad also didn't help. The conflict saw the Libyan army briefly occupy the Chadian capital, N'Djaména, in 1980 before French intervention drove it north again. It was not until 1987 that the Libyan army was finally driven back across the border.

At the end of the 1980s, the Libyan government was under considerable pressure and took steps towards greater openness by releasing the majority of political prisoners. But repression again intensified in the early 1990s, a decade which was to prove one of Libya's, and Qadhafi's, most difficult.

Lockerbie

In November 1991, the US and UK governments accused two Libyans – Abdel Basset Ali Ahmed al-Megrahi and Ali Amin Khalifa Fhimah – of the 1988 bombing of Pan Am flight 103 over the Scottish town of Lockerbie, which killed 270 people. Libya was also suspected of involvement in the 1989 bombing of a French UTA airliner over the Sahara in which 171 people were killed.

In January 1992, the UN Security Council ordered that the two men be extradited and the International Court of Justice rebuffed Libyan attempts to stop the move. The US and UK rejected a Libyan offer to hand over the suspects for trial in a neutral country. UN sanctions came into effect on 15 April 1992, six years to the day after the US air strikes on Tripoli and Benghazi.

As early as 1994 Qadhafi accepted The Hague as an appropriate venue for any trial and also Libya's 'general responsibility' for the 1984 death in London of WPC Fletcher. All of these overtures were rejected. At the same time reports began to emerge of tensions between the Libyan leadership and the Al-Megraha tribe, one of the most powerful in Libya and which was holding out against any deal (Abdel Basset Ali Ahmed al-Megrahi belongs to the Al-Megraha tribe). A key powerbroker and member of the original Revolutionary Command Council, Major Abd as-Salam Jalloud, also of the Al-Megraha tribe, reportedly clashed with Qadhafi over the Lockerbie issue. To complicate matters, Basset Ali Ahmed Ali is the son of one of Qadhafi's deputies. In October 1993, according to some accounts, there were small-scale army rebellions around Misrata and Tobruk in which sections of the army split along tribal lines.

Muammar Qadhafi – The Man with Many Names

Muammar Qadhafi is many things to many people. Leaving aside the fact that the transliteration of his name from Arabic into English can reportedly be done in over 600 different ways, the self-proclaimed 'Leader of the Masses' has been called just about every name under the sun. Ronald Reagan decided that the Libyan leader was a 'mad dog', while Yasser Arafat dubbed him the 'knight of the revolutionary phrases'. In more recent times, African diplomats have been known to call him the 'father of African unity', while Western media analysts prefer 'Libya's ageing *enfant terrible*'. To trendy young Libyans in Tripoli, their leader is known simply as 'the man', while many travellers visiting Libya are told to give their best regards to 'the Colonel'.

Everyone seems to have an opinion about Mr Qadhafi but very few know anything about the man himself. He was born in 1942 in the Libyan desert near Sirt. As with many things about him, the exact place of Qadhafi's birth is shrouded in mystery, although the homeland of the Al-Qaddhafa tribe is the area around Al-Jufra. Much political mileage has been made from the fact that he was born in a tent. His father, Mohammed Abdul Salam bin Hamed bin Mohammed (Abu Meniar), and his mother, Aisha, were poor Bedouins. By all accounts, the future leader of the revolution was a serious, pious child. He attended primary school in Sirt until the age of 14 and became the first member of his family to learn how to read and write. His childhood was a difficult one, with reports that he was ridiculed by his classmates because of his impoverished background and that he slept in a mosque during the school week, returning home on weekends.

Stung by these experiences and caught up in the Arab nationalist fervour of the day, Qadhafi was politically active from an early age. After attending secondary school for a time in Sebha, he was expelled because of his political activities. He completed his schooling in Misrata and his heroes were Omar al-Mukhtar and the Egyptian president Gamal Abdel Nasser. In 1961, he organised a demonstration against Syria for breaking the unity agreement with Egypt and proceeded to a military academy in Benghazi, from which he graduated in 1965. In 1966, he was sent to England for further training, including four months at Beaconsfield learning English, then with the Royal Armoured Corps at Bovington in Dorset. It was a difficult experience for the young Libyan and he became angry at the racial discrimination and prejudice he suffered.

When he seized power in 1969, at the age of just 27, few expected him to last the distance, a prediction he has proven wrong by outliving many of his critics. Indeed, it is for his survival – and his alternately eccentric and revolutionary behaviour – that Qadhafi will be most remembered. His capacity to recover from bitter defeats (domestic opposition, the war with Chad and the obsessive vilification by the West) and reinvent himself (eg as the saviour of Africa) is central to his endurance. For all his transformations, he has remained steadfast on a number of fronts: his implacable opposition to Israel, support for revolutions against conservative regimes, his pursuit of unity with Arab and African neighbours, and his visceral hatred of imperialism.

In 1995, and again in 1998, assassination attempts were made on Qadhafi by militant Islamic groups based in Cyrenaica. The government's edginess was also brought to the fore on 9 July 1996 when the bodyguards of Qadhafi's son fired on a crowd reportedly chanting anti-government slogans at a football match in which he was playing; up to 50 people were killed.

In 1997, with international support for the embargo waning, cracks began to appear in the facade of international unity. South African President Nelson Mandela flew into Libya in defiance of the ban and a number of African leaders followed suit. In early 1999 a deal was brokered, with the international community accepting the procedural proposals that Libya had effectively been making since 1992. The suspects were then handed over and UN sanctions were immediately lifted, although unilateral US sanctions still remained in place at the time of writing.

European governments made a beeline for Tripoli, keen to re-establish diplomatic and economic ties. In March 2001, a French court finally shelved all attempts to pursue Colonel Qadhafi and Libya over the 1989 UTA bombing. By this stage, Libya was well on the road to rejoining the international community.

Lockerbie – Conspiracy or Justice?

The Lockerbie trial in The Hague raised more questions than answers. The Scottish judges acquitted Fhimah but found Al-Megrahi guilty, sentencing him to life imprisonment in a Scottish jail. To Western governments, the verdict was justification for their isolation of Libya. From the Libyan perspective, the whole process was a show trial, part of an international conspiracy to apportion blame to a country and leader who had already been tried in the world's media. All eyes are on the outcome of Al-Megrahi's appeal. Regardless of the outcome, Libyans and others in the Arab world remain convinced that double standards apply.

Professor Robert Black, the Scottish legal expert who devised the unusual trial (unusual because it was the first time that a country handed its citizens over for trial, outside of UN tribunals, by a foreign court and because that court was set up outside Scottish territory) confessed to being 'absolutely astounded' at the outcome, which he claimed was based on a 'very weak, circumstantial case' which couldn't convict anyone, 'even a Libyan'. Even some of the grieving families of the victims expressed doubts over the verdict.

Syria was the original suspect. But when Syria supported the Allies in the Gulf War against Iraq, suspicion shifted to Libya. One of the most credible theories was that the bombing had been ordered by Iran in retaliation for the shooting down of an Iran Air airbus by a US warship in the Persian Gulf on 3 July 1988. The story goes that the bombing was carried out by members of the Palestinian Front for the Liberation of Palestine–General Command (PFLP–GC) who have sheltered in Syria since the bombing. Also yet to be refuted are the claims that the flight was being used to courier drugs for a US-backed international operation, meaning that security checks of the aircraft were waived. Immediately after the crash US investigators instantly secreted away an unidentified body which crash investigators were never allowed to see.

One sobering footnote on this matter appeared in February 2001, when Bassam and Saniya al-Ghussein, a Palestinian-Lebanese couple, went public with their attempts to bring the US government to court for the death of their 18-year-old daughter, Rafaat, who was killed by the US raid on Tripoli in 1986. The parents had a question for the international community: 'Just a simple admission. . . Or is it that the US government has a licence to kill?'

For the full text of the Lockerbie verdict, go to www.ltb.org.uk.

Libya today

There are two public preoccupations that dominate Libya today. One is the Lockerbie verdict, unfinished business that takes some of the gloss off Libyan efforts to rebuild the economy and international reputation. It's an issue that continues to trouble the national soul.

The other is Qadhafi's shift in attention from pan-Arab ideals to a messianic crusade to unify the disparate nations of Africa.

Another question simmers beneath the surface of Libyan society, one that Libyans are only willing to express unease over: What happens after Qadhafi? No-one knows the answer, and many of the surrounding states seem to believe that, for all his faults, the Libyan leader has provided stability and been a defence against the spread of Islamic fundamentalism. Fearful of the alternative, most are quite happy for the Libyan leader to stay in power for the foreseeable future.

Turning towards Africa

Having spent a lifetime trying to forge unions with Arab countries who could never quite bring themselves to share his vision of a united pan-Arab nation, Colonel Qadhafi shifted his focus to Africa. In 1999, the Libyan leader hosted a Conference of African Heads of State at a cost of some US$30 million. Officially the reason was to thank the African nations for their support during the embargo, but, never one to miss an opportunity, Qadhafi unveiled his plans for a United States of Africa. In February 2001, 41 nations signed the Constitutive Act of African Union and 13 ratified it. The agreement replaces the troubled and politically fractured Organization of African Unity (OAU) and paves the way for a future Africa-wide federation similar to the European Union. Possible outcomes include an African army, a single currency and parliament, and even a single African passport – although such ideas are a long way from being realized.

In July the gains were cemented and Colonel Qadhafi has been revelling in the accolades. It is the acclaim for which he has been searching for much of his life.

Religion

More than 95 per cent of Libya's population are Sunni Muslims. The country has small communities of Kharijites and Christians (Roman Catholics, Coptic Orthodox and Anglicans), who number around 50,000.

Islam

Islam shares its roots with the great monotheistic faiths that sprang from the unforgiving and harsh soil of the Middle East – Judaism and Christianity – but is considerably younger than both. Muslims believe in the angels who brought God's messages to humans, in the prophets who received these messages, in the books in which the prophets expressed these revelations and in the last day of judgement. The Quran (the holy book of Islam) mentions 28 prophets, 21 of whom are also mentioned in the Bible; Adam, Noah, Abraham, David, Jacob, Joseph, Job, Moses and Jesus are given particular honour, although the divinity of Jesus is strictly denied.

For Muslims, Islam is the apogee of the monotheistic faiths, from which it derives so much. Muslims traditionally attribute a place of great respect to Christians and Jews as *ahl al-kitab,* 'the people of the Book', and it is usually considered to be preferable to be a Christian or Jew than an atheist. However, the more strident will claim Christianity was a new and improved version of the teachings of the Torah and that Islam was the next logical step and therefore 'superior'.

Mohammed, born into one of the trading families of the Arabian city of Mecca (in present-day Saudi Arabia) in AD 570, began to receive the revelations in AD 610 from the Archangel Gabriel and after a time began imparting the content of Allah's message to the Meccans. The revelations continued for the rest of Mohammed's life and they were written down in the Quran (from the Arabic word for 'recitation') in a series of *suras* (verses or chapters). To this day, not one dot of the Quran has been changed, making it, Muslims claim, the direct word of Allah. The essence of it was a call to submit to God's will ('islam' means submission). By Mohammed's time, religions such as Christianity and Judaism had become complicated by factions, sects and bureaucracies, to which Islam offered a simpler alternative. The new religion did away with hierarchical orders and complex rituals, and instead offered believers a direct relationship with God based only on their submission to God.

Not all Meccans were terribly taken with the idea. Mohammed gathered quite a following in his campaign against Meccan idolaters and his movement especially appealed to the poorer levels of society. The powerful families became increasingly outraged and by AD 622 had made life sufficiently unpleasant for Mohammed and his followers to convince them of the need to flee to Medina, an oasis town some 300 kilometres to the north and now Islam's second-most holy city. This migration – the Hejira – marks the beginning of the Islamic calendar, year 1 AH (AD 622).

In Medina, Mohammed continued to preach and increase his supporter base. Soon he and his followers began to clash with the Meccans, possibly over trade routes. By AD 630 they had gained a sufficient following to return and take Mecca. In the two years until Mohammed's death, many of the surrounding tribes swore allegiance to him and the new faith.

Upon Mohammed's death in AD 632, the Arab tribes spread quickly across the Middle East with missionary zeal, quickly conquering what makes up modern Jordan, Syria, Iraq, Lebanon, Israel and the Palestinian territories. By AD 643 Libya had been conquered.

The initial conquests were carried out under the caliphs, or Companions of Mohammed, of whom there were four. They in turn were followed by the Umayyad dynasty (AD 661–750) in Damascus and then the Abbasid line (AD 749–1258) in the newly built city of Baghdad (in modern Iraq). Given that these centres of Islamic power were so geographically removed from Libya, the religion of Islam may have taken a hold, but the political and administrative control which accompanied Islamic rule elsewhere was much more tenuous in Libya.

The occasion of breaking the fast at the conclusion of Ramadan (when the moon is sighted) is a time of great celebration. In the 1930s, the Danish traveller Knud Holmboe described the scene in Tripoli:

> 'It ought to be tonight,' said a young Arab who stood next to me, as he scanned the sky eagerly. Hour after hour passed, and it was beginning to look as if Ramadan would have to be continued over the next day when suddenly the cry went up: 'El Ahmar, el Ahmar!' (The moon, the moon!) The festival began. The long month of fasting was over. All night they danced and ate to their heart's content in the Medina.
>
> Knud Holmboe, *Desert Encounter*

The orthodox Sunnis divided into four schools *(madhab)* of Islamic law, each lending more or less importance to various aspects of religious doctrine. In Libya, the Maliki rite of Sunni Islam predominates. Founded by Malik ibn As, an Islamic judge who lived in Medina from AD 715 to 795, it is based on the practice which prevailed in Medina in the 8th century. The Maliki strand of thought preaches the primacy of the Quran (as opposed to later teachings). In this sense, orthodox Islam in modern Libya bears strong similarities to the teachings of the Sanusi sect, which ruled Libya for a number of centuries.

There is also a small population of Kharijites, a sect whose name literally means 'seceders' or 'those who emerge from impropriety'. Their doctrine that any Muslim could become caliph (they believed that only the first two caliphs were legitimate), which questioned the Arab monopoly over Muslim legitimacy, naturally appealed to the Berbers when Islam arrived in Libya.

Islamic customs

In everyday life, Muslims are prohibited from drinking alcohol and eating pork (as the pig is considered unclean), and must refrain from fraud, usury, slander and gambling.

Language

Arabic is the national language of Libya and all signs are in Arabic – not even motorway signs are translated. English signs have been declared illegal in a bid to safeguard against the diluting of Arab culture, although signs in English are springing up in some parts of the country. Nevertheless, these are rare and some knowledge of Arabic is extremely helpful, especially if you're navigating on your own.

The Arabic spoken in Libya has some similarities to the Bedouin Arabic spoken in southern Tunisia; it is, however, more closely akin to Egyptian Arabic. Most published writing and speeches are delivered in Standard Arabic, which is understood throughout the country.

Outside the main cities, where some English or Italian is spoken, few people speak a foreign language. The exception is Ghadhames or Ghat, where some French is spoken. Unusually (but helpfully) for an Arab country, numbers are almost always written in Western script, even if the rest of the sign is in Arabic.

In the Jebel Nafusa and parts of Cyrenaica, many Berbers speak their own Berber language (eg Mazir). Berber languages represent a series of related dialects. All stem from the Afro-Asiatic language family and are distantly related to Arabic, but most Berber dialects have not developed a written form. The Tuareg of the south speak Tamashek, which is related to Berber and with many of the same words. The Toubou language is Tebu, which belongs to the Nilo Saharan language family, although, in keeping with the diffuse nature of Toubou society, there are many different dialects. In Libya, however, these are all secondary languages and with all publications and broadcasts in Arabic, it is very rare to find someone who is not fluent in Arabic.

Appendix 4

The Green Book[1]

The following extracts from *The Green Book* by Muammar Qadhafi, published on 3 April 1975, are included here to provide Western readers with an insight into the philosophy that has shaped the Libyan economy and business environment.

Part One: The Solution of the Problem of Democracy

The Instrument of Governing

'The Instrument of Governing is the prime political problem which faces human communities.' Even the conflict within the family is, often, the result of this problem.

'This problem has become serious since the emergence of modern societies.' Peoples, nowadays, face this persistent problem and communities suffer from various risks and grave consequences to which it leads. They have not yet succeeded in solving it finally and democratically.

The GREEN BOOK presents the final solution to the problem of the instrument of governing.

All political systems in the world today are the product of the struggle for power between instruments of governing. The struggle may be peaceful or armed, such as the conflict of classes, sects, tribes, parties or individuals. The result is always the victory of an instrument of governing – be it an individual, group, party or class and the defeat of the people, i.e. the defeat of genuine democracy.

Political struggle that results in the victory of a candidate with 51 per cent of the votes leads to a dictatorial governing body disguised as a false democracy, since 49 per cent of the electorate is ruled by an instrument of governing they did not vote for, but had imposed upon them. This is dictatorship. Besides, this political conflict may produce a governing body that represents only a minority, for when votes are distributed among several candidates, one of them polls more than any

[1] The full text of *The Green Book* is available, free, on www.geocities.com/Athens/8744/mylinks1.htm[/fn]

other candidate. But if the votes polled by those who received less are added up, they can constitute an overwhelming majority. However, the candidate with fewer votes wins and his success is regarded as legitimate and democratic! In actual fact, dictatorship is established under the cover of false democracy. This is the reality of the political systems prevailing in the world today. They are dictatorial systems and it seems clear that they falsify genuine democracy.

Popular Congresses & People's Committees

Popular congresses are the only means to achieve popular democracy. Any system of government other than popular congresses is undemocratic. All the prevailing systems of government in the world today are undemocratic, unless they adopt this method. Popular congresses are the end of the journey of the masses' movement in its quest for democracy. Popular congresses and people's committees are the final fruit of the people's struggle for democracy.

Popular congresses and people's committees are not creations of the imagination so much as they are the product of human thought which has absorbed all human experiments to achieve democracy. Direct democracy is the ideal method, which, if realised in practice, is indisputable and non-controversial. The nations departed from direct democracy because, however small a people might be, it was impossible to gather them all together at one time in order to discuss, study and decide on their policy. Direct democracy remained a Utopian idea, far from reality. It has been replaced by various theories of government, such as representative assemblies, parties, coalitions, and plebiscites. All led to the isolation of the people from political activity and to the plundering of the sovereignty of the people and the assumption of their authority by the successive and conflicting instruments of governing, beginning with the individual, on through the class, the sect, the tribe, the parliament and the party.

The Green Book announces to the people the happy discovery of the way to direct democracy, in a practical form. Since no two intelligent people can dispute the fact that direct democracy is the ideal – but its method has been impossible to apply – and since this Third Universal Theory provides us with a realistic experiment in direct democracy, the problem of democracy in the world is finally solved. All that the masses need do now is to struggle to put an end to all forms of dictatorial rule in the world today, to all forms of what is falsely called democracy – from parliaments to the sect, the tribe, the class and to the one-party, the two-party and the multi-party systems.

Democracy has but one method and one theory. The disparity and dissimilarity of the systems claiming to be democratic is evidence that they are not democratic in fact. The people's authority has only one face and it can be realised only by one method, namely, popular congresses and people's committees. No democracy without popular congresses and committees everywhere.

First, the people are divided into basic popular congresses. Each basic popular congress chooses its secretariat. The secretariats together form popular congresses, which are other than the basic ones. Then the masses of those basic popular congresses choose administrative people's committees to replace government administration. Thus, all public utilities are run by people's committees, which will be responsible to the basic popular congresses and these dictate the policy to be followed by the people's committees and supervise its execution. Thus, both the administration and the supervision become popular and the outdated definition of democracy – Democracy is the supervision of the government by the people – comes to an end. It will be replaced by the right definition – Democracy is the supervision of the people by the people.

All citizens who are members of those popular congresses belong, professionally and functionally, to categories. They have, therefore, to establish their own unions and syndicates in addition to being, as citizens, members of the basic popular congresses or the people's committees. Subjects discussed by basic popular congresses or the people's committees, syndicates and unions, will take their final shape in the General People's Congress, where the secretariats of popular congresses, people's committees, syndicates and unions meet. What is drafted by the General People's Congress, which meets annually or periodically, will, in turn, be submitted to popular congresses, people's committees, syndicates and unions. The people's committees, responsible to the basic popular congresses will, then, start executive action. The General People's Congress is not a gathering of members or ordinary persons as is the case with parliaments. It is a gathering of the basic popular congresses, the people's committees, the unions, the syndicates and all professional associations.

In this way, the problem of the instrument of governing is, as a matter of fact, solved and dictatorial instruments will disappear. The people are the instrument of governing and the problem of democracy in the world is completely solved.

Part Two: The Solution of the Economic Problem: 'Socialism'

The Economic Basis of the Third Universal Theory

Important historical developments have taken place which contribute to solving the problem of work and wages, i.e. the relationship between the workers and the employers, between the producers and the owners.

THE AUTHORITY OF THE PEOPLE

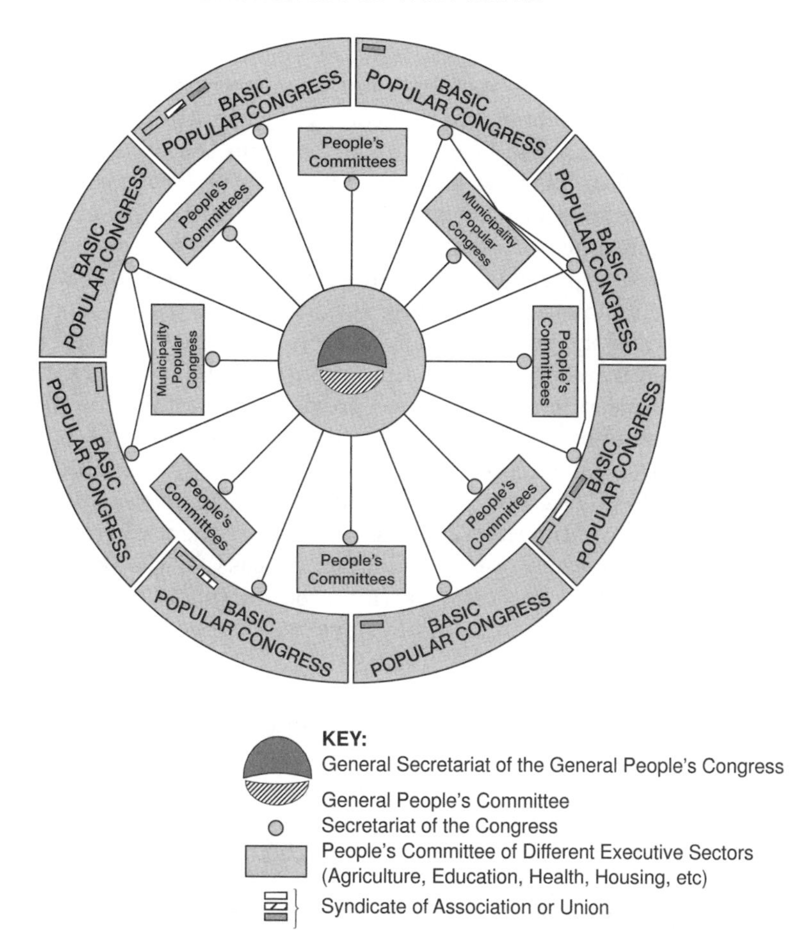

The developments include fixed working-hours, wages for additional work, different types of leave, minimum wages, profit sharing and participation in administration. In addition, arbitrary dismissal has been outlawed and social security has been guaranteed, along with the right to strike and whatever other provisions are found in almost all modern labour laws. Of no less significance are the changes in the field of ownership such as the emergence of systems limiting income or outlawing private ownership and transferring it to the state.

Partners not Wage Workers

Despite all these not inconsiderable developments in the history of the economic problem, nevertheless the problem still basically exists. The modifications, improvements, provisions and other measures have made the problem less severe than it was in past centuries by gaining many advantages for the workers. Yet, the economic problem has not been solved. All the attempts which have concentrated on ownership have not solved the problem of producers. They are still wage-workers, even when ownership has been transferred from the extreme right to the extreme left or has been given various intermediate positions.

Attempts to improve wages are as important as those which lead to the transference of ownership. The benefits received by workers, guaranteed by legislation and protected by Trade Unions are all that have been achieved in tackling the problem of wages. Thus the hard conditions of the producers immediately after the Industrial Revolution have been transformed, and, in the course of time workers, technicians and administrators have gained previously unattainable rights. However, the economic problem still, in fact, exists.

This attempt confined to wages was certainly not a solution at all. It is an artificial attempt, aimed merely at reform, more of a charity than a recognition of the right of workers. Why are the workers given wages? Because they carry out a production process for the benefit of others who hire them to produce a certain product. In this case, they have not consumed their production, but have been obliged to surrender it for a wage. The sound rule is:

'He who produces is the one who consumes.'

Wage-workers are a type of slave, however improved their wages may be.

The wage-worker is like a slave to the master who hires him. He is even a temporary slave, since his slavery lasts as long as he works for wages from the employer, whether the latter is an individual or a state. The workers' relationship with the owner of the productive establishment as regards their own interests is one and the same . . . Under all conditions prevailing now in the world they are wage-workers, even though ownership varies . . . from the right to the left. The public economic establishment itself gives to its workers only wages and other social benefits; and these do not differ from the charity granted to the workers by the rich, the owners of private economic corporations.

The argument that, in the case of public ownership, income reverts to society, including the workers, in contrast to the case of the private corporation where income reverts only to its owner, is valid. This is so provided that we take into consideration the general interests of the society rather than the particular interests of the workers, and provided that we assume that the political authority which monopolizes ownership is the authority of all the people, that is to say the authority of the people in their entirety, as practised through their popular congresses, people's committees and professional syndicates rather than the authority of one class, one party, group of parties, sect, family, tribe, individual or any other representative authority. However, what is received directly by the workers, as regards their own interests, in the form of wages, percentage of the profit or social benefits, is the same as is received by the workers in the private corporation. That is to say, workers in both public and private establishments are equally wage-workers though the owners differ. Thus the change in ownership from one type to another has not solved the problem of the workers' right in what has been produced directly by himself, and not by society or for wages. The proof is that the producers are still wage-workers despite the change in ownership.

The ultimate solution is to abolish the wage-system, emancipate man from its bondage and return to the natural law, which defined relationships before the emergence of classes, forms of government and man-made laws. The natural rules are the measure, the reference book and the sole course in human relations.

Natural law has led to natural socialism based on equality among the economic factors of production and has almost brought about, among individuals, consumption equal to nature's production. But the exploitation of man by man and the possession by some individuals of more of the general wealth than they need is a manifest departure from natural law and the beginning of distortion and corruption in the life of the human community. It is the beginning of the emergence of the society of exploitation.

If we analyse the economic factors of production from ancient times till now we always find that they are composed of these essentials: raw materials, an instrument of production and a producer. The natural rule of equality is that each of the factors has a share in this production, for if any of them is withdrawn, there will be no production. Each factor has an essential role in the process of production and without it production comes to a halt. As long as each factor is essential and fundamental, they are all equal in their essential character within the process of production. Therefore they all should be equal in their right to what is produced. The encroachment of one factor on another is opposed to the natural rule of equality, and is an attack on the right of others. Each factor, then, has a share regardless of the number of factors. If we find a process of production which can be performed by only two factors, each factor shall have half of the production. If it is carried out by three factors, each shall have a third of the production and so on . . .

Applying this natural rule to both ancient and modern situations we find the following:

In the state of manual production the productive process involved raw materials, and man, the producer. Later, an instrument of production intervened between the two and man used it in the productive process. The animal may be considered as an example of the instrument as a power unit. It, then, developed and the machine replaced the animal. Raw materials increased in kind and quantity, from cheap simple materials to valuable complex ones. Likewise man developed from an ordinary worker into a technician and an engineer and a large number of workers began to be replaced by a few technicians. Although the factors of production have quantitatively and qualitatively changed, the essential role of each factor has not changed. For example, the iron-ore which is one of the factors of production, both past and present, was primitively manufactured by the ironsmith to produce a knife, an axe or a spear . . . etc. The same iron-ore is now manufactured in big furnaces, and from it engineers and technicians produce machines, engines and all kinds of vehicles. The animal – the horse, the mule or the camel and the like – which was one of the factors of production has now been replaced by the vast factory and huge machines. The means of production which were formerly primitive tools have now become sophisticated technical equipment. The essential natural factors of production are basically stable despite their great development. The essential stability of the factors of production makes the natural rule sound. It is inevitable, after the failure of all previous historical attempts, which disregarded natural law, to return to it in order, finally, to solve the economic problem.

The previous historical theories tackled the economic problem either from the angle of the ownership of one of the factors of production only or from the angle of wages for production only. They have not solved the real problem, namely the problem of production itself. Thus the most important characteristic of the economic systems prevailing in the world today is the wage system which deprives the worker of any right in his production whether it is produced for society or for a private establishment. The industrial establishment is based on raw materials, machines and workers. Production is the outcome of the workers' use of the machines in the factory to manufacture raw materials. In this way, the finished goods pass through a process of production which would have been impossible without the raw materials, the factory and the workers. So if we take away the raw materials, the factory cannot operate; if we take away the factory, the raw materials will not be manufactured and if we remove the producers, the factory comes to a halt. The three factors are equally essential in the process of production. Without these three factors there will be no production. Any one factor cannot carry out this process by itself. Even two of these factors cannot carry it out. The natural rule in this case requires that the shares of the three factors in the production be equal, i.e. the production of such a factory is divided into three shares, a share for each of the factors of production. It is not only the factory which is important, but also those who consume its production. The same is the case in the process of agricultural production. That which involves man and land without a third factor, the instrument, is exactly like the manual process of industrial production. Here production is only divided into two shares in accordance with the number of factors of production. But if an agricultural machine or the like is used, production is divided into three shares: the land, the farmer and the instrument used in the process of agriculture.

Thus a socialist system is established to which all processes of production are subjected, by analogy with this natural rule. The producers are the workers. We call them 'producers' because the words 'workers', 'employees' or 'toilers' are no longer applicable. The reason is that workers, according to the traditional definition, are quantitatively and qualitatively changing. The working class is continually declining as science and machines develop.

Strenuous tasks which previously had to be performed by a number of workers are now done by machines. To run a machine requires a smaller number of workers. This is the quantitative change in the labour force, while the qualitative change necessitated the replacement of a physical force by technical skill.

A power which is totally concerned with producing has now become one of the factors of production. As a result of these developments the workers have changed from a multitude of ignorant toilers into a limited number of technicians, engineers and scientists. Consequently, Trade Unions will disappear to be replaced by professional and technical syndicates because scientific development is an irreversible gain to humanity. Through such scientific development, illiteracy will be eradicated and the ordinary worker as a temporal phenomenon will gradually disappear. However, man, in his new form, will always remain an essential factor in the process of production.

Need

Man's freedom is lacking if somebody else controls what he needs. For need may result in man's enslavement of man. Need causes exploitation. Need is an intrinsic problem and conflict grows out of the domination of man's needs.

The house is a basic need of both the individual and the family. Therefore, it should not be owned by others. There is no freedom for a man who lives in another's house, whether he pays rent or not. All attempts made by various countries to solve the problem of housing are not solutions at all. The reason is that those attempts do not aim at the radical and ultimate solution of man, which is the necessity of his owning his own house. The attempts have concentrated on the reduction or increase of rent and its standardization, whether at public or private expense. In the socialist society no one, including the society itself, is allowed to have control over man's need.

No one has the right to build a house, additional to his own and that of his heirs, for the purpose of renting it, because the house represents another person's need, and building it for the purpose of rent is an attempt to have control over the need of that man and 'In Need Freedom is Latent'.

The income is an imperative need for man. Thus the income of any man in the society should not be a wage from any source or a charity from anyone. For there are no wage-workers in the socialist society, only partners. Your income is a form of private ownership. You manage it by yourself either to meet your needs or to share in the production, where you are one of its main factors. Your share will not be used as a wage paid for any person in return for production.

The vehicle is a necessity both to the individual and the family. Your vehicle should not be owned by others. In the socialist society no man or any other authority can possess private vehicles for the purpose of hiring them out, for this is domination of the needs of others.

Land

Land is no one's property. But everyone has the right to use it, to benefit from it by working, farming or pasturing. This would take place throughout a man's life and the lives of his heirs, and would be through his own effort without using others with or without wages, and only to the extent of satisfying his own needs.

If possession of land is allowed, only those who are living there have a share in it. The land is permanently there, while, in the course of time, users change in profession, in capacity and in their presence.

The purpose of the new socialist society is to create a society which is happy because it is free. This can be achieved through satisfying the material and spiritual needs of man, and that, in turn, comes about through the liberation of these needs from outside domination and control.

Satisfaction of these needs must be attained without exploiting or enslaving others, or else, it will contradict the purpose of the new socialist society.

Man in the new society works for himself to guarantee his material needs, or works for a socialist corporation in whose production he is a partner, or performs a public service to the society which provides his material needs.

Economic activity in the new socialist society is productive activity for the satisfaction of material needs. It is not unproductive activity or an activity which seeks profit in order, after satisfying material needs, to save the surplus. That is impossible under the rules of the new socialism.

The legitimate purpose of the individual's economic activity is solely to satisfy his needs. For the wealth of the world has limits at each stage as does the wealth of each individual society. Therefore no individual has the right to carry out economic activity in order to acquire more of that wealth than is necessary to satisfy his needs, because the excess amount belongs to other individuals. He has the right to save from his needs and from his own production but not from the efforts of others nor at the expense of their needs. For if we allow economic activity to extend beyond the satisfaction of needs, one person will only have more than his needs by preventing another from obtaining his. The savings which are in excess of one's needs are another person's share of the wealth of society.

To allow private production for the purpose of acquiring savings that exceed the satisfaction of needs is exploitation itself, as in permitting the use of others to satisfy your own needs or to get more than your own needs. This can be done by exploiting a person to satisfy the needs of others and making savings for others at the expense of his needs. Work for a wage is, in addition to being an enslavement of man as mentioned before, work without incentives because the producer is a wage-worker rather than a partner. Whoever works for himself is certainly devoted to his productive work because his incentive to production lies in his dependence on his private work to satisfy his material needs. Also whoever works in a socialist corporation is a partner in its production. He is, undoubtedly, devoted to his productive work because the impetus for devotion to production is that he gets a satisfaction of his needs through production. But whoever works for a wage has no incentive to work. Work for wages failed to solve the problem of increasing and developing production. Work, either in the form of services or production, is continually deteriorating because it rests on the shoulders of wage-workers.

Examples of labour for wages for society; of labour for a private activity; and labour for no wages

First example:

(a) A worker who produces ten apples for society. Society gives him one apple for his production. The apple fully satisfies his needs.

(b) A worker who produces ten apples for society. Society gives him one apple for his production. The apple is not enough to satisfy his needs.

Second example:
A worker who produces ten apples for another person and gets a wage of less than the price of one apple.

Third example:
A worker who produces ten apples for himself.

The conclusion
The first (a) will not increase his production for whatever the increase might be, he will only get an apple for himself. It is what satisfies his needs. Thus all those working for such a society are always psychologically apathetic.

The first (b) has no incentive to production itself, for he produces for the society without obtaining satisfaction of his needs. However, he has to continue to work without incentive because he is forced to submit to the general conditions of work throughout the society. That is the case with members of that society.

The second does not initially work to produce. He works to get wages. Since his wages are not enough to satisfy his needs, he will either search for another master and sell him his work at a better price or he will be obliged to continue the same work just to survive.

The third is the only one who produces without apathy and without coercion. In the socialist society, there is no possibility for private production exceeding the satisfaction of individual needs, because satisfaction of needs at the expense of others is not allowed. As the socialist establishments work for the satisfaction of the needs of society, the third example explains the sound basis of economic production. However, in all conditions, even in bad ones, production continues for survival. The best proof is that in capitalist societies production accumulates and expands in the hands of a few owners who do not work but exploit the efforts of toilers who are obliged to produce in order to survive. However, The Green Book not only solves the problem of material production but also prescribes the comprehensive solution of the problems of human society so that the individual may be materially and spiritually liberated . . . a final liberation to attain his happiness.

Other examples
If we assume that the wealth of society is ten units and its population is ten persons, the share of each in the wealth of society is 10/10 – only one of the units per person. But if some members of society possess more than one unit, then other members of the same society possess nothing. The reason is that their share of the units of wealth has been taken by others. Thus, there are poor and rich in the society where exploitation prevails.

Suppose that five members of that society possess two units each. In this case the other five possess nothing, i.e., 50 per cent are deprived of their right to their own wealth because the additional unit possessed by each of the first five is the share of each of the second five.

If an individual in that society needs only one of the units of the wealth of society to satisfy his needs then the individual possessing more than one unit is, in fact, expropriating the right of other members of the society. Since this share exceeds what is required to satisfy his needs, estimated at one of the units of wealth then he has seized it to hoard it. Such hoarding is only achieved at the expense of others' needs, i.e., through taking others' share in this wealth. That is why there are those who hoard and do not spend – that is, they save what exceeds the satisfaction of their needs – and there are those who beg and are deprived – that is, those who ask for their rights in the wealth of their society and do not find anything to consume. It is an act of plunder and theft, but open and legitimate under the unjust and exploitative rules which govern that society.

Ultimately, all that is beyond the satisfaction of needs should remain the property of all the members of society. But individuals only have the right to save as much as they want from their own needs, because the hoarding of what exceeds their needs involves an encroachment on public wealth.

The skilful and industrious have no right to take hold of the share of others as a result of their skill and industry. But they can benefit from these advantages. Also if a person is disabled or lunatic, it does not mean that he does not have the same share as the healthy in the wealth of the society.

The wealth of the society is like a corporation or a store of supply which daily provides a number of people with a quantity of supply of a definite amount which is enough to satisfy the needs of those people during that day. Each person has the right to save out of that quantity what he wants, i.e., he can consume or save what he likes from his share. In this he can use his own skill and talents. But he who uses his talents to take an additional amount for himself from the store of the public supply is undoubtedly a thief. Therefore, he who uses his skill to gain wealth that exceeds the satisfaction of his needs is, in fact, encroaching on a public right, namely, the wealth of the society which is like the store mentioned in this example.

In the new socialist society differences in individual wealth are only permissible for those who render a public service. The society allocates for them a certain share of the wealth equivalent to that service.

The share of individuals only differs according to the public service each of them renders, and as much as he produces. Thus, the experiments of history have produced a new experiment, a final culmination of man's struggle to attain his freedom and to achieve happiness by satisfying his need, warding off the exploitation of others, putting an ultimate end to tyranny and finding a means for the just distribution of society's wealth. Under the new experiment you work for yourself to satisfy your needs rather than exploiting others to work for you, in order to satisfy yours at their expense; or working to plunder the needs of others. It is the theory of the liberation of needs in order to emancipate man.

Thus the new socialist society is no more than a dialectical consequence of the unjust relations prevailing in this world. It has produced the natural solution, namely private ownership to satisfy the needs without using others, and socialist ownership, in which the producers are partners in production. The socialist ownership replaced a private ownership based on the production of wage-workers who had no right in what they produced. Whoever possesses the house you dwell in, the vehicle you ride or the income you live on, takes hold of your freedom, or part of your freedom, and freedom is indivisible. For man to be happy, he must be free, and to be free, man must possess his own needs. Whoever possesses your needs controls or exploits you. He may enslave you despite any legislation outlawing that.

The material needs of man that are basic, necessary and personal, start with food, housing, clothing and transport . . . These must be within his private and sacred ownership. They are not to be hired from any quarter. To obtain them through rent or hire allows the real owners, even society in general, to interfere in his private life, to have control over his basic needs, and then to dominate his freedom and to deprive him of his happiness. The owner of the costumes one has hired could interfere to remove them even in the street and leave one naked. The owner of the vehicle could interfere, leaving one in the middle of the road. Likewise, the owner of the house could interfere, leaving one without shelter.

It is ironic that man's basic needs are treated by legal administrative or other measures. Fundamentally, society must be founded on the application of the natural law to these needs.

The purpose of the socialist society is the happiness of man which can only be realized through material and spiritual freedom. Attainment of such freedom depends on the extent of man's ownership of his needs; ownership that is personal and sacredly guaranteed, i.e., your need must neither be owned by somebody else, nor subject to plunder by any part of society. Otherwise, you will live in a state of anxiety which will take away your happiness and render you unfree, because you live under the apprehension of outside interference in your basic needs.

The overturning of contemporary societies, to change them from being societies of wage-workers to societies of partners, is inevitable as a dialectical result of the contradictory economic theses prevailing in the world today and is the inevitable dialectical result of the injustice to relations based on the wage system, which have not been solved.

The threatening power of the Trade Unions in the capitalist world is capable of overturning capitalist societies of wage-workers into societies of partners.

It is probable that the outbreak of the revolution to achieve socialism will start with the appropriation by the producers of their share in what they produce. The objective of the workers' strikes will shift from a demand for the increase of wages to a demand for sharing in the production. All that will, sooner or later, take place under the guidance of The Green Book.

But the final step is when the new socialist society reaches the stage where profit and money disappear. It is through transforming society into a fully productive society and through reaching, in production, the level where the material needs of the members of society are satisfied. In that final stage profit will automatically disappear and there will be no need for money.

The recognition of profit is an acknowledgement of exploitation. The mere recognition of profit removes the possibility of limiting it. Measures taken to put a limit to it through various means are mere attempts at reform, which are not radical, in order to stop man's exploitation by man. The final solution is the abolition of profit. But as profit is the driving force of economic activity, its abolition is not a decision that can be taken lightly. It must result from the development of socialist production which will be achieved if the satisfaction of the material needs of society is realised. The endeavour to increase profit will ultimately lead to its disappearance.

Part Three: The Social Basis for the Third Universal Theory

The social, i.e. national, factor is the driving force of human history. The social bond which binds together each human group, from the family through the tribe to the nation, is the basis for the movement of history.

Heroes in history are persons who have made sacrifices for causes. But for what causes? They have made sacrifices for others. But which others? They are those who have a relationship with them. The relationship between an individual and a group is a social relationship, i.e. the relationship between the members of a nation. For nations are founded on nationalism. Those causes, therefore, are national causes and national relationship is the social relationship. The social relationship is derived from society, i.e. the relationship between the members of a society, just as nationalism is derived from the nation, i.e. the relationship between the members of a nation. The social relationship is, accordingly, the national relationship and the national relationship is the social relationship. For the group is a nation and the nation is a group even if they differ in number, leaving aside the extended definition of the group which means the provisional group regardless of the national relations of its members. What is meant by the group here is the group which is permanent by virtue of its own national relations.

Besides, historical movements are mass movements, i.e. group movements for its own interests . . . for its independence from a different group. Each group has its own social structure which binds it together. Group movements are always movements for independence in order that subjugated or oppressed groups may attain self realisation. As for the struggle for power, it occurs within the group itself down to the family level, as expounded in Part One of the Green Book, which deals with the Political Basis of the Third Universal Theory. A group movement is a nation's movement for its own interests. By virtue of its national structure, each group has common social needs which must be collectively satisfied. These needs are in no way individualistic. They are collective needs, rights, demands, or objectives of a nation which is bound by a single nationalism. That is why these movements are called national movements. Contemporary national liberation movements are themselves social movements. They will not come to an end before every group is liberated from the domination of another group, i.e. the world is now passing through one of the regular cycles of the movement of history, namely, the national struggle in support of nationalism.

In the world of man, this is the historical reality, as it is a social reality. That means that the national struggle – the social struggle – is the basis of the movement of history, because it is stronger than all other factors since it is the origin . . . the basis . . . it is in the nature of the human group . . . the nature of the nation. It is the nature of life itself. Other animals, apart from man, live in groups. Indeed, the group is the basis for the survival of all groups within the animal kingdom. So nationalism is the basis for the survival of nations.

Nations whose nationalism is destroyed are subject to ruin. Minorities, which are one of the main political problems in the world, are the outcome of a social cause. They are nations whose nationalism has been destroyed and torn apart. The social factor is, therefore, a factor of life . . . a factor of survival. It is the nation's natural innate momentum for survival.

Nationalism in the world of man and group instinct in the animal kingdom are like gravity in the domain of mineral and celestial bodies. If the mass of the sun were smashed so that it lost its gravity, the gases would blow away and its unity would no longer exist. Accordingly, the unity is the basis for its survival. The factor of unity in any group is a social factor, i.e. nationalism. For this reason a group struggles for its own national unity, because its survival lies in that.

The national factor, which is the social bond, works automatically to impel the nation towards survival, in the same way that the gravity of an object works to keep it as one mass around the nucleus. The diffusion and dispersion of atoms in the atomic bomb are the result of the explosion of the nucleus which is the focus of gravitation for the atoms around it. When the factor of unity in those components is broken into pieces and gravity is lost, every atom is dispersed. This is the nature of matter. It is an established law of nature. To disregard it or collide with it is damaging to life. Thus man's life is damaged when he begins to disregard nationalism . . . the social factor . . . the gravity of the group . . . the secret of its survival. There is no rival to the social factor in influencing the unity of one group except the religious factor, which may divide the national group or unite groups with different nationalisms. However, the social factor will eventually gain sway. This has been the case throughout the ages. Originally, each nation had one religion. This was harmony. In fact, however, differences arose which became a genuine cause of conflict and instability in the life of the peoples throughout the ages.

The sound rule is that every nation should have a religion. The contrary to that is the abnormal. Such an abnormality creates an unsound situation which becomes a real cause for disputes within a national group. There is no other solution but to be in harmony with the natural rule that each nation has one religion. When the social factor is compatible with the religious factor, harmony is achieved and the life of groups becomes stable and strong and develops soundly.

Marriage is a process that exercises negative and positive effects on the social factor though both man and woman are free to accept whom they want and reject whom they do not want as a natural rule of freedom. Marriage within a group, by its very nature, strengthens its unity and brings about collective growth in conformity with the social factor.

Appendix 5

Information for the Visitor

Visas

Visitors require a visa, normally valid for 3 months and to be used within 45 days of issue. Visa allocation is carefully controlled. The business visitor will require a letter of invitation (a fax will do) from a local company or government organization plus entry approval from the Libyan Immigration Authority in Libya. Once approval has been granted in Libya, your nearest People's Bureau will be informed and the traveller(s) are then required to complete the local visa application process and pay the appropriate fees. Local visa processing can be quite swift but can also take many weeks to complete. An express service is available for an additional fee. Other travellers are advised to seek the help of a tour company. As always, be patient and allow for unscheduled delays.

Embassies and consulates

Embassies and consulates in Libya

Below is just a selection of embassies and consulates in Libya. The number of countries opening up diplomatic offices in Libya is steadily increasing. Postal addresses are in brackets where different from the street address.

Belgian
Dhat al-Ahmat Tower 4
Level 5
Tripoli
Tel: 021 335 0115
Fax: 021 335 0116

British
Burj al-Fateh
Level 24
Tripoli
Tel: 021 335 1084
Emergency: 091 214 7316
Fax: 021 335 1425

Dutch
20 Sharia Galal Bayar
(PO Box 3801)
Tripoli
Tel: 021 444 1549
Fax: 021 444 0386

French
Sharia Beni al-Amar
Hay Andalus (Gargaresh)
(PO Box 312)
Tripoli
Tel: 021 477 4892
Fax: 021 477 8266

German
Sharia Hussan al-Mashai
(PO Box 302)
Tripoli
Tel: 021 333 0554
Fax: 021 444 896

Greek
18 Sharia Galal Bayar
(PO Box 5147)
Tripoli
Tel: 021 333 6978
Fax: 021 444 1907

Italian
1 Shara Uahara
(PO Box 912)
Tripoli
Tel: 021 333 4131
Fax: 021 333 1673

Japanese
Dhat al-Ahmat Tower 4
Level 1
(PO Box 3265)
Tripoli
Tel: 021 335 0056
Fax: 021 335 0055

Spanish
Sharia al-Amir Abd al-Kader al Jezayir
Garden City
(PO Box 2302)
Tripoli
Tel: 021 333 6797
Fax: 021 444 3743

USA
c/o Belgian Embassy
(details above)

Libyan People's Bureaux and consulates abroad

Austria
Balaustrasse 33
1109 Vienna
Tel: +43 (0) 1 367 7639

Belgium
Ave Victoria 28
B-1050 Brussels
Tel: +32 (02) 649 1503

Denmark
Rosenvaengets Hovedvej 4
2100 Copenhagen
Tel: +45 35 26 36 11

France
2 rue Charles Lamoureux
75116 Paris
Tel: +33 (0) 1 47 04 71 62

Germany
Beethovenalle 12a
53173 Bonn
Tel: +49 (0) 0228 822 0090

Greece
Vironoz 13
152–154 Psychikon
Athens
Tel: +302 (0) 1 0674 1843

Italy
Via Nomentana 365
Rome 00 162
Tel: +39 06 86 32 09 51

Malta
Dar Tarek
Tower Road
Sliema
Tel: +356 34947

Netherlands
Parkweg 15
1285 GHS-Gravanhaga
Amsterdam
Tel: +31 (0) 20 355 8886

Spain
Pisuerga No 1–2
28002 Madrid
Tel: +34 91 5644 675

Switzerland
Travelweg 2
CH-3006 Bern
Tel: +41 31 351 3076

UK
54 Ennismore Gardens
London SW7 1NH
Tel: +44 (0) 20 7486 8250
Fax: +44 (0) 20 7589 6120

USA
309 East 48th Street
New York
NY 0201
Tel: +1 202 752 5775

Hotels

Tripoli
Bab Al-Baher Hotel: 021 608051
Bab Al-Madina Hotel: 021 608000/9
Corinthia Bab Africa Hotel: 021 3351990
Kabir Hotel (Grand Hotel): 021 4445940/57
Mahari Hotel: 021 3334091/6
Safwa Hotel: 021 3334592/4443257
Wadan Hotel: 021 606014

Sirte
Madina Hotel: 054 60160/3
Mahri Hotel: 054 60100/4
Qasr al-Mu'tamarat Hotel: 054 60165

Benghazi
Ouzo Hotel: 061 95160/66
Tibesti Hotel: 061 9802931/31, 061 92033/34

Misrata
Goztiek Hotel: 051 614614/613333

Fixed public holidays

3 March	Declaration of the Authority's Power
28 March	Evacuation Day (British)
11 June	Evacuation Day
23 July	Revolution Day
1 September	National Day
7 October	Evacuation Day

Islamic holidays 2004

New Year	22 February
Prophet's Birthday	2 May
Ramadan	15 October – 14 November*

Eid al Fitr	14 November
Eid al Adha	2 February

*Ramadan and other Islamic days of celebration are set by the actual sighting of the new moon and then by the lunar calendar. So, depending on local viewing conditions, these dates can vary. Accordingly, the dates move approximately 10 days back each year against the Gregorian calendar.

Time zone

GMT+2. There is no summer time clock change.

Telephones

International	+218
Mobiles	091 (no 0 when dialling from abroad)
Al Zawiya	23
Benghazi	61
Misuratha	51
Sabratha	24
Tripoli International Airport	22
Tripoli	21

General information

For weather reports and forecasts, immunization suggestions, currency exchange rates and other up-to-the-minute information go to www.geocities.com/LibyaPage.travel.

Appendix 6

Web sites

Over the past two years there has been a plethora of Web sites of value to those with an interest in Libya. Happily, one maintains a complete listing of all Web sites for the Libya-watcher; over 600 are listed on: www.pclibya.com/libyansites.

For news we recommend www.libya1.com. For business news we recommend www.meed.com.

Appendix 7

Suggested Reading List

Ashiurakis, Ahmed (1993) *Libyan Proverbs*, Dar Al-Fergiani, Tripoli
Ashiurakis, Ahmed 1992) *Your Guide to Libya Past and Present*, Dar Al-Fergiani, Tripoli
Azema, James (2001) *Libya Handbook*, Footprint Guides
Davis, John (1987) *Libyan Politics: Tribe and Revolution*, University of California Press, Berkeley, CA
Economist Intelligence Unit (2001) *Country Profile: Libya 2001*, EIU, London
Economist Intelligence Unit, *Quarterly Report: Libya*, EIU, London
Ham, Anthony, (2002) *Lonely Planet Guide to Libya*, Lonely Planet Publications, Victoria*
Haynes, D E L, (1965) *The Antiques of Tripolitania*, Darf, London
Muscat, Frederick (1980) *My President My Son*, Edam Publishing House, Malta
National Authority for Information and Documentation (1999) *Libya, Taqrir al-Tanmiya al-Bashiriya 1999*
Pelt, Adrian (1970) *Libyan Independence and the United Nations: A Case of Planned Decolonization*, Yale, New Haven, CT
Polidori, Robert *et al* (1999) *Libya, The Lost Cities of the Roman Empire*, Könemann Verlagsgesellschaft mbH, Cologne
Qadhafi, Muammar (1980) *The Green Book*, vols 1–3, Green Book Centre, Tripoli*
Qadhafi, Muammar (1999) *Escape to Hell and Other Stories*, Blake Publishing, London
United Nations Development Programme (2001) *Human Development Report 2001*, Oxford University Press, Oxford
Vandewalle, Dirk (1998) *Libya Since Independence: Oil and State-Building*, Tauris

When in Tripoli, be sure to visit Fergiani's bookshop on Sharia 1st September, 100 metres up from Green Square, on the right. Telephone 021 4444873. Mohammed Fergiani and his son, Hisham, stock many hard-to-find books and are a mine of information which will be imparted with good grace and delicious coffee.

* Essential reading

Appendix 8

Contributor Contact Details

Academy of Graduate Studies
Al Hadhba District
PO Box 72331
Tripoli
Libya
Tel: +218 21 487 0168/487 3100
Fax: +218 21 487 3075
E-mail: info@alacademia.org
Web site: www.alacademia.org
Contact: Milad Saad Milad
Director International Affairs

Arab Development Institute
Tripoli
Libya
Tel: +218 21 334 0300
Contact: Dr Mustafa Attir
E-mail: moattir@yahoo.com

British Arab Commercial Bank
Head Office
8–10 Mansion House Place
London EC4N 8BJ
UK
Tel +44 (0)20 7648 7777
Fax: +44 (0)20 7600 3318
Web site: www.bacb.co.uk

Consultancy Support (Libya) Ltd
18 The Crescent
Frinton-on-Sea
Essex C013 9AP
UK
Tel: +44 (0) 7050 174 175
Fax: +44 (0) 1255 677 073
Web site: www.consultancysupport.co.uk

EWM, Malta
Regent House, 55, 5th Floor
Bisazza Street
Sliema SLM 15
Malta
Tel: +356 21 342134
Fax: +356 21 3300280
E-mail: ey.malta@mt.ey.com
Contact: Mario P. Galea
Managing Partner

EWM
That El Emad Towers
Tower 5, Level 9
Tripoli
PO Box 91873
Tel: +218 335 0468
Fax: +218 335 0470
E-mail: ewm@lttnet.net

Eversheds Frere Cholmeley
8 Place d'Iena
75116 Paris
France
Tel: +331 55 734000
Fax: +331 55 734011
Web site: www.eversheds.com

IHS Energy Group
24 Chemin de la Mairies
PO Box 152
1258 Perly
Geneva
Switzerland
Tel: +41 22 721 1717
Fax: +41 22 721 1919
Web site: www.ihsenergy.com

Lonely Planet plc
Web site: www.lonelyplanet.com.au

Maghur & Partners
20 Khaled Ben El Waled Street
PO Box 2111
Dahra Area
Tripoli
Libya
Tel: +218 21 3331312
Fax: +218 21 3337851
Web site: www.maghurandpartners.com

Marat Terterov
c/o Kogan Page Ltd
120 Pentonville Road
London N1 9JN
Fax: +44 (0) 20 7837 6348
Mobile: 07931 383 336
E-mail: m-terterov@ftnetwork.com
Web site: www.globalmarketbriefings.com

MEC International
132–135 Sloane Street
London
SW1X 9AX
UK
Contact: Oliver Miles
Tel: +44 (0) 20 7591 4816
Fax: +44 (0) 20 7591 4801
E-mail: mec@meconsult.co.uk
Web site: www.mec@meconsult.co.uk

Oliver Miles
See MEC International

Mukthtar, Kelbash & Elgharabli
12, El Fateh Road
Suite No. 5
PO Box 1093
Tripoli
Libya
Tel: +218 21 333 26 65/444 44 26
Fax: +218 21 333 16 50
E-mail: mke_law@yahoo.com; mke@mail.lttnet.net

Sahara International Consulting
Contact: Dr Abdul Nasser Nageh
Kahlifa Zaidi Street
Tripoli
Libya
Tel: +218 21 3611 566
Fax: +218 21 444 2862
E-mail: hakimnag@yahoo.de

Salem El-Maiar
Brown & Root North Africa
Hill Park Court
Springfield Drive
Leatherhead
Surrey KT22 7NL
UK
Tel: +44 (0) 1372 863064
Fax: +44 (0) 1372 863064
E-mail: salem.elmaiar@halliburton.com

Jonathan Wallace
Al Anqaa Communications Company
26 Kenilworth Road
London NW6 7HJ
UK
Tel: +44 (0) 20 7624 3609
E-mail: al-anqaa@lineone.net

Index

Index of Advertisers

Other Titles in this Series from Kogan Page

Doing Business with Azerbaijan
Doing Business with Bahrain
Doing Business with China
Doing Business with Croatia
Doing Business with Cyprus
Doing Business with the Czech Republic
Doing Business with Egypt
Doing Business with Estonia
Doing Business with Georgia
Doing Business with Germany
Doing Business with Hungary
Doing Business with India
Doing Business with Kazakhstan
Doing Business with Lithuania
Doing Business with Malta
Doing Business with Oman
Doing Business with Poland
Doing Business with Qatar
Doing Business with the Russian Region of Krasnodar Krai
Doing Business with Saudi Arabia
Doing Business with Slovenia
Doing Business with Slovakia
Doing Business with Spain
Doing Business with South Africa
Doing Business with Turkey
Doing Business with Ukraine
Doing Business with the United Arab Emirates